W9-BLT-106

MARGARET ATWOOD AND THE FEMALE BILDUNGSROMAN

For my parents – Maura and Thady

Margaret Atwood and the Female Bildungsroman

ELLEN McWILLIAMS
Bath Spa University, UK

ASHGATE

Published by
Ashgate Publishing Limited
Wey Court East
Union Road
Farnham
Surrey, GU9 7PT
England

Ashgate Publishing Company
Suite 420
101 Cherry Street
Burlington
VT 05401-4405
USA

www.ashgate.com

British Library Cataloguing in Publication Data
McWilliams, Ellen
Margaret Atwood and the Female Bildungsroman.
1. Atwood, Margaret, 1939 – Criticism and interpretation. 2. Bildungsroman, Canadian – History and criticism. 3. Bildungsroman – Women authors.
I. Title
813.5'4

Library of Congress Cataloging-in-Publication Data
McWilliams, Ellen.
Margaret Atwood and the female bildungsroman / Ellen McWilliams.
p. cm.
Includes bibliographical references.
1. Atwood, Margaret, 1939 – Criticism and interpretation. 2. Women and literature – Canada – History – 20th century. 3. Bildungsroman, Canadian – History and criticism. I. Title.
PR9199.3.A8Z745 2009
818'.5409–dc22 2009003066

ISBN 978-0-7546-6027-9

Printed and bound in Great Britain by
TJ International Ltd, Padstow, Cornwall

Contents

Abstract

This book examines Margaret Atwood's work in the context of the complex history of the Bildungsroman, or novel of development. It looks at the ways in which the Bildungsroman – a term first used to describe a distinctly German genre – has developed to assume new meanings far removed from its exclusively masculine heritage, exploring in particular how, in Atwood's work, the Bildungsroman is refracted through the prism of feminist, and Canadian nationalist, discourses. The book demonstrates that Atwood's early work, her own "coming of age" fiction – that is her unpublished novel, *The Nature Hut* (1966), *The Edible Woman* (1969), *Surfacing* (1972), and *Lady Oracle* (1976) – both engages with and works against the paradigms of identity which are traditionally associated with the genre. It argues that these novels serve to expose rather than to uphold conventional models of growth and development, both artistic and personal. Drawing on critical work by Atwood (as well as unpublished manuscripts in the Atwood Collection), the book will uncover the influences shaping Atwood's fashioning of identity in her early novels, paying particular attention to her preoccupation with survival as a key symbol of Canadian literature, culture, and identity. What emerges is that Atwood is a writer who self-consciously and deliberately invokes and then undercuts the traditions associated with the Bildungsroman. This renegotiation, then, may be read as a means of at once interrogating and perpetuating the Bildungsroman.

The book goes on to consider the afterlife of the genre – which follows its gendered and nationalized reshaping – in Atwood's own work, and in works by other Canadian women writers. It examines the ways in which Atwood's later novels, namely *Cat's Eye* (1988), *The Robber Bride* (1993), *The Blind Assassin* (2000), and *Moral Disorder* (2006), revisit and develop the formulations of selfhood and identity put forward in her early fiction. Atwood's reshaping of the genre is demonstrated by the impact that she had on the development of the Canadian novel in later years; the book traces these afterlives by way of a survey of those writers most clearly influenced by Atwood.

A Note on the Text

The Atwood texts cited are mainly Virago editions, unless otherwise specified in the Works Cited. References to the Margaret Atwood Collection will take the following form throughout: Collection No.:Box No.:File No.:Page No. The material in the Margaret Atwood Collection has been presented by the author to the Thomas Fisher Rare Book Library, University of Toronto, from 1970 to the present. The transcriptions of these materials are my own and interpolations are indicated in square brackets. Unless otherwise stated, translations from German to English are my own.

Acknowledgements

I have been particularly lucky in having been encouraged and inspired by a number of kind and gifted teachers: Dr Lee Jenkins (Department of English, University College Cork), Professor Patricia Coughlan (Department of English, University College Cork), Dr Joachim Beug (Department of German, University College Cork), Professor Reingard Nischik (University of Constance, Germany) and Dr Rowena Fowler (St Peter's College, Oxford).

I would like to thank my colleagues in the School of English and Creative Studies at Bath Spa University for making me so welcome during the past year and for their support during the final stages of the project. Many thanks also to Brenda McWilliams for her kindness and excellent advice.

Financial support for this research was given, in the early stages, in the form of research scholarships, by University College Cork, the University of Constance, the National University of Ireland, and later by the University of Bristol and the International Council for Canadian Studies. I am grateful to the Canadian High Commission for a Faculty Research Award, which enabled me to spend time doing valuable research in Ottawa and Toronto. I am also very grateful to the British Association for American Studies and the Eccles Centre for North American Studies at the British Library for the award of a Visiting Fellowship.

I would like to thank Christian Corbet for kindly allowing me to use his portrait of Margaret Atwood, "Margaret Atwood Idea-Idea", which is on permanent exhibition at the University of Western Ontario, as the cover image of the book. I would also like to thank Dennis Lee for his permission to reproduce extracts from his correspondence with Margaret Atwood, and Donald Shields for allowing me to draw on material in the Carol Shields Archive at the Canadian National Library in Ottawa.

Finally, I would like to express my sincere gratitude to Margaret Atwood for her generous permission to reproduce unpublished material from the Atwood Collection at the University of Toronto and to the staff and librarians at the Thomas Fisher Rare Book Library, where the archive is housed, for being so helpful.

An earlier version of the material on *The Edible Woman* in Chapter 4 was first published as "Margaret Atwood's Canadian Hunger Artist: Postcolonial Appetites in *The Edible Woman*" in *Kunapipi: Journal of Postcolonial Writing* 28.2 (2007): 63–72 and a version of Chapter 6, "Keeping Secrets, Telling Lies: Fictions of the Artist and Author in the Novels of Margaret Atwood", first appeared in *Atlantis: A Women's Studies Journal* 32.1 (2007): 25–33.

My greatest debt is to my parents, Maura and Thady, who worked so hard to give me every chance. There are no adequate words to express my gratitude to my husband, John, for his understanding and support during the writing of this book and, far more vitally, for the happiness of the last decade.

PART 1
Margaret Atwood and the Canadian Female Bildungsroman

Introduction

In reading Margaret Atwood's work in relation to an established literary tradition, this book examines the coming of age of a writer, a genre, and a national literature. It is mainly concerned with Atwood's reclamation of a colonized national and female identity and the effect of that reclamation on a subsequent generation of Canadian women writers. The idea of the Bildungsroman has developed as a literary concept from its eighteenth-century German origins and gained new currency amongst women writers in the second half of the twentieth century. While some writers were most concerned with appropriating a tradition that had previously excluded women, others – and I want to argue that Atwood is the best example of this – were less interested in perpetuating the genre in its traditional form than in contesting and renegotiating its problematic prescriptions of femininity and its investment in an ideal of exclusively masculine perfectibility.

"Great Unexpectations" is the title of an article by Margaret Atwood in which she considers some of the challenges to being a writer of woman-centred fiction in Canada in the 1960s. This article is examined in more detail later, but its title – a pointed engagement with the title of what is possibly the most famous Bildungsroman in English literature – encapsulates many of the issues under investigation in this book, which focuses on how Atwood renegotiates the Bildungsroman as a literary model. Margaret Atwood's early fiction is the best example of this renegotiation, and shows how Atwood contests the traditional expectations of the genre. One of the more striking illustrations of this, something that is frequently commented on in Atwood criticism, is in the way that Atwood replaces conventional narratives of cohesive, singular development, with sometimes outrageous narratives of multiple identity. As a feature of her work, this has been a particular preoccupation of critics with an interest in Atwood as a postmodern writer.

Atwood's early phase of writing, however, is also contemporaneous with a problematic and crucial period in Canadian literature. From our current perspective, not only is Canada a major player in the literary world, but Atwood seems to be an established international, and perhaps internationalist, writer, both in terms of the reception of her work and the imaginative landscapes of her fiction. But Atwood's early novels (that is, those of the 1960s and 1970s) evince a genuine struggle with identities, and are far removed from the current confidence of Canadian literature. The fact that Atwood's "coming of age" as a writer coincides with, and is informed by, the literary renaissance in Canada in the 1960s and 1970s is something that will be considered in detail in Chapter 2 of the book. As an aspiring woman writer in Canada during this period, Atwood encountered a number of obstacles to literary development: the absence of an inherited literary tradition and the general assumption that Canadian literature was a contradiction in terms were perhaps the most challenging of these. Thus, Atwood's early development as a writer was framed by her involvement in promoting a distinctive Canadian literature. Indeed, the fashioning of identity in her early fiction and her contribution to the developing female Bildungsroman were particularly influenced by her formative experiences as a writer at a time of radical cultural change in Canada.

Chapter 1 of this book offers a survey of the historical and theoretical background of the Bildungsroman and revisits a number of key critical debates, thus setting the background for Atwood's later engagement with the genre. In terms of theory, it argues for an inclusive approach to the genre, in particular including the kind of subversion of the genre which Atwood achieves. The chapter's history of the genre opens with a summary of the German origins of the Bildungsroman, before briefly going on to show the ways in which the tradition was taken up by writers in English. Most crucially, the chapter examines Bildungsromane by and about women in the second half of the twentieth century and investigates a number of framing discourses, including feminist contexts and postmodern concepts of subjectivity. It goes on to develop a working definition of the *female* Bildungsroman and suggests examples of models of female development and related inflections that characterize the genre in its contemporary form. This chapter, then, is concerned with how the female Bildungsroman responds to its controversial heritage and how it reanimates the genre by renegotiating the early paradigm, thus setting up a relevant context for the consideration of Atwood's own versions of the genre. Chapter 2, following on from this, establishes the relevance of Atwood's own critical preoccupations to the issues described in Chapter 1. Most important is her identification (as an historian and a literary critic) of survival and endurance as key symbols of Canadian literature and culture in texts such as *Survival: A Thematic Guide to Canadian Literature* (1972). To this end, this chapter makes extensive use of Atwood's unpublished correspondence, essays, and speeches deposited in the Atwood Collection at the University of Toronto. As we shall see, access to these materials provides a valuable insight into her early career and her formative years as a writer. The chapter contends that Atwood's published critical writing, as well as miscellaneous unpublished material, provides a unique insight into her fiction. It offers another slant on Atwood's creative process, providing a fuller and significantly different picture of Atwood's development as a writer and cultural critic.

Reingard M. Nischik in her introduction to *Margaret Atwood: Works and Impact*, a landmark publication launched to coincide with Atwood's sixtieth birthday, draws attention to Atwood's importance in Canadian public life:

> In a work published in 1997 by two Canadian historians, Rawlinson's and Granatstein's *The Canadian 100: The 100 Most Influential Canadians of the Twentieth Century*, Margaret Atwood is ranked in fifth place, a gratifyingly high position for someone who is neither a politician nor an industrial magnate, but a writer by profession. (1)

This contemporary image of Margaret Atwood contrasts starkly with her formative experiences as a writer. In an interview with Joyce Carol Oates, in 1978, Atwood remarked that: "The Canadian literary scene has been likened (by myself, in fact) to a group of figures dancing with considerable vigor and some grace on the edge of a precipice" (*Waltzing Again: New and Selected Conversations with Margaret Atwood* 52). Chapter 2 will focus on how this position would seem to impact upon Atwood's Bildungsroman; the combination of precariousness, vigour, and grace is something that speaks to many of her characters as they struggle to come to terms with their own personal histories.

Chapter 3 focuses on Atwood's signature novel, *Surfacing* (1972), and a draft of an earlier unpublished novel, *The Nature Hut* (1966), which makes for a most valuable companion text to *Surfacing*. Both of these novels are Bildungsromane that conflate the search for an autonomous female identity with the quest for a meaningful national identity. Informed by theoretical inquiries into national identity, my discussion will focus on Atwood's engagement with received ideas and images of Canada and suggest that her early work interrogates as well as invests in the narrative processes involved in imagining national identity.

Chapter 4 examines *The Edible Woman* (1969) and *Lady Oracle* (1976), paying particular attention to how these novels undercut the characteristics associated with the Bildungsroman. Both novels are primarily concerned with selfhood under threat and both protagonists find unconventional ways of taking control of their lives. This discussion will focus, in particular, on the correlation between actual and literary consumption in these novels, as the main characters have a particularly complex and difficult relationship with the process of establishing their place in the world. Each in turn refuses to be a martyr to imposed scripts, whether ordained by social discourses or by literary convention. *Lady Oracle*, in particular, marks a departure in Atwood's writing in the way that it emphasizes the creative possibilities of strategies for survival over its more negative implications and takes a more flamboyant approach to writing the female Bildungsroman.

Chapter 5 includes extended analyses of two of Atwood's later novels, namely *The Robber Bride* (1993) and *Alias Grace* (1996). These novels are representative of another pivotal moment in Atwood's work where female and Canadian national identity are closely related as, in reclaiming the personal histories at the centre of these novels, Atwood revisits crucial moments in the history of English-Canadian culture. These novels also add a new dimension to the power and pleasure of storytelling, particularly the telling of women's life stories. Chapter 6 looks at the Atwoodian Künstlerroman, or novel of the artist (a near relative of the Bildungsroman), in more detail, and examines in particular the artistic and creative models that emerge in *Cat's Eye* (1988) and *The Blind Assassin* (2000). This will be set against Atwood's longstanding critical interest in the image of the writer throughout literary history (particularly in *Negotiating with the Dead: A Writer on Writing* (2002)). Chapter 7 goes on to look at Atwood's most recent novel, *Moral Disorder* (2006), perhaps her most experimental Bildungsroman to date, one that further distances itself from its original form and holds up a mirror to Atwood's fictional oeuvre. It will look at how *Moral Disorder* responds to earlier moments in her writing career and show how enduring Atwoodian preoccupations regarding writing the self are given new expression. These later chapters will take particular care to relate the developments in Atwood's more recent writing to issues that arise from her early work, and will also prepare the way for a discussion of Atwood's key influence on her Canadian contemporaries.

The book seeks to show, amongst other things, how Atwood's sophisticated response to the Bildungsroman is, in part, determined by her position as a writer campaigning for the future of Canadian literature. The realization of this future will be examined in the Postscript to the book, with particular focus on Atwood's influence and the development of Canadian female Bildungsroman in the last three decades. The Postscript to the book, then, draws from the range of contemporary Canadian fiction in English, and shows how strongly Atwood's influence – especially her reanimation of the Bildungsroman – is written onto these works. The Atwood that emerges from this book is one who not only enters into a productive dialogue with a venerable genre but also effectively changes that genre in the process.

Atwood's most recent collection of short prose, *The Tent* (2006), opens with a piece called "Life Stories", which explores what happens when the expected conventions of life narratives are abandoned: "Once you get started it's fun. So much free space opens up. Rip, crumple, up in flames, out the window. *I was born, I grew up, I studied, I loved, I married, I procreated, I said, I wrote*, all gone now. … Only a paragraph left, only a sentence or two, only a whisper. *I was born. I was. I.*" (4–5, italics in original). The almost gleeful abandonment of the verbs that signify order and progress in the telling of a life story is representative of one of the most pressing concerns in Atwood's work; the "Life Stories" at the centre of Atwood's fiction are subject to a similarly disruptive interest in thinking outside the limits of such conventions.

Chapter 1
The Coming of Age of the Female Bildungsroman

The German Bildungsroman: Origins, History, and Controversies

Any attempt to study the relationship of a work of literature to a given genre necessitates an investigation into the history of, and expectations borne by, that tradition. In other words, in order to locate a text (or set of texts) in relation to an extended discourse, an appreciation of the paradigms of that discourse is essential: it can allow us to develop a reading that identifies a tenable relationship between text and tradition, although we must also be wary of resorting to crude extractions of meaning or grasping at tenuous connections. The problem is that every genre inevitably proves to be beset by uncertainties and contradictions, and the Bildungsroman is no exception; indeed, it might be said especially to frustrate any attempt at a working definition. Dictionary entries, which usually encapsulate the genre as the chronicle of a young man's development and striving towards maturity, fail to acknowledge the controversy that surrounds the tradition, and are therefore incomplete. Thus, while many critics use the term without reference to its complex history, to bypass this controversy, and launch into a reading of Margaret Atwood's novels as female Bildungsromane, would be to isolate the term from its heritage. It would also be to miss precisely the complexity of the genre on which Margaret Atwood builds. This book will show how Atwood is a writer interested in the complexities and contradictions of the genre, not one who unthinkingly takes on the straightforward dictionary definitions just mentioned. It is exactly because the term is so loaded with meanings from the past that its application needs to be made with some acknowledgement of those templates. While this may not guarantee a solution to the problems posed by the Bildungsroman, it at least establishes a point of reference in contextualizing and analyzing more recent developments in the tradition and, furthermore, illuminates Atwood's contribution to the reconceptualization of the genre.

The problems with defining the Bildungsroman – even if we for a moment limit our attentions to its German context – are nicely summarized by Todd Kontje in his helpful study *The German Bildungsroman: History of a National Genre*: "at least three factors combine to produce the history of the Bildungsroman over time: the changing reception of the old literature, the production of the new, and the effort to situate the new literature in the context of the growing literary tradition" (13). An appreciation of these three elements is crucial to any effective strategy for approaching the Bildungsroman. It entails a delicate balancing act of keeping a keen revisionist eye on the works of literature that constitute the early canon of the genre, while simultaneously focusing on the anxious relationship between more recent Bildungsromane and the prototype; it involves a chronological survey of the genre and related critical approaches, and an investigation of the status and validity of the Bildungsroman as a genre. It is with this in mind – and in order to establish more firmly what is at stake in Atwood's evocation of the Bildungsroman – that I briefly sketch the history of the genre and revisit the key critical questions that surround it.

The political and social developments of eighteenth-century Germany are very often highlighted by historians as the cornerstones of the modern era in German society, providing the conditions that allowed the development of the Bildungsroman as a distinct literary genre. As described by Todd Kontje, in nineteenth-century readings of the early tradition, the idea of *Bildung* was appropriated as a national as well as individual model of development:

> The literary historians transferred the concept of *Bildung* from the individual human being to the national literature, which records the ripening of the German spirit. Thus, the Bildungsroman becomes the privileged genre of German literature: the organic development of the hero toward maturation and social integration reproduces in miniature the movement of German literature towards its maturity, and this literature in turn, is to inspire the unification of the German nation. (*The German Bildungsroman* 28–9)

Thus, clear links were established between literary and national conceptions of *Bildung*.

Johann Wolfgang von Goethe's *Wilhelm Meister's Apprenticeship* (1795–96) is at the centre of the German tradition, as well as the tradition as it spread throughout the world, and as such it holds a highly privileged position in literary history. It is an epic record of human experience at a pivotal time in Germany's history and casts a formidable shadow over all subsequent developments in the Bildungsroman genre. In Bildungsroman studies, all roads lead back to Wilhelm Meister and his odyssey to maturity. Every writer who attempts a Bildungsroman and every scholar of the genre pays homage to *Wilhelm Meister* as the archetype. *Wilhelm Meister's Apprenticeship* marked a turning point in the genesis of the genre, exerting an influence over all models of the Bildungsroman that followed in its wake. The novel chronicles the experience of a young man, the "unfledged merchant's son" (2) that we meet at the beginning of the novel, who leaves his comfortable but limiting bourgeois surroundings to pursue his dreams of working in the theatre. His passion for the theatre is appropriately inspired by a childhood toy, a puppet theatre, which sows the seeds of his enthusiasm for the dramatic arts. Wilhelm's poetic sensibility is offended by the apparent crassness of his merchant father's commercial interests and he imagines himself as "The Youth at the Crossroads" of the title of one of his early literary efforts (18). While he sees his engagement with the theatre as a means of momentarily escaping his bourgeois origins and indulging in an alternative fantasy life he soon becomes disillusioned and withdraws from theatrical life. However, in spite of his disappointment and failed ambition, he is reassured by a stranger who he meets (a disguised member of an aristocratic circle – his secret mentors in the course of his journey of self-discovery) that "everything that happens to us leaves its traces, everything contributes imperceptibly to our development" (257). With full ceremony, Wilhelm is eventually issued with a "Certificate of Apprenticeship" and the seal of approval of his collective of guardians: "Hail to you, young man. Your apprenticeship is completed, Nature has given you your freedom" (304). He is finally restored to his son Felix (the product of a passionate but thwarted love affair) and becomes engaged to the beautiful and worthy Natalie, and the novel concludes, full of promise that harmony has been restored.

If *Wilhelm Meister* is the blueprint for the Bildungsroman, then it can be argued that every subsequent manifestation of the genre engages with the original of the species. In his essay, "The German Bildungsroman for Nonspecialists: An Attempt at Clarification", Jeffrey Sammons provides a succinct synopsis of the ebb and flow of the Bildungsroman: "the German Bildungsroman emerges in the late eighteenth century, flourishes briefly in the age of Goethe and Romanticism, goes largely underground in the nineteenth century except for a handful of scattered examples … and then re-emerges in the modernist neo-Romantic revival in our own century" (32). Bildungsromane, of course – as we shall see in detail throughout this book – do not always slavishly follow Goethe's model. The nineteenth century in Germany saw a considerable increase in novels that interrogated the genre through irony and parody, most notably in the suggestively titled *The Life and Opinions of the Tomcat Murr* (1820–22) by E.T.A Hoffmann, the full title of which reads *The Life and Opinions of the Tomcat Murr (together with a fragmentary Biography of Kapellmeister Johannes Kreisler on Random Sheets of Waste Paper*), which contains deliberately teasing chapter headings such as "My Youthful Experiences", "My Apprentice Months", and "Beneficial Consequences of a Superior Education". A satiric twentieth-century relative to Hoffmann's novel, appeared in the form of Robert Musil's modernist monument *The Man Without Qualities*, which he started writing in 1924 (it was published in its most complete form in 1978). It would seem that, by this point, far removed from the sincerity of Wilhelm Meister and his earnest journey of discovery, the Bildungsroman was being tested and challenged by self-conscious, experimental parodies of the form. Coupled with the fact that the novel as a whole, in the early decades of the twentieth century, faced a new challenge in the form of literary modernism – one that was highly suspicious of realist narratives – the Bildungsroman must have appeared particularly under siege.

However, rather than being abandoned as a historical curiosity, the genre underwent, in the first instance, a (highly regrettable) rebirth in the context of Nazi Germany, where the genre's close association with nation-building was given a new and sinister dimension (Mayer, *Der Deutsche Bildungsroman* 272). Decades later, Günter Grass's *The Tin Drum* (1959) would respond to this in a revolutionary contribution to one of Germany's most important and valorized literary categories. It conveys the unfolding events of the Second World War from the perspective of an unlikely *Bildungsheld*, Oskar Matzerath, who, as stressed by Kontje, "like Wilhelm Meister and Heinrich Lee before him … is a child of his century: a drummer, a cripple, and an idiot" (*The German Bildungsroman* 59). Oskar Matzerath's macabre, fantastical, and frequently sacrilegious adventures are far removed from the idealism of his literary predecessors. Narrating his life story from a lunatic asylum, he describes the unfolding events in Germany and Poland between the 1920s and the 1950s to the accompaniment of his tin drum. Here, parody of the Bildungsroman climaxes in a grotesque fantasy based on the premise that "there are no more individualists, because individuality is a thing of the past" (3). The key conventions of the Bildungsroman are exploded, particularly in Oskar's determined refusal to grow beyond the height of a three-year-old: "I remained the precocious three-year-old, towered over by grownups but superior to all grownups, who refused to measure his shadow with theirs, who was complete both inside and outside, while they, to the very brink of the grave, were condemned to worry their heads about 'development'…" (46). *The Tin Drum*, excoriating as it does the genre's privileging of individual progress and "development", should surely have been a nail in the coffin of the Bildungsroman. This subversive assault has divided critics; it has been viewed by some as marking a decisive end to the genre and by others as self-consciously sustaining it. For example, while Hans Magnus Enzensberger, in an essay on Günter Grass first published in 1959, cites *The Tin Drum* as a prime example of the genre, thus ratifying Martin Swales's insistence that "even the non-fulfillment of consistently intimated expectation can, paradoxically, represent a validation of the genre by means of its controlled critique" (12), David Miles, in dramatic contrast, suggests that Grass's novel signals an end to the Bildungsroman as "The figure of the dwarf on the cover of Grass's novel, characteristically more clown than Bildungsheld, seems to be mocking his entire literary parentage of the last two hundred years – the picaros, the confessors and the various tragicomic inversions of both" (990). And yet it proved to be a tenacious animal, as it was to find a new creative expression in socialist engagements with the genre.

One of the most pointed Socialist renegotiations of the classic model of the Bildungsroman is Ulrich Plenzdorf's *The New Sorrows of Young W* (1973), which engages explicitly with Goethe's literary sensation *The Sorrows of Young Werther* (1774). *The New Sorrows of Young W* charts the growing disillusionment of the son of a factory director with the repressive, paranoid realities of life in the GDR. In its turn, this surge of interest in the Bildungsroman reanimated a number of critical debates about the nature of the genre and its defining features.

Even though, for some time, the Bildungsroman seemed a genre on the brink of extinction, interest in its usefulness as a literary category has seen it undergo varied and sometimes unexpected revivals. Ultimately, for the purpose of literary critics, the most useful, inclusive definition of *Bildung* can be taken as a physical, intellectual, or indeed spiritual process of cultivation and transformation. This extends to definitions of the Bildungsroman as a literary term and underpins most interpretations of the genre.

As will be addressed in the next section, feminist and other readers have been, at times, vociferous in their objections to the genre on account of its often unapologetic investment in masculine, bourgeois ideologies. I would like briefly to consider how iconoclastic arguments made in favour of abolishing the term are fuelled by the problematic closeness of multiple varieties that prove to be central, rather than peripheral, to the genre as a literary category. It is also necessary to take into account the debate as to whether the term should be applied only in a German context and if and how it might be seen to be relevant to other national literatures – this is an issue which is discussed in detail in the following section, where it will be argued that this German model has much to say to other national literatures.

Notwithstanding the slightly unfortunate disciplinary finger-pointing, Frederick Amrine cuts to the crux of potential problems with classifying the genre when he challenges that:

> if one takes "Bildung" in its strict and limited historical sense, then nothing is a *Bildungsroman* – not even *Wilhelm Meisters Lehrjahre*; but if one takes it in the loose sense, something like "development of the protagonist," then *everything* is a Bildungsroman. Either horn of this dilemma alone would be sharp enough, but we have arrived at an even worse impasse, and must face both: German Departments having effectively rejected the strict definition, English Departments have sallied forth to champion the vague. (127)

Critics have responded to this in different ways, dividing into what look like two directly opposed schools of thought. Jeffrey Sammons is at the forefront of the lobby to have the Bildungsroman purged from literary terminology:

> it seems clear that if the term is to be applicable to the whole universe of discourse of general literature, the claims made for its peculiar Germanness in its initial introduction dissolve. One may be tempted to ask, what of it? Well, one consequence, it seems to me is to introduce an uncontrollable arbitrariness into the usage of the term that, in turn, raises the question why we should retain it at all. (34–5)

James Hardin concurs when he suggests that the term be replaced with something free from the burden of the ideologies of a past age (x). Over time, different critics have gone in search of and canvassed for a more appropriate alternative term. Hartmut Steinecke has suggested *Individualroman* [Novel of the Individual] (94) as a more neutral substitute for Bildungsroman while Norbert Ratz makes a similar attempt with his coinage *Identitätsroman* [Novel of Identity] (4). In his essay "Zum Deutschen Antibildungsroman" [On the German Anti-Bildungsroman] (1974), Gerhart Mayer introduces the idea of an *Antibildungsroman*, claiming that it would allow the critic to make reference to the genre whilst maintaining a distance from its troubled history (41–6). The problem with the *Antibildungsroman*, however, is that it suggests a pointed and conscious confrontation with the genre when most re-workings in parody and irony tend to be more subtle than this implies. Another difficulty with these arguments is that they risk losing the distinction of a highly fecund literary and critical term; the Bildungsroman has developed a palimpsest of meanings, one that cannot be easily erased. Far more helpful, then, are Francois Jost (125) and Lothar Köhn (87–8), both of whom stress the usefulness of the term. Jost is especially reluctant to issue the "death certificate" (125) of the Bildungsroman, a position that resonates with Todd Kontje's undogmatic idea of the Bildungsroman as an "umbrella concept" (xi). As will become apparent, Kontje's and others' allowing arguments in relation to the term are particularly relevant to the application of the term to literature in English, given that many important studies of novels that engage with the genre are published in Britain or the United States, and, indeed, concern English novels (see the following section). Also, in the field of Bildungsroman scholarship, both in a Germanist context and in relation to other literatures, British and North American critics such as Jerome H. Buckley, Martin Swales, Todd Kontje, and James Hardin have emerged as key contributors to the debate. It would seem, then, that the genre is more suited to migration than previously imagined and that it retains – and perhaps extends – its importance as a creative and interpretative category when removed from its native origins. As I will explore later in this chapter, evidence of this transnational aspect of the genre can be found in the increasingly diverse applications of the Bildungsroman as a literary category, perhaps most unexpectedly in relation to women's writing and the feminist reclamation of female literary history.

All of these issues lead back to the same question of how the genre can be applied in a way that is convincing without yielding to too rigid or too vague a definition. The most helpful advice offered, in this case, comes from Martin Swales:

> I want to insist that the genre works *within* individual fictions in that it is a component of the expectation to which the specific novels refer and which they vivify by their creative engagement with it. The degree to which the expectation is or is not fulfilled is not the criterion for participation in the genre construct. As long as the model of the genre is intimated as a sustained and sustaining presence in the work in question, then the genre retains its validity as a structuring principle within the palpable stuff of an individual literary creation. In other words, the notion of a genre must, in my view, operate as a function of the imaginative literature written with reference to that concept; it is not a petrified, extraliterary thing. (12)

Swales's reading of genre as a site where literary conventions and expectations are contested finds sympathy in Tzvetan Toderov's assessment of "The Origin of Genres":

> The fact that a work "disobeys" its genre does not mean that the genre does not exist. It is tempting to say "quite the contrary", for two reasons. First because, in order to exist as such, the transgression requires a law – precisely the one that is to be violated. We might go even further and observe that the norm becomes visible – comes into existence – owing only to its transgressions. (196)

This offers a more optimistic slant on apparently "disobedient" engagements with genre, one which is very relevant to the misbehaving fictions found in novels such as Margaret Atwood's *Lady Oracle*.

Swales's assertion, positive as it is, invites the question: what is to be sustained in order to maintain the relationship between genre and individual work of literature? This idea of a "sustaining presence" seems to imply consciousness on the part of the author in deliberately mirroring and simultaneously challenging, subverting, and recasting the established structures of the genre. It is impossible to determine this level of consciousness, as there is no straightforward answer to the question of whether the author determines the generic paradigms within which s/he chooses to work or whether the work is equally guided by the invisible but powerful influence of history and the canon of the genre. It is perhaps more useful to think of this "sustaining presence" in terms of signifiers or indicators that bear a relation to the genre. This does not necessarily mean resorting to tabulating episodes or events but could be used as one of a number of guides in locating a text in relation to the genre. For example, in Atwood's female Bildungsroman, such indicators are often established only to be turned on their head. A particularly striking instance of this is the way in which marriage, a frequent turning point or climax of the Bildungsroman, is turned into the ritual sacrifice of a home-baked effigy of the bride-to-be in Atwood's first novel, *The Edible Woman*. This book will argue for the continuing aptness, indeed fecundity, of the term *Bildungsroman* – especially in relation to the work of Atwood – and thus acts as a counter to those critics who would relegate the term to the past.

In this project this book is not alone: above the din of iconoclastic voices, there exists strong and convincing support for maintaining the genre. While, for some critics, the idea of using the term as a shorthand for novels that investigate human development and transformation is to risk causing further confusion, it may also be appreciated – particularly, perhaps, in a postmodern context – as a flexible and valuable tool for investigative, exploratory purposes. While former varieties of the genre are neither to be forgotten nor ignored, the Bildungsroman has reached a new stage in its history particularly in the emergence of the idea of the female Bildungsroman. As I will explore in the next section, it has in the process of its naturalization into English taken on a new meaning, partly removed from the ideology of its past. Similarly, while some might consider its adoption by the feminist movement in the 1970s and 1980s to be problematic, to my mind the outward expansion of the genre and the retention of the term Bildungsroman is not something for which apology is necessary. Certainly, an understanding of the history of the genre from a Germanist perspective is very helpful, but what is more important at this point is that, for better or worse, the Bildungsroman is recognized throughout the world as a synonym for exploring aspects of human progress and development. As will emerge later in this chapter, the idea of the female Bildungsroman is, for some critics, doubly problematic. Again, there are various schools of thought that present the concept as a bankrupt and jaded oxymoron but, as will be shown here, the Bildungsroman is not simply defined by resemblance to the classic template, but is rather sustained in the mapping of an odyssey of selfhood in which the internal machinations of the self are foregrounded; in this way the female Bildungsroman reinvigorates the genre. My interest, from this point, is further to expound how and why women writers have selected the Bildungsroman as a literary model for narratives of female development. These developments strongly suggest that the Bildungsroman and its currency as a literary term cannot be disregarded as, in spite of its problematic heritage, it has been adapted as a cogent mode of expression for contemporary women writers.

The Tradition in English: History and Critical Reception

What is missing from the above sketch of a genre, of course, is an acknowledgement of the powerful ways in which writers in English appropriated the Bildungsroman, particularly in the nineteenth century: many points of contact and contrast have been noted between the emergence of the Bildungsroman in Germany in the eighteenth century and the rise of the English novel. Although Atwood, as will become clear, engages with the German tradition (perhaps indirectly), it is this English tradition which is most directly relevant to her work. This section will briefly consider this important relationship, drawing particular attention to those works which bear a special relationship to Atwood's writing.

In his important study of the early English novel, *The Rise of the Novel: Studies in Defoe, Richardson and Fielding* (1957), Ian Watt describes how the privileging of individual experience emerged as a distinctive feature of the novel (13). While critics such as Michael McKeon have since reconsidered and suggested modifications to Watt's model, it remains, nevertheless, very compatible with the prime interests of the Bildungsroman. In 1930, in considering the early tradition of the genre, Susanne Howe concluded that the Bildungsroman failed to achieve the same significance on English soil (6). However, Jerome H. Buckley's later study, *Season of Youth: The Bildungsroman from Dickens to Golding* (1974), made a powerful case for the existence of a canon of Bildungsromane in English. Buckley insists that there is a clearly identifiable sequence of development and influence in the Bildungsroman in English and includes Dickens, Eliot, Hardy, Lawrence, and Joyce on this continuum (viii). Acknowledging the influence of the Romantics' interest in individual experience and the interior, emotional life of the individual, Buckley's study takes the early Victorians as its point of departure. He suggests that novels dating to this period are most compatible with the Bildungsroman's preoccupation with middle-class progress, aspirations, and frustrations (20).

Buckley also provides a breakdown of the principal elements of the traditional Bildungsroman: "childhood, the conflict of generations, provinciality, the larger society, self-education, alienation, ordeal by love and the search for a vocation and a working philosophy – answers the requirements of the Bildungsroman as I am here seeking to describe and define it" (18). Since the appearance of Buckley's *Season of Youth*, Bildungsroman studies have flourished in English speaking countries, as has interest in the genre's influence on literature in English. The growing internationalism of the genre and use of the term in relation to other literatures has become commonplace, as the Bildungsroman, although laden with the burden of its history, moves beyond its native borders and takes on a new relevance in relation to other national literatures.

The relevance of this English tradition to Atwood's own work will become clear in due course, but an interesting fact – revealed in an interview Atwood gave in 1978 – suggests the extent to which this relevance is highly self-conscious on Atwood's part. In that interview, she describes how her primary motivation for going to study at Harvard in the early 1960s was the reputation of Jerome H. Buckley (*Conversations* 78). Buckley was also Atwood's PhD supervisor from 1966 to 1973 – letters to and from Buckley regarding her studies and the completion of her thesis ("Nature and Power in the English Metaphysical Romance of the Nineteenth and Twentieth Centuries") can be found in the Atwood Papers (MS Coll. 200:1:20; MS Coll. 200:50:5).

This is further consolidated in Nathalie Cooke's biography of Atwood:

> During Atwood's time, Buckley taught a large undergraduate lecture class (of 350 to 500 students) on the bildungsroman, which covered "Dickens through to Joyce and Woolf". When I contacted Professor Buckley, I expected him to tell me that Atwood, as a graduate student, had been a teaching assistant for the course – which he did." (89)

In response to Cooke's questions as to whether he thought Atwood's work had been influenced by the genre, Buckley replied: "[Atwood] may, as you say, have drawn some notion of the scope of the "novel-of-development" from the Bildungsromane she taught, but of course, [she] has such a fertile imagination of her own that it is hard to say what themes or techniques she has borrowed" (89). Atwood's relationship with a scholar responsible for a seminal history of the Bildungsroman in English seems especially relevant given that she was to take up and challenge the tradition so productively in her own writing. And yet Atwood's characters, most particularly the authors and artists that inhabit her fiction, contribute something radically new to the Künstlerroman tradition, particularly in the way that the artist emerges as deeply involved in day-to-day living but is also capable of creating self-protecting personae that jostle for position within the text. This is far removed from the idea of the artist that Atwood encountered as a young woman, which was formed by the archetypal literary portrait of the artist, as is acknowledged in her critical investigation of historically-privileged images of the author in *Negotiating with the Dead.*

It might be argued that the tradition in English begins not with Dickens, as Buckley suggests, but with the narratives of development of eighteenth-century fiction, such as Henry Fielding's *Tom Jones* (1749) – already, of course, a brilliant exposure of the genre – and Laurence Sterne's *The Life and Opinions of Tristram Shandy* (1759–67). However, Atwood – in a Buckleyan tradition, one might suspect – draws particular attention to Dickens as providing a model of development and progress, which she confronts in her own work. It is, therefore, useful to consider the tradition of the Bildungsroman in English that pre-exists Atwood's writing as both her fiction and her criticism gesture towards the conventions of that genre in the nineteenth century.

The two early English Bildungsromane already mentioned, *Tom Jones* and *The Life and Opinions of Tristram Shandy,* are examples of coming-of-age narratives that predate the generic expectations of the German tradition. While, as discussed earlier, this tradition (as both a literary and a theoretical phenomenon) was most concerned with the organic development of the individual (which also served to complement the manifest destiny of the German nation), coming-of-age narratives in English in the eighteenth century provide an interesting contrast to this agenda. The farcical and picaresque adventures of *Tom Jones* are far removed from the serious endeavour that is coming of age in the German Romantic tradition, and *Tristram Shandy* presents an even more striking contrast, given that it is a narrative that is extraordinarily self-conscious about its own endeavour of "writing a life". The narrator mocks the idea of the cohesive development of both the subject and the narrative by attempting to begin at the moment of his conception and deliberately subverting any notion of plot consistency and continuity by means of outrageous digressions and uncharacteristic features such as diagrams, changing typefaces, and other devices. As a narrative that is acutely aware of its own artifice, it also draws attention to the complex processes that are involved in writing a life. As will be seen later in this chapter and book, this self-consciousness and self-referentiality has much in common with the paradoxes and predicaments of writing the self in postmodern fiction such as that of Margaret Atwood.

Nevertheless, Buckley himself contends that English tradition of the Bildungsroman begins with the Victorian novel, which was also one of the central focuses of Atwood's PhD thesis under Buckley's supervision. Charles Dickens, in particular, stands out as having a particular interest in "growing up Victorian" and played a crucial role in the popularization of the form in the Victorian period. Dickens's novels show signs of an enduring preoccupation with the idea of the self as narrative that find resonance with Atwood. Atwood's article "Great Unexpectations" – a commentary on the dilemmas of being an aspiring woman writer in Canada in the 1960s – may seem an explicit subversion of Dickens, but her fiction, in fact, shows a Dickensian interest in the complexities and challenges of writing a life. *Great Expectations* (1861) constitutes a political interrogation of class privilege and the effects of capital and capitalism on the social construction of the self, but it is also very much interested in the relationship between language and identity; the tension between Pip, the mature experienced narrator and Pip the narrated subject is particularly compelling in this respect.

Another hugely important meta-narrative which emphatically records this kind of challenge – and further illustrates how the Bildungsroman is both taken up and subverted in English – is *David Copperfield* (1849–50). Again the novel immediately foregrounds how narrative does not simply record biography or history but is capable of rewriting it: "Whether I shall turn out to be the hero of my own life, or whether that station will be held by anybody else, these pages must show" (49). What is striking about these lines is the fact that there is no guarantee that the ensuing narrative will make the narrator the "hero" of his own life. Thus, the novel is poised between "real life" and life as narrative, and the first paragraph draws further attention to this issue with the words: "To begin my life with the beginning of my life". The double meaning, indeed the duplicity, of the word "life" becomes, for Charles Dickens (and for David Copperfield – of course a version of Charles Dickens himself), a source of anxiety about the possibility of successfully narrating lived experience. This is not the place for an extended reading of Dickens's novels, but these brief comments certainly suggest the complexity of the most famous English exponent of the Bildungsroman with whom Atwood engages. Thus, while in her play on *Great Expectations* in "Great Unexpectations" Atwood seems to assert herself against the Dickensian tradition of writing a life, in fact, as will become apparent, the acute awareness that her work displays of the possibility for subversive strategies in writing a life is not so far removed from Dickens's own preoccupations.

However, there is another feature of the Bildungsroman in English that is crucial to Atwood's work. Jerome H. Buckley, in *Season of Youth*, identifies one of the most important, and unifying, concerns of the Bildungsroman in English: the hero as artist. He notes that "its hero, more often than not, emerges as an artist of sorts, a prose writer like David Copperfield or Ernest Pontifex, a poet like Stephen Dedalus, an artisan and aspiring intellectual like Hardy's Jude, a painter like Lawrence's Paul Morel or Maugham's Philip Carey" (13). Of these examples, Joyce's Stephen Dedalus in *A Portrait of the Artist as a Young Man* (1916) is the most important influence on Atwood's writing. This is seen in a comic but revealing engagement with the "portrait of the artist" archetype in a cartoon strip, "Portrait of the Artist as a Young Cipher", that the young Atwood drew for one of the University of Toronto's student newspapers. A self-effacing recollection of the precocity (and pretentiousness) of the aspiring writer, it takes no prisoners in tackling the mystique of the artist prescribed by the Stephen Dedalus archetype (MS Coll. 335:20:1). Furthermore, as will be examined in detail in the next chapter on the Canadian literary imagination in the 1970s, in the introduction to *Survival: A Thematic Guide to Canadian Literature* (1972), Atwood invokes a Joycean model in thinking about Canada's need to assert a cohesive national identity and reformulates in Canadian terms Stephen Dedalus's aspiration "to forge in the smithy of my soul the uncreated conscience of my race" (*Portrait*

276). It is easy to see why *A Portrait of the Artist as a Young Man* and Joyce as an icon of a new phase in Irish writing in English would have held such appeal for Atwood. For Atwood, as a young writer concerned with breaking free from past and present colonial influences and forging a distinct Canadian literary tradition in English, Joyce provides a powerful postcolonial role model. At the same time, in *Negotiating with the Dead: A Writer on Writing*, Atwood draws attention to how "James Joyce's well-known triple-barreled slogan, 'silence, exile, and cunning,' had a distinct resonance for aspiring Canadian writers" (68) at that time in Canadian cultural history. Also, as will be seen in later chapters, her fiction is especially interested in the plight of the female artist and responds to the *Portrait* archetype in a way that reveals alternative possibilities for the female author and artist.

Women in the Bildungsroman, Women Writing the Bildungsroman

Thus far we have a thumbnail sketch of a male, indeed distinctly masculine, genre. But Atwood responds not only to a male tradition of writing, but to an equally vibrant – although often oppositional – female tradition of the Bildungsroman. This necessitates a brief consideration of the German tradition, as well as a more extended examination of the English precedents, in terms of women in, and women writing, the Bildungsroman. In *The German Bildungsroman*, Todd Kontje poses a potentially troubling question regarding the usefulness of seeking out the female Bildungsroman: "given the incessant terminological debates surrounding the Bildungsroman and its implication in the German ideology, why would one want to rediscover forgotten texts by women only to associate them with this dubious tradition?" (104). Considering the apparently unbridgeable chasm between the theoretical ideal and literary reality that has been a feature of the genre since its eighteenth-century infancy, the idea of trying to assimilate the problem of gender into the equation could seem like a further complication in an already unworkable situation. It is, however, because, rather than in spite of, this perversity that the female Bildungsroman has such an interesting and potentially revealing relationship with the established literary tradition. More than any other narrative of development, it dismantles a genre trammelled by an exclusively patriarchal heritage and becomes the means of its perpetuation in a new context.

Before looking in detail at the recent history of, and critical debates surrounding, the female Bildungsroman in the second half of the twentieth century, it is helpful first to consider briefly the nineteenth-century literary models of female development central to the evolution of the Bildungsroman in English. Annis Pratt and Barbara White explore how novels of development written in English in the eighteenth and early nineteenth century tend to offer models for "growing down" (14) rather than for successful "coming of age". Furthermore, in the introduction to *The Voyage In: Fictions of Female Development*, Abel, Hirsch, and Langland reveal how Jerome Buckley's definition of the key constituents of the Victorian

Bildungsroman collapses when applied to the female Bildungsroman (8). Perhaps the most incisive assessment of the female Bildungsroman in the nineteenth century is Esther Kleinbord Labovitz's assertion that in such novels female potential and aspirations are foiled by "ambivalent endings" (6).

Many self-improving heroines can be found in nineteenth-century fiction. Fanny Price in Jane Austen's *Mansfield Park* (1814), Elizabeth-Jane Henchard in Hardy's *The Mayor of Casterbridge* (1886), Dorothea Brooke in George Eliot's *Middlemarch* (1871–72) and Maggie Tulliver in Eliot's *The Mill on the Floss* (1860) are all prime examples of a typical pattern of female aspiration and development in this period. In Victorian literature, Mary Barton in Mrs Gaskell's eponymous novel (1848) and Tess in Hardy's *Tess of the D'Urbervilles* (1891) stand out as characters whose development and self-realization is at every turn influenced by the pressures and constraints of Victorian social and political realities. All of these characters also suffer the compromise of "ambivalent endings" to some degree. The work of the Brontë sisters is crucial here, most eminently Charlotte Brontë's *Jane Eyre* (1847). This text, in particular, has a special relationship with Atwood's work, as will become clear later. *Jane Eyre* has been powerfully and aptly read as a feminist text, indeed has an iconic place in women's literary history, and has been a major source of feminist inspiration and debate. In particular, it represents the apotheosis of the nineteenth-century interest in female narratives of self-realization. Its relevance to Atwood's work – especially, for example, *Lady Oracle* – will become apparent in later chapters. More generally, *Jane Eyre* has held an important position in the feminist imagination of the last 30 years, and one of the most influential books of feminist literary criticism – Gilbert and Gubar's *The Madwoman in the Attic* – takes its title from a famous crux in *Jane Eyre*, and summarizes the novel as:

> a story of enclosure and escape, a distinctively female Bildungsroman in which the problems encountered by the protagonist as she struggles from the imprisonment of her childhood toward an almost unthinkable goal of mature freedom are symptomatic of difficulties Everywoman in a patriarchal society must meet and overcome: oppression (at Gateshead), starvation (at Lowood), madness (at Thornfield), and coldness (at Marsh End). (339)

What is especially curious about Gilbert and Gubar's summary is that, in boiling down the key feminist elements of *Jane Eyre*, they announce the novel to be a female Bildungsroman. Thus in asserting the importance of *Jane Eyre* to the feminist imagination, they fix their manifesto to a genre that, in spite of its dubious history, remains powerfully associated with a new understanding of how women arrive at maturity and come to own their lives.

While Jane's exclamation in the final pages "Reader, I married him" remains an unresolved controversy – it can be read as a capitulation to heterosexual romance mythologies or an announcement of a union based on autonomy – the novel is also invested with a realistic understanding of female need for agency and assertiveness that makes Gilbert and Gubar's invocation of the Bildungsroman all the more appropriate: Jane only returns to Rochester after she achieves personal independence, after living independently as a school teacher, and after Jane Eyre becomes Jane the Heiress, having realized her connection to the Rivers family. When she agrees to marry Rochester, she is seemingly no longer alone in the world and has acquired an unprecedented level of confidence and self-knowledge.

The unrivalled status of *Jane Eyre* in the woman-centred or feminist imagination may be seen in the way that women writers, most famously Jean Rhys in *Wide Sargasso Sea* (1966), have engaged with the text. Rhys presents the narrative of Bertha Mason as a means of answering narrative elisions in the original novel, but other engagements, such as Margaret Drabble's *The Waterfall* (1969), have been more discreetly conceived. As will be seen in later chapters, Atwood's writing, in particular the gothic parody of *Lady Oracle* – but also the complex narratives of female progress throughout her oeuvre – takes up the challenges presented by *Jane Eyre* in particularly fertile and interesting ways.

As we have already seen, a close relative of the Bildungsroman is the Künstlerroman, or novel of the development of an artist, and while the Stephen Dedalus type is well established in literature in English, his female counterpart is notable for her absence. As with the female Bildungsroman, the novel of development of the female artist in the nineteenth century is riddled with pitfalls that seem to deem the downfall of the protagonist inevitable. In the mid-nineteenth century Elizabeth Barrett's Browning's *Aurora Leigh* (1856) spent much time articulating the "anxiety of female authorship" as defined by Gilbert and Gubar (49), while towards the end of the century these anxieties were expressed in fiction in the work of Charlotte Perkins Gilman and Kate Chopin's "The Awakening" (1899). In "The Awakening", Edna Pontellier's progress is relayed in terms of her aspiration and development as an artist. The indictment of capitalist patriarchy in this text exposes how the constraints under which she lives are impediments to both her personal and artistic growth. In "The Awakening" the mantra "the artist must possess the courageous soul that dares and defies" (176) is analogous to Edna's desire to "swim far out, where no woman had swum before" (73).

Virginia Woolf's work is crucial in relation to the female Bildungsroman, not least in its own development from conventionality to something more radical. Her first novel, *The Voyage Out* (1915) – an archetypal female Bildungsroman – ends with the sacrifice of the heroine to Victorian convention. However, her later critical writings, most famously *A Room of One's Own* (1929), and her portrayal of the female artist in *To the Lighthouse* (1927), provide a powerful counterpoint to the Stephen Dedalus figure. Dedalus's coming of age, which is based on a series of epiphanies and separations from family, nation, and religion, is undercut by Woolf, whose narratives specifically refuse such progressive development. For Dedalus, art is a religious vocation that demands the kind of detachment from life that feminist thinkers have found to be incompatible with the realities of life for the female artist. In *To the Lighthouse*, however, there is a synchronicity between life and art – for example, in the way that Lily finds a domestic muse in the figure of Mrs Ramsay.

This synchronicity has more than an aesthetic function and is often described as being borne out of necessity or duty in descriptions of the woman writer at work; this can be observed in accounts of another important literary foremother – Charlotte Brontë. Elizabeth Gaskell's description of Charlotte Brontë at work in the kitchen at Haworth, assisting an elderly servant whose fading sight made her break from her writing to carry out the most routine of domestic tasks, is especially evocative of this inventive juggling of creative and domestic enterprise:

> Miss Brontë was too dainty a housekeeper to put up with this; yet she could not bear to hurt the faithful old servant, by bidding the younger maiden go over the potatoes again, and so reminding Tabby that her work was less effectual than formerly. Accordingly she would steal into the kitchen and quietly carry off the bowl of vegetables, without Tabby's being aware, and breaking off in the full flow of interest and inspiration in her writing, carefully cut out the specks in the potatoes, and noiselessly carry them back to their place. This little proceeding may show how orderly and fully she accomplished her duties, even at those times when the "possession" was upon her. (233–4)

Atwood's work does not lose sight of the complicated relationship between art and domesticity in novels such as *Lady Oracle* and *Cat's Eye*.

The notion that "the woman artist is a missing character in fiction" (Spencer 247), examined in further detail in Linda Huf's *A Portrait of the Artist as a Young Woman* (5), is one that Atwood powerfully contradicts, although more often than not Atwood's women artists adopt a camouflage or maintain a carefully chosen mask. Atwood's "portrait of the artist" contributes something new to the image of the female artist in fiction, and reveals more radical strategies for the female artist's survival; these issues will be discussed in the later stages of the book and will pay particular attention to how Atwood's artists are far removed from the aggrandized image of the male artist described in classic studies such as Maurice Beebe's *Ivory Towers and Sacred Founts: The Artist as Hero in Fiction from Goethe to Joyce* (1964).

A number of feminist critics such as Esther Kleinbord Labovitz and Rita Felski see the emergence of the female Bildungsroman as directly tied to women's new-found public and political agency in the twentieth century and particularly in the 1970s and 1980s. As early as 1972, Ellen Morgan identified the female Bildungsroman as a platform for female empowerment and development:

> Thus the female Bildungsroman appears to be becoming the most salient form for literature influenced by neo-feminism. The novel of apprenticeship is admirably suited to express the emergence of women from cultural conditioning into struggle with institutional forces, their progress toward the goal of full

> personhood, and the effort to restructure their lives and society according to their own vision of meaning and right living. (185)

From this highly politicized version of female *Bildung*, more recent studies of the genre have focused less on the female Bildungsroman as a straightforward appropriation of the traditional form and have placed greater emphasis on how contemporary female Bildungsromane challenge and renegotiate the traditional paradigm. One of the major complications of this approach to the female Bildungsroman does not relate to gender but to the attack on the humanist ideal of authentic selfhood. Abel, Hirsch, and Langland agree in their discussion of writing from this period that "Although the primary assumption underlying the *Bildungsroman* – the evolution of a coherent self – has come under attack in modernist and avant-garde fiction, this assumption remains cogent for women writers who now for the first time find themselves in a world increasingly responsive to their needs" (13). Rita Felski takes up this argument in favour of the possibilities of organic development valorized in the classic Bildungsroman in her important essay "The Novel of Self-Discovery: A Necessary Fiction?" in insisting that the question "who writes?" although no longer fashionable in current critical thinking is one that should not be casually overlooked in discussions of women's writing (145).

Thus, in keeping with some of the conclusions drawn previously, the female Bildungsroman seems to work both within and against postmodern trends. On the one hand, the idea of the cohesive self moving towards clarity and a secure place in the world continues to be (as Martin Swales identifies) the "sustaining presence" of the genre and, in this respect, the genre seems to contradict the main tenets of postmodernism. On the other hand, it might be argued, the idea of the cohesive self is intimated only to be rendered in a new form removed from the measured, linear development propounded in the early Bildungsroman and related theory. This is certainly the dynamic at work in Atwood's fiction, which seems to offer a point of compromise whereby the unquestioning investment in the conventional ideology of the genre is avoided and yet the Bildungsroman is not abandoned altogether.

In spite of various attacks on the Bildungsroman as a literary concept, either explicitly or implicitly, a number of contemporary women authors have returned to the traditional premise of the genre. Determining inflections in these novels include, as previously suggested, gender, age, class, ethnicity, and nationality. From novels of childhood and adolescence to chronicles of transformation in middle age such as Doris Lessing's *The Summer Before the Dark* (1973), the temporal boundaries of the female Bildungsroman are fluid. They can, however, usually be drawn along moments of crisis so that change is prompted by turning points, such as the onset of puberty, imminent marriage, or the prospect of children leaving home. The structure of the novels themselves varies with the possibility of dual *Bildung*, as in the novels of Margaret Drabble and A.S. Byatt, which frequently depict the fraught relationship of two sisters, whose *Bildungsweg*, or course of progress, collides. This is the case in Drabble's *A Summer Bird-Cage* and, to a lesser degree, Byatt's *The Game*. The *Bildung* of an individual may also emerge as an indicator of social change, as in the novels of Edna O'Brien in which the female protagonist's struggle against and eventual escape from the suffocating parochialism of Ireland in the 1950s can be read as heralding the social and cultural change of the decades that followed.

Perhaps most noticeable is the centrality of ethnicity to the female Bildungsroman, particularly in North American literature. It would seem that in spite of the ideological limitations foregrounded by many critics, the Bildungsroman is destined to remain a medium of expression for new generations of emerging voices, whether in relation to gender and sexuality or to ethnicity and race. Its movement outward in increasing concentric circles from its German origins has made it a truly supranational genre. This book will argue that Atwood's differences from this recent groundswell in the female genre are as important as her similarities, and yet a brief description of this phenomenon will serve to place Atwood in the context of the genre revitalized far in time and place from its origins.

Common to all studies of the multicultural Bildungsroman, whether in the context of Commonwealth, African-Caribbean, Asian, or African-American literatures, is the recognition that, although the Bildungsroman is "a literary form that has outlived its usefulness and become virtually defunct in the European context", it has assumed "a new and viable identity overseas" (Butcher 261). This is something that is at the centre of Martin Japtok's comparative reading of the genre in *Growing Up Ethnic: Nationalism and the Bildungsroman in African American and Jewish American Fiction* (2005), in which he emphasizes the communal dimension of the genre in its new contexts: "What may be called the ethnic Bildungsroman consists, then, of a development away from the more exclusively personality-oriented plot of the traditional Bildungsroman and towards a more political and social vision" (27). Bonnie Hoover Braendlin takes up this theme in her article "Bildung in Ethnic Women Writers", as does Geta LeSeur in her study *Ten is the Age of Darkness: The Black Bildungsroman* (1995). For LeSeur, the regeneration of the Bildungsroman by African-American and Caribbean writers is indicative of how "The shift of focus from the English form is symptomatic of a more general shift in the use of the form among postcolonial writers, particularly Black writers of the United States and the British Caribbean, to enunciate their special condition" (30). As will be considered in the Postscript to this book, the Bildungsroman – partly as a result of the influence of Atwood's work – is also an important literary tool in the forging of Canadian identity, particularly in relation to Native Canadian and immigrant Canadian fiction. For Braendlin, the female Bildungsroman in American literature is a vital mode of expression for marginalized voices:

> it expresses their struggle for individuation and a part in the American dream, which society simultaneously proffers and denies to them. This new *Bildungsroman* asserts an identity defined by the outsiders themselves or by their own cultures, not by the patriarchal Anglo-American power structure; it

> evinces a revaluation, a transvaluation of traditional *Bildung* by new standards and perspectives. (75)

Criticism concerning the multicultural female Bildungsroman, in line with revisions of feminist theory, is suspicious of casual assumptions about "female experience". In her study of two of the most important recent practitioners of the female Bildungsroman – Maxine Hong Kingston and Toni Morrison – Pin-chia Feng suggests that Abel, Hirsch, and Langland's oft-cited, groundbreaking collection of essays on the genre is based on an exclusively Eurocentric foundation (13). Other Chinese-American and African-American writers who have contributed to the expansion of the genre and have been the focus of more recent studies of the female Bildungsroman include Amy Tan and Alice Walker, while the Chicana writer Sandra Cisneros's *The House on Mango Street* (1989) can also be studied in this context. Maxine Hong Kingston's *The Woman Warrior* (1977) and Amy Tan's *The Joy Luck Club* (1989) explore complex issues of cultural identity as the young women depicted in these fictions try to forge a sense of self that reconciles their ethnic origins with their present lives in America. Toni Morrison's *Sula* is an especially interesting example of a Bildungsroman in which the identities of the main characters Nel and Sula merge. Nel's newfound sense of self, "'I'm me,' she whispered. 'Me.'" (28), which emerges early on in the novel, is at every turn affected by and bound up in her intimate relationship with Sula. While more recent developments in this vein, such as Gish Jen's *Who's Irish?* (1999), mark a new departure in explorations of multicultural diversity in America and highlight the chasm between the expectations and values of first and second generation Chinese-Americans, many of the previously mentioned novels played an important role in expressing the frustrations and fears of the earlier immigrant experience.

Jamaica Kincaid's *Annie John* (1985) and *Lucy* (1990) explore the vicissitudes of life for a young woman growing up in, and later self-exiled from, Antigua and at the same time interrogate the postcolonial legacy of the island. This doubling of individual and collective progress can also be found in other Commonwealth fiction such as Doris Lessing's *Martha Quest* (1964). This novel centres on the development of its eponymous protagonist, but also explores the tensions in a colonial community in Africa. In the same tradition, Nadine Gordimer's *Burger's Daughter* (1979) explores coming of age under apartheid in South Africa – Rosa Burger's early life is punctuated by her left-wing parents' arrest, trial and imprisonment as her own maturation is inextricably bound up in the traumatic events unfolding in her country.[1]

In addition to emphasizing the necessity of an alternative approach to reading the multicultural female Bildungsroman (one which avoids the imposition

---

[1] For a bibliography of the female Bildungsroman, please see Laura Fuderer's *The Female Bildungsroman in English: An Annotated Bibliography of Criticism* (1990), which provides an alternative list of novels that might be read as female Bildungsromane and offers a comprehensive survey of the critical reception of the genre.

of limited critical assumptions) Pin-chia Feng insists on an open, expansive understanding of the multicultural female Bildungsroman as "any writing by an ethnic woman about the identity formation of an ethnic woman, whether fictional or autobiographical in form" (15). Thus, regardless of the protests outlined earlier in the chapter, the only possible definition of the contemporary Bildungsroman is one that is inclusive of all narratives of formation that are based on biography and history. Insisting on a definition based on Enlightenment philosophy, or rejecting the genre out of hand because of the burden of its history, leaves no room for the current inflections that characterize the genre and the significance attributed to it by feminist critics. Such a protest is in fact futile because the genie has, generically speaking, clearly escaped from the bottle.

While the relationship of women to the eighteenth-century Bildungsroman – particularly in Germany itself – is, unsurprisingly, peripheral, the genre has re-emerged in the second half of the twentieth century as giving expression to new literary voices in Germany. These voices provide an interesting and useful counterpoint to how Atwood takes up the genre in her own national context. To return briefly to the moment of the genre's conception, it quickly becomes clear that women writers in eighteenth-century Germany were largely ignored in the process of canon formation; the Bildungsroman, both as an emblem of Germany's development towards a unified nation, and as a literary genre in its own right, was defined as an essentially masculine concern. As highlighted by Todd Kontje: "if *Bildung* and the *Bildungsroman* were for men only, then the construction of a national literature was also essentially, and not accidentally, masculinist. … The German fatherland was just that: a nation of patriarchs, a land of fathers, where women – at least in theory – played a subordinate, silent, private role" (*Women, the Novel and the German Nation* 10). A recent collection of essays, *A History of Women's Writing in Germany, Austria and Switzerland*, edited by Jo Catling, although it does not offer an extended consideration of the Bildungsroman, touches on many of its co-ordinates in meaningful ways. Lesley Sharpe explains that while literacy amongst women improved dramatically in the course of the eighteenth century, the literature being produced reinforced problematic stereotypes such as the *Schöne Seele* or the "beautiful soul" as featured in *Wilhelm Meister's Apprenticeship* (48). In *The Voyage In*, Marianne Hirsch takes up this theme and examines in detail the story of female development, "Confessions of a Beautiful Soul", interpolated into the sixth book of *Wilhelm Meister's Apprenticeship*. The role of women in the Goethean model of the Bildungsroman seems to confine them to acting as a foil to the affirmative development of the young hero. Alternatively, female characters are presented as catalysts in, or potential obstacles to, the hero's development. A spectrum of types, from Natalie, a paragon of feminine virtue to Mariane, the fallen woman, and the feckless Philine, described by Laertes as "the real Eve, the progenitrix of the whole female race. They're all like her, though they won't admit it" (55) may be identified in *Wilhelm Meister*. Women in *Wilhelm Meister* are clearly accessories to the central preoccupation with the hero's development. They exist as hinges in the plot or as a convenient conduit for the hero's gradual self-realization. Even if by the end of the century, attitudes towards women and education were beginning to change, there seemed little possibility of expanding the German literary tradition to include women: "Whereas the male hero goes into the world as a kind of representative figure and grows to maturity and insight through experience, the openness to change and receptivity to life that are the preconditions of the maturing process in men are presented as problematic and even hazardous for women" (Sharpe 65).

More recently the female Bildungsroman in German has come to prominence in rather unlikely and regrettable circumstances. Under National Socialism, the genre was effectively revamped with a new profile of Germany's female population in mind:

> we meet heroines who are deeply rooted in a German landscape and who understand their roles in terms of an essential "Muttersein der Seele" (motherhood of the soul). In an often single-handed struggle against war, famine, and the invasion of "red-hordes" these heroines protect the purity of their race against all kinds of opposition from outsiders, people of "different race" or "different ideas". (Cardinal 148)

Subsequent to this troubling misappropriation of female Bildung, Christa Wolf, in line with her GDR contemporaries, drew on the Bildungsroman as a literary model to express a growing disillusionment with socialism. *The Quest for Christa T* (1968) is centrally preoccupied with the "*long and never-ending journey toward oneself.* The difficulty of saying 'I'" (174, italics in original). This "difficulty" was given similar expression in Virginia Woolf's landmark essay *A Room of One's Own*, where the authoritative first-person voice of the rational, cohesive male subject and author looms like a shadow across the page: "One began to be tired of 'I'. Not but what this 'I' was a most respectable 'I'; honest and logical; as hard as a nut, and polished for centuries by good teaching and good feeding" (115). The narrator of *The Quest for Christa T* overcomes this difficulty and the formidable expression of "I" described by Woolf, by reconstructing the life of Christa T through alternative sources: manuscripts, letters, diaries, and the even less reliable sources of her own memories of (and speculations about) her friend's life. Her representation of Christa T centres on Christa's private disillusionment in the face of the disappointing and sometimes devastating realities that lurk behind the utopian possibilities of socialism.

More recently still, it would seem that quest or odyssey has emerged as an important medium of expression for emerging national identities amongst German women writers. In the case of Turkish-German women writers, the exploration of an identity suspended between the "'Orient' and the Occident" (Kuhn 247), frequently figures the navigation of a path to self-discovery that does not attempt naïvely to reconcile juxtaposed cultural identities but serves to explore the possibilities of plural identity in a modern German context. There are clear indications that these novels – interested as they are in progress towards self-determination – may be considered as representing a new kind of Bildungsroman.

One of the novels mentioned by Anna Kuhn in her discussion of recent transitional developments in contemporary women's writing in German, and a powerful example of a Turkish-German woman writer drawing on the Bildungsroman as model for the expression of identity, is Emine Sevgi Özdamar's semi-autobiographical novel *Die Brücke vom Goldenen Horn* [*The Bridge of the Golden Horn*] (1998). Set in Berlin and Istanbul in the politically volatile climate of the late 1960s, the novel filters the main character's isolation and disorientation through issues of language and translation. In her early days as a *Gastarbeiterin*, in her jobs as a factory worker in Berlin, the protagonist's only opportunity to learn German is through the newspaper titles she learns off by heart on her way to and from work at the factory. The novel plays with her Turkish pronunciation of words so that "Wohnheim" [residence] becomes and remains "Wonaym" throughout the text. She arrives in Berlin – in distinctly Goethean fashion – carrying the complete works of Shakespeare and with ambitions to save money from her work in the factory to train to become an actress in German theatre (the echoes of Wilhelm Meister's passion for theatre are very telling). What follows is an education in literature (the director of the Turkish women's residence in which she lives gives her Wilde, Joyce, and Chekhov to read), and a political education directed by the young, left-wing student activists that she meets in Berlin. While the character's political consciousness is raised by her contact with the Berlin student movement, she remains wary of Europe's relationship to her homeland, as suggested in her conclusion: "Europa war ein Stock, mit dem man sich gegenseitig die Köpfe einschlug. 'Wir sind zu sehr à la Turca', sagten die Türken und wussten nicht, dass selbst dieser Ausdruck aus Europa kam" ["Europe was a stick we used to beat ourselves with. 'We're too à la Turca' say the Turks and don't know that this expression came from Europe"] (250).

Herta Müller's *Reisende auf einem Bein* [*Travelling on One Leg*] (1989) is another striking example of the contemporary German female Bildungsroman. It tells the story of a German-Romanian woman's escape from Ceaucescu's Romania and arrival in West Germany. Central to the novel are evocations of the poverty and disappointment that Irene encounters in Berlin and her frustration in the face of German administration and bureaucracy as she awaits asylum. As a member of Romania's German minority, the character feels lost to what she repeatedly describes as "das andere Land" [the other land]. Her only remaining connection with her home place takes the form of letters from her friend Dana, which arrive censored by Ceaucescu's secret police. Bound up with the failure of her romance with the German man who persuaded her to come to Germany is her feeling of disorientation and displacement in the country which, as an ethnic German, she should have been able to consider home.

While detractors of the female Bildungsroman are sceptical about the apparent dissemination of the genre, John H. Smith finds the notion a "contradiction in terms" for other reasons:

> Much women's literature addresses, in fact, the inappropriateness of male developmental models for women in the patriarchy. … My tendency for now, however, would be to reserve the term *Bildungsroman* for those works that illustrate narratively the cultivation and discontent of *Bildung* understood as the engendering of the male subject in the modern patriarchal Symbolic order. (221)

However, as addressed earlier, identifying the inappropriateness of these models does not necessarily imply that disconnection is the only means of responding to this incongruity: "inappropriateness" often emerges positively in the female Bildungsroman in terms of subtle and sophisticated textual and narrative ploys.

If we accept the possibility of the female Bildungsroman – as I have argued we certainly should – the next stage in attempting to formulate any kind of working definition of the genre involves assessing some of the more prevalent genre-based criticism that has emerged over the last 30 years. As with the male Bildungsroman, the female Bildungsroman both overlaps and competes with a number of closely related genres. The closest relative or potential substitute for the Bildungsroman, put forward by Susan Rosowski, is the "Novel of Awakening". Her idea of awakening is based on the notion of an "awakening to limitations": "Each presents a resolution only at great cost to the protagonist … each presents the dilemma of the individual who attempts to find value in a society that relegates to her only roles and values of the woman, ignoring her needs as a human being" (68). While Rosowski establishes the "Novel of Awakening" as a counterpart to the female Bildungsroman, as mentioned previously Rita Felski considers them two different strands of the more general Novel of Self-Discovery. It might be more useful to think of the "awakening" epiphany described by Rosowski as one element of the Bildungsroman: limitations must be acknowledged before they can be overcome. This is certainly the case in Doris Lessing's *The Summer Before the Dark* (1973) and Joan Barfoot's *Gaining Ground* (1978); in both novels, the protagonist reaches a crisis point and recognizes and contests various patriarchal constraints to the way she lives. In *Beyond Feminist Aesthetics: Feminist Literature and Social Change*, Felski identifies these narrative types as some of the most important modes for women's writing in the late twentieth century. Quest and odyssey are at the heart of these forms, as individual narratives attempt to articulate collective experience. These texts played an important role in foregrounding the particularity of individual women's experience while attempting to retain some collective resonance.

In *Beyond Feminist Aesthetics*, Felski briefly charts the progression in literature from woman's marginalization and subjugation in the eighteenth century (marriage or death seeming to be the only possibilities available to her) through to the smothered potential portrayed in the nineteenth-century novel (133). She goes on to address the comparatively subversive dimensions of the contemporary female Bildungsroman. The more important aspects of the genre are, for Felski, its refusal of the heterosexual romance plot and its ability to critique contemporary society without sacrificing the female protagonist. Felski, however, is conscious that the survival of the protagonist does not necessarily mark harmonious closure in the novel but rather signifies a new beginning: "The heroine's new self-knowledge creates a basis for future negotiation between the subject and society, the outcome of which is projected beyond the bounds of the text" (133). As will later be examined, this projection of a possible outcome beyond the ending of the text is a familiar feature of Atwood's novels.

In focusing on what Felski identifies as the "feminist Bildungsroman", she makes considerable headway towards articulating the generic expectations of the woman-centred Bildungsroman:

> For my present purposes, the Bildungsroman can be construed as *biographical*, assuming the existence of a coherent individual identity which constitutes the focal point of the narrative; *dialectical*, defining identity as the result of a complex interplay between psychological and social forces; *historical*, depicting identity formation as a temporal process which is represented by means of a linear and chronological narrative; and *teleological*, organizing textual signification in relation to the projected goal of the protagonist's access to self-knowledge, which will in practice be realized to a greater or lesser degree. (*Beyond Feminist Aesthetics* 135)

In an earlier essay, "The Novel of Self-Discovery: A Necessary Fiction?", she emphasizes the act of necessary separation that the female Bildungsroman shares with the male tradition. This separation or negation at the beginning of the novel marks the beginning of the protagonist's personal odyssey, which is thereafter characterized by outward movement into uncharted social territory ("The Novel of Self-Discovery" 132). Thus compared to the idea of the Novel of Awakening, which involves "a voyage inward rather than outward" (*Beyond Feminist Aesthetics* 141), the female Bildungsroman relies largely on a gradual process of self-realization through interaction and engagement with social and cultural paradigms. That said, however, the two very often overlap as the female *Bildungsweg* is frequently marked by moments of clarity that direct the course of the protagonist's development and engagement with their environment. While Felski's model based on biography, history, and teleology provides a useful starting point, what has to be included in the equation is the possibility of inversions and subversions of this model.

Feminist Contexts

As has become apparent, the challenge of locating the female Bildungsroman in relation to the masculine tradition of the Bildungsroman tradition is both awkward and intriguing: awkward, because at first it seems that the minefield of theoretical and ideological issues presented by the seminal versions of the genre is rendered doubly difficult to navigate by the idea of a female Bildungsroman, but intriguing in the way that it serves as an example of the complex process of rehabilitating the gender politics of established generic forms. Moreover, feminism (perhaps a somewhat unlikely Knight in Shining Armour) has, unexpectedly, come to the rescue of the Bildungsroman and ensured its place as a critically interesting literary category in the second half of the twentieth century. In suggesting that the genre is subject to the same interrogation as all writing either identified as feminist or bearing particular relevance to female experience, this book is necessarily interested in a number of themes and debates that are central to feminist literature and criticism. These debates also prove to be central to Atwood's own work, both as writer of fiction and as feminist literary critic, and so it is fruitful to examine them here.

The idea of reclaiming or revitalizing the silent legacy of women's writing, so important to feminist criticism in the 1970s and 1980s, and the plotting of a strategy for recuperating a dispossessed tradition, is in itself fraught with possible problems. It might, for example, lead to a view of women's writing as an ancillary to the patriarchal literary canon, and therefore run the risk of fortifying the ideological structures that support the disenfranchisement of women writers. Yet, an important feature of the female Bildungsroman is its responsiveness to its patriarchal heritage. This responsiveness manifests itself in two ways: imitation and subversion. While the next section briefly considers examples of the female Bildungsroman that appropriate the conventions of the masculine genre, Atwood's fiction is subversive because it challenges the patriarchal hegemony inscribed in the tradition and plays with its main assumptions in a way that is creatively productive. For many feminist critics, particularly the French feminist tradition, such rehabilitative strategies are inadequate. However, Atwood's work suggests that subtle textual ploys are the most engaging and effective means of at once exposing embedded patriarchal assumptions and renegotiating the place of women in the genre.

The conflicting expectations of different feminist traditions regarding the points of confluence between literature and social reality are most apparent in the differences between French feminism and Anglo-American feminism. For Toril Moi, in her landmark survey *Sexual/Textual Politics*, early Anglo-American literary criticism runs the risk of overstating the authority of the author (70). She challenges the theories propounded by Annette Kolodny and Elaine Showalter in the early 1980s; Moi finds Kolodny's idea of feminist pluralism ill-defined (73) and refutes Showalter's investment in the potentially oppressive idea of literature as: "an excellent instrument of education: by reading 'great works' the student will become a finer human being. The great author is great because he (occasionally even she) has managed to convey an authentic vision of life; and the role of the reader or critic is to listen respectfully to the voice of the author as it is expressed in the text" (77). As explored previously, the idea of the Bildungsroman as educative (and thus as exerting an influence over the reader) can be dangerous, given its potential to reinforce the kind of tyrannous relationship between author and reader that Moi describes. However, Patrocinio P. Schweickart is similarly assertive in establishing the author as the determining force of the text: "Feminist criticism, we should remember is a mode of praxis. The point is not merely to interpret literature in various ways; the point is to *change the world.* We cannot afford to ignore the activity of reading, for it is here that literature is realized as praxis. Literature acts on the world by acting on its readers" (161, italics in original). As pointed out by Moi, the problem of such an approach is that it resurrects the humanist tradition of faithfully representing and communicating experience through writing. The early Bildungsroman adheres closely to this tradition and in some cases the female Bildungsroman also emulates aspects of this practice. Thus, examples of the female Bildungsroman from the late 1960s and 1970s seem at odds with developments in contemporary literature and theory that banish the author from the text. This chapter will later examine reasons why this phase of development seems to invest in, rather than to expose or undermine, the traditional paradigms of the genre. In fact, what is most interesting about Atwood's work is the way her early novels run contra to the trajectories of development common in the fiction of many of her contemporaries. Rather than adopting narrative structures that aggrandize the author and suggest a linear formula for self-development, she displays a striking consciousness of the complex processes involved in writing a life in fiction. I will return to this critique later in the chapter by addressing the idea of the self as narrative (an idea more recently expounded by critics such as Kim Worthington, who builds on postmodern theories in her investigation of the relationship between narrative and subjectivity) and the apparent disinclination of French feminism to contribute constructively to thinking about woman as a political agent capable of engaging with and exerting an influence over social processes and discourses.

This book, in part, seeks to chart a path through the possible approaches to the female Bildungsroman. This involves interrogating the various established responses to the genre with the objective of arriving at a new understanding of its internal structures and its place in the literary canon. The problem of what has been identified as the potential divisiveness of early feminist criticism is especially relevant in this regard. More specific to the female Bildungsroman is the question of why the genre has been appropriated and granted new currency in contexts apparently remote from its origins. Also at issue is the recurring query of what might be said to comprise or represent this new revitalized idea of *Bildung*.

"Re-vision – the act of looking back, of seeing with fresh eyes, of entering an old text from a new critical direction – is for women more than a chapter in cultural history: it is an act of survival" ("When We Dead Awaken: Writing as Re-Vision" 35). Adrienne Rich's idea of "writing as re-vision" serves as an appropriate point of departure for looking at possible strategies for reclaiming female literary history. This has involved rediscovering or addressing writers of every period in literary history who have been lost, ignored, or deliberately excluded in the process of canon formation. The process of excavating new meaning and creating a new female context for studying literary history is vital not just to the politics of feminism but to any attempt to categorize woman-centred literature. This dynamic bears some relevance to almost all research being carried out on women's writing. However, it is more than just a question of filling in or papering over the gaps in literary history: as important and as fascinating are the possibilities in contemporary women's writing for debating with the male-defined models enshrined in established literary traditions.

While the process of re-reading the past poses various challenges, a dual approach encompassing Ellen Moers's assertion that "the women's movement has brought back dead writers, created new writers, changed established writers, and summoned old writers to literature again" (preface xiii), along with a new awareness of the possibilities of re-working, expanding, and playing with tradition, formed the basis of feminist criticism and theory in the 1970s and 1980s. Some critical methodologies, such as the model of "Gynocriticism" put forward by Elaine Showalter in 1979, suggest that the objective of feminist criticism should be to isolate writing by women from the male-centred literary past.

A number of problems have been identified with this idea of a new, independent female tradition. First of all, in suggesting a purely self-referential order of women's writing, this position relies on an aggressively oppositional foundation which can only impede the development of critical approaches to women's writing and leaves little room for the exuberant pluralism advocated by Annette Kolodny in "Dancing Through the Minefield": "whatever our predilection, let us not generate from it a straightjacket that limits the scope of possible analysis. Rather, let us generate an ongoing dialogue of competing potential possibilities – among feminists and, as well, between feminists and nonfeminist critics" (19). It is this ongoing dialogue of "competing potential possibilities" that is both productive and fruitful when applied not just to criticism, but to the actual writing process. Kolodny's admission that "the many tools needed for our analysis will necessarily be largely inherited and only partly of our own making" (19) might be read, not as defeatist resignation or passive acceptance of the formidable shadows cast by patriarchal tradition, but as an acknowledgement of the potential released in the possibilities for re-working and rehabilitating that tradition. Kolodny appreciates the possibilities released in the tension between the established order and new emerging voices in female literature without resorting to unhelpful oppositional politics.

When pressed about the work of other critics, Atwood has always been very reluctant to commit herself to any kind of feminist or critical allegiance with the exception of an admission, in an interview in 1985, that she considered Annette Kolodny's work to be particularly insightful and progressive (*Conversations* 187). Certainly, Atwood's and Kolodny's work as critics seems compatible, particularly in their shared emphasis on feminist pluralism; for them, the celebration of dialogue between various discourses remains a more productive alternative to the potentially disempowering influence of more isolationist feminist politics. Ellen Moers's refreshing image of women's literature as "an undercurrent, rapid and powerful" (42) that modifies the established course of the mainstream expresses how literature by women can productively destabilize and challenge the literary status quo. Linda Anderson agrees that "Women cannot be simply added on to history – expanding the boundaries of historical knowledge empirically – without putting under pressure the conceptual limits that excluded them in the first place" ("The Re-Imagining of History in Contemporary Women's Fiction" 130). The manifestation and effect of this pressure exerted against such predetermined conceptual limits will be examined in considerable detail in relation to Atwood's fiction.

One of the greatest challenges in this process, and a key preoccupation of both Anglo-American and French feminist criticism, lies in locating the female tradition of writing in relation to the established literary canon and arriving at a new understanding of female difference in literature. Whilst in the 1970s, feminist criticism emphasized the oppression of women in collective terms, later decades showed a greater interest in the process of dispersal and the emergence of "feminisms" rather than a single, prescriptive, potentially divisive doctrine that insisted upon intractable definitions of feminist politics and literature. Mary Eagleton, in her introduction to her anthology *Feminist Literary Theory*, describes this new diversity and plurality in literature and criticism as a "dense network of charge and counter-charge, positionings and repositionings, alliances and oppositions" (218). What constitutes "female" and what comprises women's literature and feminist literature was interrogated in the 1980s, as critics became increasingly aware of the danger of appropriating the very prejudices and policies of exclusion that they were trying to challenge. The emergence of "feminisms" is often described in terms of fracturing, splitting, and dispersal, which seems to connote a dissemination of power and energy; in fact the very opposite was true as new dissenting voices emerged both in feminist criticism and literature by women.

This new consciousness of the feminist potential to alienate or overlook the experience of certain groups of women and replace the old dominant narratives with new equally homogenous discourses marked a turning point in the acknowledgement and development of coexisting traditions in women's literature and is resonant with Annette Kolodny's foregrounding of pluralism as a constructive model for feminist dialogue and debate. In sympathy with these developments, Bonnie Zimmerman and Adrienne Rich provided two of the earliest critiques of the heterosexism and failure of mainstream schools of feminism to include and appreciate the diversity of female experience in essays such as Zimmerman's "What has Never Been: An Overview of Lesbian Feminist Criticism" (Showalter 200–24). Hence, assumptions about the universality of female experience and the idea of feminist theory as equally relevant to all women were dramatically exposed as naïve and even dangerous. Far from being confined to ethnicity and sexuality, inflections of age, class, nationality, and history came to be considered equally important factors in the diversity of female experience. One of the most interesting aspects of the female Bildungsroman, as we have already seen, is the way that, more than any other genre, it seems to lend itself to this diversity. These various debates are important to the female Bildungsroman as it is almost unique in the way that it has appropriated and dismantled and yet in so many ways sustained the Bildungsroman beyond its native borders.

The complex intersection of gender and genre is informed by the blurring of generic boundaries characteristic of much contemporary literature, and the more recent identification of a number of genres, most particularly science fiction, romance, and utopia, that lend themselves particularly well to the expression of female experience and emancipation. This controversial confluence of genre and gender in literary studies is most dramatically manifest in the novel. From the earliest designation of the novel as a genre suitable for the woman writer on account of its being less public than, for example, drama, and more compatible with domestic pursuits, what Mary Eagleton somewhat ruefully describes as the "time on her hands" theory (137), the potentialities of genre from a gender perspective has been of particular interest to critics. While the latter is a rather gloomy example of this interrelationship, there exist more positive instances that foreground the possibilities of various genres as compatible with emerging female literary voices. K.K. Ruthven insists that the exploration of "'gender generics' leads away from names and forms and into those exclusionist practices which, in the past, have obliged women to avail themselves of genres deemed marginal to an androcentric culture, and therefore non-canonical in status" (117). Here, Ruthven implies that women writers have enjoyed most success when engaging with genres that might be considered less privileged in literary studies. This has been expressed in more optimistic terms by a number of feminist critics, as such genres appeal to a large, wide-ranging readership; the appropriation of popular, heretofore non-canonical, genres can be read as savvy literary practice rather then being seen purely in terms of marginalization and subordination (Cranny-Francis 2–3).

In *Feminist Fiction*, Anne Cranny-Francis investigates the challenge posed by this development to the established narratives defined by patriarchal meanings and interpretation: "In feminist fiction, including feminist genre fiction, feminist discourse operates to make visible within the text the practices by which conservative discourses such as sexism are seamlessly and invisibly stitched into the textual fabric, both into its structure and into its story, the weave and the print" (2). As will be explored in detail in Chapter 5, this stitching and unstitching is given very vivid expression in Atwood's *Alias Grace*. The engagement of women writers with historically male-centred genres frequently involves a delicate unpicking or unravelling of the naturalized ideological assumptions embedded in the history of the tradition. If genres such as science fiction have thus been established as being particularly open to female, and feminist, appropriation, what then of the Bildungsroman?

The Bildungsroman may at first seem like an unlikely candidate for this treatment. It might be expected to resist appropriation given the classical version's very specific German Enlightenment context and the genre's preoccupation with the trials and progress of the young hero. Yet from the late 1960s and indeed in more recent literature, it emerges as a medium sympathetic to new female literary voices. The reason for this may be traced to the larger concept of the self-discovery narrative, which gained new currency during these decades, as it emerged as an appropriate complement to the feminist politics of emancipation. As previously discussed, these narratives of self-discovery include autobiography, confessional literature, and the novel of awakening, as well as the female Bildungsroman.

Criticism on autobiography and the range of autobiographical sub-genres has come to recognize the process of writing a life as not just an act of recording or even recounting perceived truth but as a more creative process of crafting a narrative complete with its own subjective pitfalls. The extent to which these sub-genres overlap is indicated in Leigh Gilmore's introduction to *Autobiographics*. She cites Sandra Cisneros's *The House on Mango Street* (1989) and Jamaica Kincaid's *Annie John* (1983) as examples of how the boundaries between autobiography and fiction blur. The same novels identified by Gilmore as essentially autobiographical appear frequently in discussions of the Bildungsroman. However, this overlap is a natural aspect of genre as, far from being self-contained or existing in a vacuum, the contract between reader and author in terms of fulfilling or negating generic expectations is fluid and unpredictable.

Given that the Bildungsroman, possibly more than any other genre, foregrounds the processes and dynamics of human development, it is worthwhile considering the politics of identity explored in theory and criticism most relevant to the genre. Having earlier identified the feminist tradition within which I intend to examine the female Bildungsroman, it is useful to develop this context and pay particular attention to how it intersects with key concepts of identity, particularly those which are resonant with the representation of selfhood in Atwood's fiction.

Writing the Self: Paradoxes and Predicaments

In *Concepts of the Self*, Anthony Elliott appraises the current conceptions of the self in social and political theory: "Selfhood is flexible, fractured, fragmented, decentred and brittle: such a conception of individual identity is probably the central outlook in current social and political thought" (2). As a result of the impact of theorists such as Derrida, Barthes, Foucault, and Lacan, the idea of the self as a construct bound by ideological machinations beyond its control, as a martyr to language, has had an impact on all disciplines. Post-structuralism and postmodernism frequently deny human beings the luxury of an essential selfhood, preferring to adhere to the idea of self as the product of a confluence of cultural and social vocabularies. In *Feminine Fictions: Revisiting the Postmodern*, Patricia Waugh examines how this preoccupation with textuality has been defended by postmodernists as a liberation from a bourgeois valorization of an inherited philosophy of universal, transcendental selfhood (1–4). Waugh is wary of such generalization especially with regard to what she sees as postmodernism's troubled relationship with feminism. She concludes:

> At the moment when postmodernism is forging its identity through articulating the exhaustion of the existential belief in self-presence and self-fulfilment and through the dispersal of the universal subject of liberalism, *feminism* (ostensibly,

> at any rate) is assembling *its* cultural identity in what appears to be the opposite direction. During the 1960s, as Vonnegut waves a fond goodbye to character in fiction, women writers are beginning, *for the first time in history*, to construct an identity out of the recognition that women need to discover, and must fight for, a sense of unified selfhood, a rational, coherent, effective identity. (*Feminine Fictions* 6, italics in original)

This statement has clear ramifications for the female Bildungsroman. As a genre, it would seem to meet all of the requirements for the expression of female experience and offers seemingly easy access to the previously masculine privilege of self-containment and unity. According to Waugh, this coming of age of female agency inspired narratives that "emphasized the need to 'actualize' and 'strengthen' the self-in-the-world. In particular, it emphasized the ideological production of 'femininity' as the 'other' of patriarchy and the need, therefore, for women to become 'real' subjects and to discover their 'true' selves" (9). I will later consider a number of novels by American women writers that validate Waugh's assessment. This will serve as a valuable point of contrast to Atwood's early fiction, which, for reasons that will become apparent in the next chapter, offers a more sophisticated and progressive alternative to that just described. It is, however, understandable that, as Waugh puts it, "'unity' rather than dispersal seemed to offer more hope for political change" (13), but Atwood is up to something different – and, this book will argue, more interesting – than this political agenda.

In *Self as Narrative: Subjectivity and Community in Contemporary Fiction*, Kim Worthington agrees with Waugh's assessment of the appeal of humanist ideals of selfhood to feminist writers in an otherwise anti-humanist climate. In her introduction, she traces the history of approaches to identity and selfhood from the Aristotelian ideal, which situates human beings in a predetermined role in the hierarchy of the universe, to the Enlightenment proclamation of human beings as self-contained agents capable of changing the world around them, and the Romantic valorization of the uniqueness of the individual's self-expression (1–5). From this point, Worthington launches a refreshing critique of the reduction of the self to a subject trammelled by language in challenging: "What possibility is there of autonomy or individuality if human beings are understood to be forever subjected or violated by the linguistic medium in which they know themselves or are known by others? How can socially constructed subjects ever be the agents of social change?" (12). She suggests that the more depressing conclusions drawn by such theory cannot simply be counteracted by any naïve idea of the self as transcendent of social discourse; she is more convinced by the concept of subjectivity as capable of challenging or rewriting social order from within (13). Worthington's concern is not with reinstating the humanist concept of a universal, transcendental self but with exploring the possibilities for transgression and subversion within the limits of a socially-engaged notion of selfhood and subjectivity.

Most relevant to this project is the emphasis that this alternative approach places on the potential for transgression and subversion in literature. Works that self-consciously engage in playful narratives of selfhood are similarly capable of foregrounding the contrived nature of narrative conventions. This finds particular resonance with a longstanding critical tradition of reading Atwood's work. Eleonora Rao's work on identity in Atwood's fiction and Colin Nicholson's edited collection *Margaret Atwood: Writing and Subjectivity* represent some of the most frequently cited appreciations of the significance of multiplicity in Atwood's writing. Rao suggests in a discussion of the treatment of generic conventions in *Lady Oracle* (although, as an observation, it has much to say to other Atwood novels as well) that Atwood's work can be read as foregrounding "the liberating aspects of multiple, plural subjectivity" (67). Indeed, descriptors such as "plural", "multiple", and "protean" reappear regularly in discussions of Atwood's work. Worthington, like Rao, is conscious of how metafictions in contemporary literature contribute to the kind of textual liberation that Rao endorses (although examples can almost certainly be found in any period of modern literature) and exemplify how novels can be "intrusively aware of their own processes of fictionalization" (19), particularly in relation to fictional narratives of selfhood. My interest here is in how this critical consensus on the figuring of subjectivity in Atwood's work might be productively applied to reading Atwood's novels in relation to the Bildungsroman.

Worthington emphasizes the effectiveness of such ploys to women's literature in its bid to carve out a path in literary history that is not determined by patriarchal definition. However, as is stressed in *Self as Narrative*, the difficulty lies in developing transgressive strategies that avoid placing female voices outside of recognizable discourses to the point that they cease to be meaningful. She is especially wary of the French feminist insistence upon

> a language apart from patriarchal discourse, a language with the potential to create its own meanings. It is a language that will counterpose masculine linearity and "phallic" closure with the openness of fluidity, tactility, and libidinal impulse. But the call for women to invent their own language is surely utopian within the terms of a world-view in which linguistic predetermination prevails. (110–11)

For Worthington, the idea of "a language apart" threatens further disempowerment, as it only serves to further marginalize women and endorse a divisive oppositional literary practice. However inspiring the poetic theatre of well-known examples such as Cixous's "The Laugh of the Medusa", there is a general acknowledgement of the need to remain wary of its resistance to forging any relationship to social power structures. For many Atwood critics, the interests of women's writing are better served by the idea of a female language that challenges and exposes the naturalized, frequently male-centred structures valorized in the process of canon making. It is less about removal from dangerously oppressive power structures than about questioning the nature and assertion of such power from within – something that has become synonymous with Margaret Atwood's writing.

Margaret Atwood's Formative Years in Context (1) – Piercy, Jong, and French: An Alternative Feminist Tradition

This chapter has sought to introduce the literary and critical history of the Bildungsroman (and the female Bildungsroman) in the context of a range of feminist and theoretical debates, and has hinted at ways in which Atwood's fiction provides a new perspective on the genre. Her early novels in particular introduce a subversiveness that playfully contests the humanist subject embraced by many of her more politically inclined feminist contemporaries. It is also important, however, to consider how Atwood's fiction reacts to its more immediate literary context, and to this end there follows an account of four novels by Atwood's American contemporaries that are more characteristic of the female Bildungsroman in the late 1960s and 1970s. The fact that this context is an explicitly American one is important in seeing how Atwood asserts a specifically Canadian difference in a North American context. The next chapter will further examine the importance of Canadian identity to understanding Atwood's slant on the genre and its relationship to the work of other Canadian women writers, but here I set up Atwood's oppositional relationship to her immediate American context.

Marge Piercy's *Small Changes* (1972), Erica Jong's *Fear of Flying* (1974) and *How to Save Your Own Life* (1978), and Marilyn French's *The Women's Room* (1978) are all overtly political in the way that they attack existing stereotypes and explore the possibilities for female development and self-realization. For Patricia Waugh:

> Such fictions did little to challenge the dominance of expressive realism with its consensus aesthetics: its assumption of the authority of omniscience or the veracity of personal experience in first-person narration; its coherent, consistent characters whose achievement of self-determination signifies a new maturity; its assumption of a causal relationship between the "real" inner essence of a person and the ultimate achievement of selfhood through acts in the world. (23)

While such highly-politicized fiction must be valued for its candid exploration of contemporary feminist issues, these novels ultimately offer a formula for self-realization that emulates the masculine quest narrative of genres such as the Bildungsroman. Patricia Waugh describes a common narrative technique in such work as consisting of the first person narrative of the mature self that looks retrospectively at the version of the self embroiled in a struggle to cast off socially-imposed feminine roles (26). While this technique was received by feminist critics such as Ellen Morgan as a radical appropriation of the luxury of secure selfhood and agency in the world, elsewhere its reception was more guarded.

Such examples of the female Bildungsroman often develop along the same trajectories as those associated with the masculine tradition. Recurring motifs and defining moments in the course of the protagonist's progress frequently include: separation from the constraints of marriage and domesticity, conflict with an older generation complicit in perpetuating oppressive images of femininity, deliverance into a radically different social sphere (in the case of *Small Changes* and *The Women's Room*, an academic community), where for the first time the protagonist enjoys the freedom of self-expression and the pursuit of intellectual fulfilment. Personal and sexual liberation through "consciousness raising" and participation in an exclusively female community are other favoured developmental catalysts in such fiction. While escape from the unhappy subservience of married life is often a springboard for these narratives of development, these fictions remain ever wary of the seductive lure of marriage and maternity as a means of fulfilling socially specified feminine roles.

Marge Piercy's *Small Changes* (1972) is made up of two narrative strands that conflate in the second half of the novel. Parts One and Two, "The Book of Beth" and "The Book of Miriam", trace the early development of two women and their disappointment at the realities of married life and the social roles they inherit. On her wedding day Beth describes feeling like "a wedding cake: they would come and slice her and take her home in white boxes to sleep on under their pillows" (11). Thus, she is, from the outset of her marriage to Jim, aware of herself as a commodity in relation to her husband and very quickly finds her resources depleted and sense of self diminished; books and her imagination provide her only sustenance. Beth describes the development of her relationship in terms of her husband's "expansion" in relation to her own "contraction" (28) and escapes before she is paralysed by her husband's tyrannical expectations. Her arrival in Boston and initial observation of and gradual participation in a politically conscious academic community serves as an important catalyst in her development. The other main character, Miriam, shares many points of confluence with Beth's story, particularly in relation to the feminine roles prescribed by her mother and female relatives. In contrast to Beth, Miriam fights the constraints her family tries to impose on her and resists their attempts to force her into an obedient stereotype. When the characters' lives finally intersect, Miriam is for Beth a model of autonomy, confidence, and sexual emancipation. However, as Beth slowly learns to assert herself and construct a new, meaningful life away from her high-school sweetheart turned misogynous, oppressive husband, Miriam retreats from her life as a charismatic, brilliant student, and seeks refuge in what she perceives as the potential stability of marriage. In the early chapters of the novel, following her escape from Syracuse, Beth revolts against the power politics of food, and the exhausting rituals of cooking for her father and her husband, by refusing to cook and rebelling against domesticity. It is telling that later in the novel, Miriam throws herself into cooking and baking rituals in search of the fulfilment of playing "women's roles" (195). As suggested by this example, the characters' development shares an inverse relationship that emerges more clearly in the second half of the novel. While Beth becomes increasingly political, joining a women's commune and later a feminist theatre group and declaring her bisexuality, Miriam's energy is increasingly diminished by the demands of domesticity and her husband's suppression of her spirit and energy. Even though he is initially attracted to Miriam's autonomous spirit, he ultimately finds this incompatible with his idea of Miriam as his wife. From this brief summary, it is clear that the novel seeks to explore feminism as a social revolution, and that attention to the detail of women's experience is more important than textual innovation.

Such fictions often describe, in very explicit terms, a late awakening or blossoming of female sexuality and desire, frequently prompted by the influence of a woman whose sexual fulfilment seems complete and uncompromised (Miriam in *Small Changes* and Val in *The Women's Room*). Erica Jong's Isadora Wing in *Fear of Flying* (1974) and *How to Save Your Own Life* (1977) is the voice of that "sexually liberated" woman. *Fear of Flying* recounts writer Isadora Wing's search for sexual and personal fulfilment, while *How to Save Your Own Life* examines Isadora's perspective on the reception of her semi-autobiographical heroine, Candida. This is a revealing first person narrative, another voice of experience, that draws attention to both books as politically motivated depictions of women's lives. The narrative is, at the same time, aware of its own limits in so far as the narrator admits "Everyone in the world wanted salvation. *Candida* had started the problem but hadn't begun to *solve* it. And who *could* solve it? … If I ever get the time to write another book, I thought, I am going to call it *How to Save Your Own Life* – a sort of how-to book in the form of a novel" (*How to Save Your Own Life* 34, italics in original). It is a result of this "how-to" element that such novels might be considered as much prescriptive as descriptive, although ultimately their concern is with the communication of experience rather than providing serious answers to feminist questions.

Marilyn French's *The Women's Room* (1978) is perhaps the most self-reflexive of this kind of female Bildungsroman. Drawing together the testimonies of different female characters, it focuses on Mira's progress over three decades. It examines the frustrations for young women growing up in the 1950s and the social impediments to Mira's intellectual burgeoning and later on, the drudgery of her domestic life as a young wife and mother. Much like Beth in *Small Changes*, she forges a new life for herself in a Harvard academic community, where she draws support from a community of women and recreates herself. The narrator of *The Women's Room* is another voice of experience. The tone of the narrator ranges from emotional and provocative to strident and militant with occasional explicit addresses to the reader. In Chapter 1, the narrator confides: "Perhaps you find Mira a little ridiculous. I do myself." (10). Various self-conscious commentaries within the novel show an awareness of the limits of such fictions:

> I feel like an outlaw not only because I think men are rotten and women are great, but because I have come to believe that oppressed people have the right to use criminal means to survive. Criminal means being, of course, defying the laws passed by the oppressors to keep the oppressed in line. Such a position takes you scarily close to advocating oppression itself, though. We are bound in it by the terms of the sentence. Subject-verb-object. The best we can do is turn

> it around. And that's no answer, is it? Well, answers I leave to others, to a newer generation perhaps, lacking the deformities mine suffered. (267)

This pre-empts many of the criticisms of such writing as based on the premise of transmittable experience; tellingly, the cover of *The Women's Room* declares solemnly "This Novel Changes Lives".

The emphasis here on the transmission of experience clearly suggests that *The Women's Room* sets itself up as a tool of feminist enlightenment and emancipation. However, it is a literary agenda that, as just described, is based on a reversal of "the terms of the sentence" more than innovative strategies. This is not to say that these texts do not in any way test the conceptual limits of the Bildungsroman. Early on in *The Women's Room*, the narrator confesses: "Some dramatic sense, probably culled from reading plays, or female *Bildungsromane*, which always end with the heroine's marriage, makes me want to stop here, make a formal break, like the curtain going down" (52). Again, the Bildungsroman is, without warning, introduced as a crucial mode of representing women's experience. French and writers like her push the boundaries of the female Bildungsroman as it existed up until that point. While such texts have a place in the canon of feminist literature and are very revealing of the changes taking place in the time in which they were written, more interesting is how Atwood's early fiction compares to these female Bildungsromane. Atwood's fiction is less concerned with reversing or extending existing narrative structures than in tackling the internal mechanics of generic convention. While this is most apparent in retrospect, there are indications that, in the early 1970s, Atwood and those closest to her were already aware of the need to distance her work from that of a number of her more overtly (and, in their opinion, unsubtly) politicized contemporaries. Particularly telling is a letter from one of her publishers, dated August 1973, regarding a review of Atwood's fiction and the work of other women writers: "Here is the dumb *Times* review, which I imagine you've already seen. Complete with advice on what you and everyone else should do. I hope you can manage to avoid being lumped in with Jong in the future. Jesus" (MS Coll. 200:92:5). This suggests not only that Atwood and her "camp" took such matters seriously but reveals the strength of feeling with which they addressed this important issue.

It is important, then, also to consider the relationship of the female Bildungsroman (and its contrasting manifestation in an American feminist context) to developments in Canadian writing, and this will pave the way for the consideration of Atwood's own work in this book. In situating the genre in a Canadian context, I will draw largely on Atwood's own reading of Canadian literature and a number of particularly Atwoodian insights into Canadian culture and identity. More than any other genre that explicitly identifies itself as woman-centred, the female Bildungsroman draws attention to, rather than eliding, its ideological past, and it confronts those ideologies in a way that both challenges and sustains the genre. Beyond its native borders, the female Bildungsroman in English writes back to the Fatherland in interesting and productive ways and emerges as a preferred mode of literary expression in both a woman-centred and postcolonial context. As will become apparent, twentieth-century Canadian women's writing, and Atwood's early fiction in particular, exemplifies this complementary relationship.

Chapter 2
Progress, Identity, and the Canadian Imaginative Landscape: Cultural and Critical Contexts

An examination of Atwood's relationship with the female Bildungsroman must take into consideration a number of recurring preoccupations in her fiction and criticism. As will be demonstrated in the following chapters, Atwood's re-working of the genre tests the limits of the inherited tradition. This engagement with the Bildungsroman as a literary form is invariably informed by Atwood's particular interpretation of Canadian literature and culture, the foundations of which were laid down in the 1970s. While Atwood's writing since the 1970s clearly departs from this early Canadian nationalist influence, it remains a significant framing historical context and it is worth revisiting the sometimes contentious debates surrounding Atwood's early literary criticism. Atwood's perspectives as critic and author have, from the very beginning of her career, shared a lively intertextual relationship. In "A Statement of My Intellectual Interests, Research Related Activities and Future Plans" on file in the Atwood archive (part of an application for a Woodrow Wilson Fellowship made in 1961), Atwood, then just 22 years old, asserts with considerable self-assurance: "I once thought of the creative and the academic as two opposite and mutually exclusive elements, which they may be for some writers; however, I have found that for me, they are complementary" (MS Coll. 200:1:7). In hindsight, this is a wonderfully understated description of what would indeed turn out to be a richly complementary relationship between Atwood's creative and critical writing, something that the present discussion seeks to explicate more fully. Without a doubt, from the very beginning of her career, Atwood's critical writing bore a mutually revealing relationship to her poetry and fiction. This chapter will consider a range of critical texts by Atwood that develop her theory of survival and her interest in the "Malevolent North" as an important motif in Canadian literature. Of particular interest are how these interests shape her interpretation of Canadian identity during her formative years as a writer, particularly in relation to the Canadian cultural nationalism of the 1960s and 1970s, and how such influences impact the life narratives at the heart of her fiction. These issues assert themselves, sometimes explicitly, sometimes obliquely, in all of the narratives of female progress in her early novels, but are reconsidered and reinvigorated in her later work and have considerable implications for the Atwoodian version of the Bildungsroman. In order to further contextualize Atwood's contribution to the genre, this chapter will also briefly consider the landmark female Bildungsromane of Atwood's Canadian contemporaries Alice Munro and Margaret Laurence, whose work is similarly concerned with the articulation of specifically Canadian experiences of female development at a crucial moment in Canadian literary history.

As a genre, the female Bildungsroman represents a useful model for considering Atwood's development and coming of age as a writer at a time when efforts were being made to distinguish and promote a distinctively Canadian literature. Correspondence in the Atwood Collection at the University of Toronto, dating from the mid-1960s to the mid-1970s, provides a clear sense of the serious and concerted efforts made by writers and poets to foster a Canadian literary community in this period. Letters to and from Margaret Avison, Gwendolyn MacEwen, Michael Ondaatje, and Eli Mandel as well as Canadian publishers, editors, and critics are suggestive of an emerging literary community and an ongoing dialogue between writers and poets. It is clear, then, that the central concerns of Atwood's early fiction are closely related to this project of excavating and achieving an autonomous Canadian literary identity. Her later work, though it moves on in new directions, remains connected to these early, urgent preoccupations.

Survival: Making Canadian Literature Possible

Progress in the traditional Bildungsroman is often centred on encountering and overcoming challenges and obstacles in the quest for identity. Margaret Atwood's interpretation of Canadian literature would seem, on first consideration, to render it incompatible with such an endeavour – her theory of survival might, on the first appraisal, not seem to leave much room for the cultivation of potential in striving towards maturity.

In *Survival: A Thematic Guide to Canadian Literature* (1972), Atwood attempts to define a Canadian cultural and literary community by examining the key tropes and motifs that predominate in Canadian literature. *Survival* is first and foremost an attempt to identify the distinctive "shape of Canadian literature" (13) and Atwood was not the first to express concern at its apparent amorphousness. The concern with the survival of Canadian literary culture was expressed decades earlier in the work of E.K. Brown. In 1951, in an essay called "Is a Canadian Critic Possible?" Brown concluded somewhat gloomily: "What is really lacking is not Canadian criticism in any sense of the term but an audience for it. As I have said before in this place – and expect to say again – Canadians do not care what other Canadians think" (314). In the light of this historical anxiety about the visibility and viability of Canadian literature and culture, Atwood's work marks a moment of unprecedented assertiveness and confidence in the Canadian literary tradition.

In the preface to *Survival*, Atwood famously identifies a number of victim positions evident in Canadian literature and goes on to examine these different manifestations and variations of victimhood in detail. While she classifies a wide range of works as portraying different victim positions, from denial through to creative defiance of victimhood, more often than not she returns to the conclusion that: "The central symbol for Canada – and this is based on numerous instances of its occurrence in both English and French Canadian literature – is undoubtedly Survival, *la Survivance*" (32). Atwood supports this conclusion with reference to poetry and fiction drawn from Anglo- and French-Canadian literature from the 1930s to the 1970s. Thus, survival emerges as the key preoccupation of Canadian literature with a typical narrative pattern that runs contrary to other, and in particular American, quest narratives:

> Our stories are likely to be tales not of those who made it but of those who made it back, from the awful experience – the North, the snow-storm, the sinking ship – that killed everyone else. The survivor has no triumph or victory but the fact of his survival; he has little after his ordeal that he did not have before, except gratitude for having escaped with his life. (33)

She finds evidence of this obsession with survival – and what she sees as Canadian literature's accompanying, almost pathological, fixation on victimhood – in literary representations of experiences of nature, animals, the native peoples of Canada, the Canadian family unit, the Canadian immigrant, the Canadian artist, and women in Canadian literature.

The Canadian artist, according to Atwood's thesis, faces a particularly daunting uphill struggle in the face of such inhospitable conditions. In *Survival* and in later critical writings such as *Second Words* (1984) and *Negotiating with the Dead* (2002), Atwood returns to the dilemma of the aspiring writer growing up in Canada in the 1940s and 1950s and, as will become apparent, her fiction shows a sustained interest in images of the female author and artist. She describes her growing awareness of the apparent absence of an inherited Canadian literary tradition with which she might identify. In the early 1970s, Atwood read this as a symptom of the greater problem of Canada's past and ongoing colonial subjugation, a threat to the psychological and cultural as well as economic independence and growth of the country. Decades earlier, Hugh MacLennan had already begun to articulate the frustrations of the Canadian writer in *Two Solitudes* (1945):

> Must he write out of his own background, even if that background were Canada? Canada was imitative in everything. Yes, but perhaps only on the surface. What about underneath? No one had dug underneath so far, that was the trouble. … As Paul considered the problem he realized that his readers' ignorance of the essential Canadian clashes and values presented him with a unique problem. The background would have to be created from scratch if his story was to become intelligible. He could afford to take nothing for granted. He would have to build the stage and props for his play, and then write the play itself. (329)

For Atwood, then, as for many Canadian cultural nationalists of her generation, the sociological and literary were, by necessity, closely related. Canada's struggle for an identity that was not determined by the overbearing influence of former colonisers and the United States was the driving force of her search for a unified theme in Canadian literature.

By current standards, *Survival* might seem a flawed and naïve attempt at representing a national literature and culture according to a notion of unified national character and may seem to lack critical balance with its emphasis on plot and apparent lack of concern with language and form. These and far more damning criticisms were made of the work in the years that directly followed its publication and remarkable commercial success. One of the main criticisms came from those who objected to the "thematic" approach and the idea that the literature discussed was presented according to Atwood's reading of a singular theme, one that lacked an appreciation of the aesthetic or literary value of the work. While some of these criticisms remain valid, many stubbornly overlook the context in which Atwood was writing and the audience for whom *Survival* was designed. The angrier attacks on *Survival* charged Atwood with reducing Canadian literary criticism to paraphrase and suggested that the book favoured theme over quality and showed a bias towards the then relatively new Anansi Press for which Atwood was an editor. Dramatically contradicting these claims of opportunism, Atwood was in fact most careful to limit references to her own work, as indicated in an editorial letter from fellow poet and critic Dennis Lee prior to the publication of the book:

> Your own work, it seems, is not going to be cited at nearly as many points as it should be. (I only recall one instance at the moment.) You might do yourself a trifle more justice in the preface with a line or two; you could do a nice Canadian self-deprecating thing – as a poet and novelist, you share a good many obsessions with the authors mentioned in this book and with the author of this book, but have tried not to yank that in by the heels … or something. (MS Coll. 200:51:2)

For Frank Davey, in "Atwood Walking Backwards" (1973), "culture-fixing" (83) and the "breezy journalistic style" (84) of *Survival* were Atwood's greatest crimes against Canadian literature and literary criticism. A few years later, in his rival survey of the history and potential of Canadian literature in *Canadian Literature: Surrender or Revolution* (1978), Robin Mathews also insisted that *Survival* served only to perpetuate a "'non-evaluative', colonized tradition" (120). As will become clear, this reading of *Survival* fails to appreciate its purpose in promoting an awareness of Canadian literature's differences from its inherited literary traditions, and it overlooks the political motives of the work. While remaining aware of the problems of thematic criticism, in particular the way it seems to pursue myths and symbols in literature in order to provide evidence of a unified national culture, critics such as Arnold Davidson take a more balanced view and allow for the "valuable insights" afforded by a thematic approach (Introduction, *Studies on Canadian Literature* 2).

If, in retrospect, many of these points about *Survival* seem necessary, Atwood's subsequent critical and fictional oeuvre best answers the accusations of her more damning critics. Through her fiction she emerges as one of the most interesting exponents of a complex and self-interrogating paradigm of survivalism in Canadian literature, contributing to the tradition in a way that explores, develops, and also provides relief from the apparent negativity of the idea as theorized in her early work.

Also important and something that is given full expression in Atwood's collected papers, is the way in which she herself was aware of the limitations of the project. Foundational research notes in the Atwood Collection shed new light on her intentions for *Survival*. A tentative outline of the project, found amongst her research materials and notes for *Survival*, reveals that the original title was *Survival: A Canadian Culture Handbook* (MS Coll. 200:51:1). While this may seem to support the argument of critics who complained that *Survival* mined Canadian literature for Canadian myths and symbols, it also reveals that, from the outset, Atwood made no apology for the necessity of such a guide to Canadian culture and, rather than being the academic Trojan horse that some of her contemporaries imagined it to be, *Survival* was very self-consciously designed with a public readership in mind. Furthermore, her collected papers show that she had done considerable work towards compiling a companion anthology *Survival Two: A Thematic Anthology of Canadian Literature* (MS Coll. 200:54), a further indication of the extent to which she conceived of *Survival* as an introductory reader with a very specific intention and inevitable limitations. Dennis Lee elaborates on the need for a study like *Survival* in editorial correspondence, in which (couching his suggestion in Atwood's voice) he neatly summarises the book's main objectives and achievements:

> Perhaps the most interesting discovery I have made is that Canadian writers have not been trying to write English or American books and failing; they have been trying to write Canadian books and, to an increasing degree they have been succeeding. They have been at least a century in the process; what's needed now – odd though it may sound – is for us to learn how to *read* Canadian books. A Canadian book … deals with the same subjects as books elsewhere, and it has the same range of techniques available. But it handles those things in a characteristic way, one which constitutes the stamp or signature of the people whose experience gives the book its body and substance. You cannot read that signature (nor decide when it is well written, when badly) if you are looking for a different name all along. *Survival* is one attempt to recognise our signature, so that we can read and assess our books as what they are. (MS Coll. 200:51:2)

While Atwood fully addressed the questions and objections raised to her thematic approach in published responses collected in critical anthologies such as *Second Words*, unpublished and uncollected speeches show that her public role as an advocate for Canadian literature provided her with a forum to be candid about her motivations at this time in her career. In an undated address delivered to an academic audience in Italy in the 1970s, she frankly admits:

> Mine is not the viewpoint of the detached observer but of one in the midst of a process, which is not only a literary one but an economic and political one as well. I should warn you in advance that my view of Canadian literature is exactly what it has often been accused of being: personal and biased. ... All writing is rooted in a particular environment, and that of Canada is no exception. For the writers of my generation – those who began publishing in the late 50s and early 60s – the fact that we are writing at all, much less publishing, seems like a miracle. Nothing in our education would have led us to expect this. (MS Coll. 200:56:11:2)

The "process" that Atwood alludes to includes the involvement of many writers of her generation in the establishment of publishing houses such as Coach House and Anansi, evidence of which can be seen in collected correspondence in the Atwood archive (MS Coll. 200:56:11), as well as her outspoken commitment to associations such as "The League of Canadian Poets" and the "Canadian Writers Union", founded in 1967 and 1973 respectively (MS Coll. 200:92:2, 92:10).

Atwood's dismal description of Canadian publishing in the early 1960s provides a sense of the literary climate in which she first started writing. Reflecting back on this decade in a speech delivered in 1982 called "The Improvisation of Eden", she ruefully writes:

> When I began to unearth my own literature, I discovered that – for instance – in the year 1960, there were about five novels published in the whole of English Canada. A bestseller for poetry was two hundred copies. A novelist was doing well to sell five hundred. Mordecai Richler, one of our better known novelists, published his first novel in England at this time. It sold three copies in Canada. (MS Coll. 200:74:13:3)

Looking back in 1999, Atwood herself reflects on the state of Canadian literary criticism in the early 1970s and finds a plausible explanation for the controversy that surrounded her first book of criticism: "The few dedicated academic souls who had cultivated this neglected pumpkin patch over the meagre years were affronted because a mere chit of a girl had appropriated a pumpkin they regarded as theirs, and the rest were affronted because I had obnoxiously pointed out that there was in fact a pumpkin to appropriate" ("Survival: Then and Now" 55).

In retrospect, it is easy to appreciate why *Survival* sparked such controversy, but Atwood's achievement in *Survival* is best understood in relation to the literary tradition with which she is identified as a critic. She studied under Northrop Frye as an undergraduate and the book clearly aligns her with his critical tradition. Indeed, she seems to take the conclusions that he draws in the preface to his collection of essays on the Canadian imagination, *The Bush Garden* (1971), as a point of departure for her own critical writing. In the preface to *The Bush Garden*, Frye sets out to identify the "containing imaginative forms" associated with Canada (ii). It is the fusion of the literary, cultural, and social imagination of Canada that many critics of Frye and Atwood found so unpalatable and led to accusations of "breezy journalism". And yet this criticism fails to consider the value of the function that such an approach served at that moment in Canada's cultural and literary history. Furthermore, Atwood shows herself to be very self-conscious of the limits of her approach from the outset. Indeed, in his recent reappraisal of this mode of literary criticism, "The Practice and Theory of Canadian Thematic Criticism: A Reconsideration", Russell Morton Brown draws a far more conciliatory conclusion, one that acknowledges its potential interest, while at the same time making a number of qualifications as to its value (15). I would argue that Atwood's self-awareness, as revealed most explicitly in her unpublished notes and letters, and the way she directly addresses the vulnerabilities of *Survival* as a critical enterprise from the moment of its conception, shows her to be a critic who was very conscious of the limitations to the project so often foregrounded by those sceptical of the value of her early criticism.

In the preface to *Survival*, Atwood draws attention to the urgent need to promote an awareness of a shared Canadian literary tradition by referring to the young Stephen Dedalus's scribblings in James Joyce's *A Portrait of the Artist as a Young Man*: "Stephen Dedalus, Class of Elements, Clongowes Wood School, Sallins, County Kildare, Ireland, Europe, The World, The Universe" (12). She notes that in relation to this list of "everything it is possible for a human being to write about and therefore to read about" (15), the study of representations of Canadian nationality is a luxury that is not afforded the Canadian critic. It is appropriate that she should have found inspiration in early twentieth-century Irish writing, in another literature finding its feet, though the brand of cultural nationalism evident in *Survival* and in her very early work might seem to have more of a Yeatsian than Joycean flavour, with its emphasis on the need to reinvigorate an overlooked or elided cultural history. A most powerful statement of this position can be found in an address on Canadian Nationalism delivered in March 1973, a year after the appearance of *Survival*. She begins by acknowledging it as decentred and multifaceted, but goes on to draw a definitive conclusion: "But underneath all the uproar, what *do* Canadians want? I think I can put it very simply: they want to exist. As themselves, that is. They are tired of being called, even thinking of themselves as exiled British or failed Americans" (MS Coll. 200:56:18:3). As the following chapters will show, this dilemma is one shared by many of Atwood's characters. At the same time, through all of these developments, Atwood remained a cultural nationalist of independent temper, as there are moments in her fictional oeuvre that vividly foreground the dangers of nationalism, when misconstrued to serve the purposes of insular tribalism. Stephen Dedalus is once again a revealing source of inspiration in this regard. In *Portrait*, Stephen is determined to evade the stifling determinants of Irish nationalism at the turn of the last century: "When the soul of a man is born in this country there are nets flung at it to hold it back from flight. You talk to me of nationality, language, religion. I shall try to fly by those nets" (220). In 1972, Atwood faced very different pressures as a young writer struggling to establish the determining features of Canadian identity and literature. Irish cultural nationalism at the end of the nineteenth century, caught up as it was with political and religious struggle and the effort to sustain a dying language, provides a useful contrast to Canadian cultural nationalism in the 1970s. If Irish cultural nationalism was a struggle to revive a culture and literature that had been destroyed and abandoned over centuries of colonial subjugation, Atwood's cultural nationalism is concerned with a literature that had never been fully established or appreciated and perhaps, more importantly, a literature that had yet to be written. Thus, Atwood can be understood as an active participant in the simultaneous forging of a national and literary consciousness.

What is especially significant to my reading of Atwood's work in relation to the female Bildungsroman is that these political and cultural transformations, from Canada's imported culture of the 1940s and 1950s to the radical change that gathered momentum in the 1960s and 1970s, coincided with Atwood's own coming of age as a writer. As a result, she found herself in the unusual position of playing a major role in forging the means by which she could write with confidence as a Canadian woman writer. On one level, she described the tradition to which she was to make a major contribution in the course of her writing career. Thus, it is no coincidence that, given her arrival on the Canadian literary scene at a peculiarly charged historical moment, processes of self-determination and self-invention and their relationship with larger historical narratives are so important in her early writing and remain ever-present preoccupations throughout her writing career. At the same time, she is quick to acknowledge her changing relationship with the idea of Canada in her work. In *Second Words* she describes how looking back on the early 1980s: "I see that I was writing and talking a little less about the Canadian scene and a little more about the global one" (*Second Words* 282). In an article published in 1999 she reflects: "People often ask me what I would change about *Survival* if I were writing it today. The obvious answer is that I wouldn't write it today, because I wouldn't need to. The thing I set out to prove has been proven beyond a doubt: few would seriously argue, anymore, that there is no Canadian literature" ("Survival: Then and Now" 58). In a significant footnote to Atwood's early incarnation as a cultural ambassador for Canada, those who suspected her of precocious opportunism might indeed be interested to see how she continued her early project long after her establishment as a writer of international significance. Correspondence in the Carol Shields Collection at the National Library of Canada in Ottawa, made up of letters from Atwood and Graeme Gibson, discusses the production of an anthology of Canadian writing in Spanish. One letter, dated 25 June 1996, from Gibson to Shields explains how: "Literary translators within the Union will translate the works into Spanish and return them to us. Since the Cubans have no paper for literary publishing and virtually no hard currency, we have agreed to arrange for production here in Canada. We are also finding the money to pay for it and donating our work and time" (1997–2004:59:1). No longer "a mere chit of a girl"("Survival: Then and Now" 55), a more mature Atwood continued to campaign discreetly for the dissemination of Canadian literature well into the 1990s.

For Atwood, writing in 1972, the issue of discovering a distinctive identity as a Canadian citizen – in some ways making the Canadian Bildungsroman possible – was as much a question of geography as personal history. Again she takes her cue from Northrop Frye:

> But in Canada, as Frye suggests, the answer to the question "Who am I?" is at least partly the same as the answer to another question: "Where is here?" "Who am I?" is a question appropriate in countries where the environment, the "here," is already well-defined, so well-defined in fact that it may threaten to overwhelm the individual. ... "Where is here?" is a different kind of question. It is what a man asks when he finds himself in unknown territory, and it implies several other questions. (*Survival* 17)

In fact, the extent of Frye's influence in this regard is seen in early drafts of *Surfacing*. *Where is Here* was the original working title of the novel (MS Coll. 200:21, 22). One of the "several other questions" implied by this position relates to whether or if the investment in ideas of progress and development historically associated with the Bildungsroman was possible on territory, which had yet to be given the kind of firm cultural demarcation that Frye describes.

In contrast to Canadian survivalism, Atwood identifies the primary unifying symbol of American literature (a literature which would seem to have a ready answer to Frye's question) as "The Frontier, a flexible idea that contains many elements dear to the American heart: it suggests a place that is *new*, where the old order can be discarded ... a line that is always expanding, taking in or 'conquering' ever-fresh virgin territory" (*Survival* 31). The direct opposition of the values of the American West and the Canadian North is important to Atwood's project of delineating an independent Canadian literary tradition removed from American influence. A number of recent studies such as Sherrill Grace's *Canada and the Idea of North* investigate the idea of North as a cultural construct, an important facet of the Canadian imagination. Or, as Atwood would have it: "The north focuses our anxieties. Turning to face north, face the north, we enter our own unconscious" ("True North" 33). This emphasis is resonant with the same critical tradition to which Frye and Atwood belong, whereby literary and national myth-making complement each other. These complex geo-political issues have an important place in her early fiction, most obviously in *Surfacing* but also in *The Edible Woman* and *Lady Oracle*, as well as in Atwood's later novels. While the later fictions are set largely in contemporary, urban Canada, the effects of Atwood's interest in surviving the Canadian wilderness can be seen to have a considerable impact on the imaginative landscape of these novels. It has a more explicit significance in collections such as *Wilderness Tips* (1991) and *Strange Things: The Malevolent North in Canadian Literature* (1995) where Atwood returns to the idea of North.

One of Atwood's readings of the Canadian North – as marauding and inhospitable – poses challenging questions as to how this affects the representation of progress and development and their related processes of change and transformation. Many of the motifs that Atwood identifies as essential to the Canadian literary past centre on the idea of bare endurance against the odds, or as she would have it "making it back" from life-threatening conditions. This leads us to the question: Can the form of a genre like the Bildungsroman, historically reliant as it is on the promise of teleological progress, be accommodated in such an apparently cold climate? The hostile terrain – imaginative and real – that often takes centre stage in Atwood's writing would seem to be most incompatible with the generic coordinates of the genre. However, it might be more useful to see them as forcing a reconsideration of the shape and structure of the genre.

The Canadian Identity Crisis

For the purpose of further explicating Atwood's slant on and contribution to the assertion of a Canadian literary identity, and its resonance with narratives of development and the writing of the female Bildungsroman in her own work, it is necessary to consider her work in the context of the postcolonial dimensions of Canadian literature. The confluence of postcolonial and feminist interests has been identified as a particularly Canadian phenomenon and this is most vividly seen in Atwood's own criticism and fiction. Atwood's early critical writings can be considered milestones in the Canadian cultural renaissance and what was to become a relentless process of self-interrogation for Canadian culture. Indeed, the questioning of Canadian cultural identity by no means begins with *Survival.*

In 1961, in *The Canadian Identity*, W.L. Morton pre-empted Atwood by asserting that Canada could be identified with "a common psychology, the psychology of endurance and survival" (112). Such investment in the endurance of an embattled Canadian culture and identity seems to set the tone even for very recent analysis and interpretation of cultural developments in Canada and suggests that the agonizing questioning of the existence of an autonomous Canadian culture continues to the present day. In *The House of Difference* (1999), Eva Mackey makes a valuable contribution towards explaining the permanent state of crisis of the "Canadian imagination". She considers that the Canadian formula for nation-building "specifies a (Western) *belief system* within which continuous moral and physical 'improvement' – progress – is seen as necessary and natural. The *subject* of this improvement is an 'entire governable population', which implies that diverse peoples must be *made 'governable'*" (17, italics in original). This idea of progress towards a unified idea of Canadian nationhood is, according to the discourse put forward by Mackey and other critics, incompatible with the marginalized experience of anyone outside this essentially Anglo-Canadian "belief-system". Mackey includes Frye and Atwood in what she sees as the problematic anglocentricism of traditional formulations of Canadian identity, suggesting that their representations of northern Canadianness, so important to this project "utilise a settler point of view (lost in the wilderness) which erases Aboriginal people. Yet, paradoxically, white settlers take up a subject position more appropriate to Native people, in order to construct Canadians as victims of colonialism and U.S. imperialism, and to create Canadian identity" (49).

Perhaps unsurprisingly, the bare, uninhabited landscapes of Canada's most famous artistic collective are at the centre of this discussion led by critics who question what seems to be the attempted erasure of aboriginal identity. The early twentieth-century "Group of Seven" artists, and their influential precursor Tom Thomson, are most famous for their striking Canadian landscapes. Thomson's work is largely concerned with communicating the vitality and force of different Canadian landscapes, and the dramatic northern landscapes recreated in their paintings are notably void of all human presence and influence. For critics such as Mackey, and also Jonathan Bordo in his critique of this body of work in "Jack Pine – Wilderness Sublime or the Erasure of the Aboriginal Presence from the Landscape", this is troubling because it is too typical of the settler point of view in Canadian art and literature: it is a perspective based on the elision of Native presence and experience. Atwood, however, does in fact carefully address the marginalization and typecasting of First Nations people in *Survival* and *Strange Things* and her work proves politically sensitive in this way. Moreover, as will be discussed in the next chapter, *Surfacing* and her formative unpublished work, far from being a mouthpiece for Canadian anglocentricism, openly interrogates the hazards of nation building in any form.

While *Survival* might be considered a moment of transition in the Canadian campaign against cultural imperialism, more recent studies of the state of Canadian culture such as Tom Henighan's *The Presumption of Culture* (1996) and *Ideas of North: A Guide to Canadian Arts and Culture* (1997) show signs of a continued self-consciousness and even defensiveness of a particular strand in Canadian cultural and literary criticism. *Ideas of North* begins by posing the somewhat alarming question: "Will Canadian culture survive in the twenty-first century?". It goes on to provide a careful and detailed documentary of anglophone and francophone cultural achievements in defence of a culture that is "underrated, misperceived, and currently under threat of being swallowed up by the world entertainment industry, centred in the United States" (ix).

In keeping with this continued preoccupation with the state of the arts in Canada is an ongoing pursuit of representative themes in Canadian literature and culture. Yet, in 1996, a year before the appearance of *Ideas of North*, Coral Ann Howells posed the provocative question: "Is there such a thing as the 'Canadian literary imagination'? Or is this an outdated concept of cultural nationalism, now replaced by gendered, regional, Native or ethnic imaginations in the plural?" ("Disruptive Geographies: or, Mapping the Region of Woman in Contemporary Canadian Women's Writing in English" 124). Thus there is a clear tension between the drive towards a totalizing discourse of Canadian national identity and one more appreciative of the possibilities of thinking, as Howells suggests, in the plural.

This troubled aspect of Canadian identity is, in part, a result of the tension between regional and national articulations of Canadianness. Sam Solecki, writing about the Canadian novel in English from the 1960s to the 1980s, adds yet another dimension to this; in examining this relationship between the regional and national, he sees the tension between regional and national identities as one of the reasons for the lack of certainty in a "defining self-image" (831). Atwood's *Survival* attempts to resolve this tension by placing writers who draw on very different Canadian geographies on a thematic continuum suggested by a unifying concern with survival and endurance. Linda Hutcheon modifies this approach to Canada's literary regionalism. She suggests that Canadian literature's inherent suspicion of totalizing narratives (whether geographical, ethnic, linguistic, national, political or cultural) and the process of writing back to former and current centres of power can be appreciated in a postmodern context as a valuable source of creativity ("The Canadian Postmodern: Fiction in English since 1960" 19–21). This does not necessarily contradict the position taken by Atwood as there are many moments in Atwood's fiction where the apparently marginalized victim position becomes the preferred and indeed more interesting position.

The reason for this ongoing concern with Canadian self-image becomes clearer when the relationship between Canadian postcolonialism and Canadian feminism is examined in greater detail. In *The Canadian Postmodern: A Study of Contemporary English-Canadian Fiction*, Hutcheon outlines how postmodernism's "deconstructing of national myths and identity" is "possible within Canada only when those myths and identity have first been defined" (6). This is an exact replication of the status of the female Bildungsroman in the 1960s and 1970s as explored in the previous chapter and perhaps casts a sympathetic light on the ready acceptance and appropriation of the genre by second-wave feminism. Hutcheon makes the connection to Atwood and other Canadian women writers explicit in addressing what seems to be an ongoing preoccupation with "character formation" in their work:

> The reason is that you can assume selfhood ("character formation") or "subjectivity" only when you have attained it. Subjectivity in the Western liberal humanist tradition has been defined in terms of rationality, individuality, and power; in other words, it is defined in terms of those domains traditionally denied women, who are relegated instead to the realms of intuition, familial collectivity, and submission. (*The Canadian Postmodern* 5)

In Atwood's early fiction, two compatible processes are at work as her fiction explores the limits of the female Bildungsroman in a Canadian context, bringing together issues of female and Canadian identity and autonomy. She addresses this very candidly in an essay "Playgroup on the Fringe of Empire" written during a visit to Scotland in 1979: "The problems of women writers and the problems of colonial writers, writers from culturally colonized groups, interest me about equally. As they should: they have much in common" (MS Coll. 200:56:37:6).

This intersection of gender and nationality is further complicated by the way in which Atwood's cultural nationalism frequently draws on gendered images of the nation. This is expressed most explicitly in Atwood's critical writings, as in a speech delivered in November 1987, opposing the Canada–U.S. Free Trade Agreement:

> Canada as a separate but dominated country has done about as well under the U.S. as women, worldwide, have done under men; about the only position they've ever adopted towards us, country to country, has been the missionary position, and we were not on the top. I guess that's why the national wisdom *vis a vis* Them has so often taken the form of lying still, keeping your mouth shut and pretending you like it. (MS Coll. 200:97:10:6)

This feminisation of Canada, according to Eva Mackey, is potentially misleading and inappropriately exploits an idea of Canadian victimhood (12).Thirty years on this may be a valid criticism, but it does not necessarily detract from the importance of Atwood's early criticism as representative of a crucial moment in Canadian literary history. Moreover, as emphasised by Coral Ann Howells in her seminal study of Atwood's work, Atwood remains at all times aware of her own cultural identity as "white, English-speaking, Canadian and female; but she also challenges the limits of such categories, questioning stereotypes of nationality and gender" (*Margaret Atwood* 2). It is this driving force in Atwood's work – her mode as a writer interested in and capable of challenging and reshaping categories, whether national, gendered, or literary – that is of central interest to my reading of her relationship with the Bildungsroman.

Margaret Atwood's Formative Years in Context (2) – Munro, Laurence, and Atwood: Pioneers of the Canadian Female Bildungsroman

While the pressing issue of an autonomous Canadian identity and culture are heavily inscribed in Atwood's early fiction, most relevant to this project is how those issues are played out in her renegotiation of the Bildungsroman. Linda Hutcheon is one of the very few critics who comes close to addressing this question:

> It is clear that many thematic lacunae in our literary experience are now being filled, thanks to the work of novelists such as Alice Munro, Margaret Laurence, Margaret Atwood and many others: we are finally learning what it feels like, for example, to be *female* and growing up in repressive small-town Canada. The traditional *bildungsroman* also takes on different forms and emphases when its subject is female. In other words, while critical feminism has pushed post-structuralism in directions it could not and would not have gone, so fiction by women writers, in Canada and elsewhere, has actually wrought changes in the

> novel, in its traditional forms as well as its themes. ("'Shape shifters': Canadian Women Novelists and the Challenge to Tradition" 226)

That Hutcheon should touch (if briefly) on the Bildungsroman as a form central to the telling the story of a national literature is suggestive of its peculiar hold over the literary and critical imagination, particularly in cultural contexts where the luxury of its existence has yet to be fully appreciated.

For the purpose of comparison, I will briefly examine two extremely influential novels by Laurence and Munro before beginning a detailed analysis of Atwood's fiction. While this must by necessity be a cursory treatment of the signature novels of two major Canadian writers, I will limit my focus to the patterns of female development established in these novels and how they prefigure and relate to the trajectories of progress that emerge in Atwood's writing. Laurence and Munro are appropriate choices because they, together with Atwood, number amongst the most important post-1960s Canadian women writers. The novels that I will address represent just one moment in the long and illustrious careers of these writers, but it is useful to examine how they, like Atwood, find clarity in the female Bildungsroman at a key moment in the history of the genre. This is both indicative of a sea change in Canadian women's writing, but is also in keeping with the woman-centred appropriation of the genre examined in the previous chapter. As stressed by Hutcheon, female development, in particular female artistic development and the achievement of an autonomous identity are core preoccupations of Munro's *Lives of Girls and Women* (1971) and Laurence's *The Diviners* (1974). These works were contemporaneous to Atwood's early novels, and a brief consideration of how they compare and contrast with Atwood's writing will illustrate the differing ways in which the female Bildungsroman was appropriated in Canada in this period. One of the things that is sometimes overlooked by Atwood critics is that these novels also display an awareness of many of the concerns raised in Atwood's fiction and criticism; in particular the necessity of forging a Canadian national and female literary consciousness.

Alice Munro's *Lives of Girls and Women* seems to contain all of the classic ingredients of the Bildungsroman. Munro's Bildungsroman unfolds in distinct phases each exploring and representing Del's development and growing awareness of the vulnerability and fallibility of the adults around her (in particular her mother), the code of behaviour by which her community functions and the dangers and challenges of contravening its status quo. Within these confines the conflict between her own ambitions and the limits suggested by her upbringing and origins and her sexual and emotional awakening are played out alongside of her burgeoning artistic aspirations. Published a year prior to *Survival*, Munro's novel pre-empts Atwood's concern at the lack of distinctively Canadian landscapes in Canadian literature.

As in the fiction of Margaret Laurence and other contemporaries, Munro's Wawanash County and the town of Jubilee affect Del's development at every level. From a young age Del is subject to the received wisdom and prejudice of her environment. Outside her immediate family, the scrutiny and watchfulness for any sign of individual pretentiousness, most keenly maintained by her Aunts Elspeth and Grace, ensure that Del knows better than to call undue attention to her intellectual and artistic aspirations: "Ambition was what they were alarmed by, for to be ambitious was to court failure and to risk making a fool of oneself" (38).

Most significantly, Del's development as a writer is determined by the town of Jubilee and the surrounds to the extent that Jubilee becomes the inevitable subject of her writing. In the epilogue, Del is seen to nurture an idea for a novel, a melodrama inspired by local mythology, until it becomes clear that the town itself is to fire her writer's imagination, and she is compelled to recreate Jubilee in fiction. Looking back on her anxiety to escape Jubilee, Del reflects: "It did not occur to me then that one day I would be so greedy for Jubilee. Voracious and misguided as Uncle Craig out at Jenkin's Bend, writing his history, I would want to write things down" (249). Del's relationship with her Uncle Craig's thousand-page *History of Wawanash County* is important in the assertion of her own literary pursuits. The history is a tediously detailed chronicle of ordinary, daily events and occurrences, a project that is regarded with theatrical significance by her aunts as "man's work". On the death of her uncle, Del's aunts solemnly present the incomplete history in a padlocked tin to Del, in the hope that she will complete it at some point in the future. Del removes the contents of the manuscripts and notes to use the tin to store her own efforts at writing a "few poems and bits of a novel" (62) and the original manuscript is later ruined in a cellar flood. *Lives of Girls and Women* is the replacement history of female coming of age in rural Ontario: a radically new endeavour in Canadian literature.

On account of the structure and tone of the collection, one might compare it to *A Portrait of the Artist as a Young Man*, and this comparison in turn draws attention to one of Atwood's key ambitions in *Survival*. When teaching Uncle Benny how to write, Del begins with "*Mr. Benjamin Thomas Poole, The Flats Road, Wawanash County, Ontario, Canada, North America, The Western Hemisphere, The World, The Solar System, The Universe*" (11, italics in original), effectively rewriting Stephen Dedalus's inscription on the flyleaf of his geography book in *A Portrait of the Artist as a Young Man*: "Stephen Dedalus, Class of Elements, Clongowes Wood School, Sallins, County Kildare, Ireland, Europe, The World, The Universe" (12). Drawing on Joyce's formula a year before the publication of *Survival,* Munro is already filling in the gaps to be later addressed by Atwood (McWilliams 372). *Lives of Girls and Women* brings together female development with a vision of a specifically Canadian geographical and social landscape, making an essential contribution to the resolution of the pressing question posed by Frye and Atwood: "Where is here?"

Much like Atwood's *Lady Oracle*, Margaret Laurence's *The Diviners*, the final instalment of her Manawaka series, charts a series of escapes: from the poverty and bigotry of small-town life in Manitoba, and later from a paternalistic husband, to Morag Gunn's achievement of independence as a writer. The structure of the novel, alternating between Morag's life as a writer and mother at 47 and her childhood and youth in Manawaka, has attracted much critical attention. Stories and myths of family and regional history are very important in the novel as Morag assimilates Christie Logan's stories of her ancestor Piper Gunn, a brave Scottish pioneer, as well as the conflicting stories of her Métis lover and father of her daughter, Jules Tonnerre. As in Atwood's fiction, the formation of selfhood is, in part, a process of mythmaking. *The Diviners* draws attention to the limits and ultimate unreliability of this process in Morag's "Memorybank Movie" and "Innerfilm" sequences and in the conflicting versions of the stories told according to their source. In spite of this unreliability, Morag determinedly passes her own version of these stories on to her daughter as she realises that such mythologies are indelibly inscribed on her own imagination and are crucial determinants of her identity.

In the course of the novel, Morag Gunn gradually recognises the importance of the Canadian myths and stories that have shaped her development as she comes to accept her hometown as a key influence on her artistic imagination. Like Del Jordan the young Morag Gunn realises that: "She wouldn't go back to Manawaka for all the tea in China or Assam. And yet the town inhabits her, as once she inhabited it" (185). Unlike Atwood, Munro and Laurence foreground locality and region as key components of Canadian identity. For Laurence as for Munro writing "has to be set firmly in some soil, some place, some outer and inner territory which might be described in anthropological terms as 'cultural background'" ("A Place to Stand On" 18). Atwood's early work as a writer and critic was thus fashioned by Laurence's emphasis on the need to acknowledge a distinctively Canadian "cultural background" as her primary concern as a critic in the early 1970s was with establishing a national Canadian literature while remaining respectful of Canadian literature's regional origins. At the same time, Atwood's early fiction is as concerned with imagined as real Canadian geographies.

Like Atwood's engagement with her literary heritage in her collection of poetry, *The Journals of Susanna Moodie*, Laurence situates her novelist Morag Gunn in relation to a real-life Canadian pioneer woman writer: Moodie's sister, Catherine Parr-Traill. Morag engages in a humorous dialogue with Parr-Traill and in a moment of crisis resorts to Parr-Traill's *The Canadian Settler's Guide* (1855) for guidance. Laurence is as specific and explicit as Munro in her evocation of the obstacles to her character's ambitions as a Canadian woman writer; Morag Gunn's first novel is reviewed in England as "a pleasant enough novel from the Canadian backwoods" (251). Writing in 1971, Laurence asserted on behalf of all Canadians that: "We have only just begun to value ourselves, our land, our abilities. We have only just begun to recognize our legends and to give shape to our myths" (217). A review of *The Diviners*, written by Atwood for the *New York Times* in 1974 shows acute sensitivity to this element of Laurence's work: "On yet another level, it explores the need for ancestors, legends, a past that is meaningful both personally and culturally. Morag, orphan and adopted child, rejecting the present and searching for a past she can respect and claim, is the archetypal transplanted Canadian, who must acknowledge the validity of the here and now before she can possess the myths she longs for" (MS Coll. 200:56:24:3). This, however, reveals as much about Atwood's primary concerns in the period as it does about *The Diviners* and so Atwood's ambitions find sympathy with two other hugely significant figures on the Canadian literary landscape.

The appearance of *Survival* just a year later was to serve exactly this purpose and moreover, as will become apparent in the next chapter, Atwood's early fiction – *Surfacing* in particular – reinvigorates and renegotiates such national myths and so, in keeping with her literary peers, Atwood makes a vital contribution to a new chapter in Canadian literary history.

PART 2
A Canadian Literary Apprenticeship: Atwood's Early Fiction

Chapter 3
The Canadian Bildungsroman: The "Birth of a Nation" in *The Nature Hut* and *Surfacing*

Atwood's search for a unifying Canadian symbol is a famous driving force in the narrator's journey into the Canadian wilderness in *Surfacing*. In *Surfacing*, the interior voyage of the unnamed narrator is conflated with the search for a meaningful national identity – one removed from misrepresentations and clichéd images of Canada. However, this quest does not entirely begin in 1972 with *Surfacing* and *Survival* as an earlier, unpublished novel, *The Nature Hut* (1966), displays strong signs of an awareness of the need for a fresh narrative of Canadian national identity. As with *Surfacing*, the novel presents another female protagonist charged with the hazardous task of asserting Canadian difference. With this in mind, this chapter will examine what is thought of by many as Atwood's signature novel, *Surfacing*, and the formative text, *The Nature Hut*, with particular reference to Atwood's expression of and commitment to, borrowing Benedict Anderson's phrase, the fashioning of a Canadian "imagined community".

While 1972 marked a turning point in Atwood's development as a curator and defender of the Canadian literary tradition, the questions raised in *Surfacing* and *Survival* were already to the forefront of Atwood's literary consciousness in 1966. In *The Nature Hut*, as in *Surfacing*, Atwood deploys the Bildungsroman for the purpose of contesting and re-envisioning images of Canada in a project that writes against the past and for the future of a Canadian literature. Indeed, that one of the other proposed titles for *The Nature Hut* was *Birth of a Nation* (though this is scribbled out on the draft typescript) is especially in keeping with this moment of commencement in Atwood's early career (MS Coll. 200:17:6).

The postcolonial interest in reading the nation as a narration, capable of plotting its own fictions, provides an appropriate point of entry for thinking about Atwood's writing in this period. Edward Said, in *Culture and Imperialism*, draws attention to the idea that:

> nations themselves *are* narrations. The power to narrate, or to block other narratives from forming and emerging, is very important to culture and imperialism, and constitutes one of the main connections between them. Most important, the grand narratives of emancipation and enlightenment mobilized people in the colonial world to rise up and throw off imperial subjection; in the process, many Europeans and Americans were also stirred by these stories and

> their protagonists, and they too fought for new narratives of equality and human community. (xiii)

Said's investment in the power of literary narrative to change the world is, on the one hand, very powerful and inspiring, yet also somewhat idealistic in its aspirations. However, the period of Canadian cultural renaissance explored in the previous chapter relied upon exactly such a faith in the possibility for change – and the refusal to be a victim – and so the compelling idea that nations rely on and are made up of the stories that nations tell about themselves is especially relevant to reading Atwood's early fiction. More than this, in Atwood's early work, the coming of age of her female characters is, at every turn, bound up with a transitional reading of Canada.

Said's idea of the "nation as narration" responds to the work of another postcolonial theorist, Homi Bhabha. As intimated in his introduction to the suggestively entitled *Nation and Narration*, Bhabha is more interested in the narratives and stories that make up a national identity than in the notion that there is anything essential about such an identity. For Bhabha, as for Said, the idea of the nation is an unstable one, dependent on narratives, which are in turn guided by varied and different narrative perspectives (3). This speaks to the heart of Atwood's cultural mission in the late 1960s and 1970s, something that is most explicitly stated in the manifesto of *Survival*, but is also evident in the subtexts of *The Nature Hut* and *Surfacing*. Of particular interest in this chapter is how the Bildungsroman seems to offer Atwood an appropriate vehicle for the expression of a new idea of Canada. As is emphasized by historians of the genre such as Todd Kontje, the Bildungsroman was seen, in its original German context, as presenting a reliable model for nationhood (*The German Bildungsroman* 29). The Canadian version is far less willing to commit to the same totalizing narrative. Atwood's Canadian Bildungsroman seems concerned with the positive possibilities of conflating self and nation, but does so in a way that necessarily resists the genre's original faith in a teleological idea of national progress. Atwood's novels, although they contain distinctively Canadian inflections, show, at the same time, a real sensitivity to the dangers of discourses of national identity that leave national myths and symbols unquestioned.

Anthony D. Smith's definitive survey of the concept and theory of national identity emphasizes the importance of "shared memories, myths and traditions" (14) in sustaining collective identities. The importance of myth is evidently something that is at the forefront of most meditations on national identity. In his essay "The Functions of Myth and a Taxonomy of Myths" in *Myths and Nationhood*, George Schöpflin's discussion very quickly comes around to the idea that "Myth is one of the ways in which collectivities – in this context, more especially nations – establish and determine the foundation of their own being" (19). Atwood's *The Nature Hut* and *Surfacing* are fundamentally preoccupied with the making of such myths. Critics who considered *Survival* too absolute in its interest in coming up with a definitive critical model by which to read Canadian literature do not always acknowledge that, in the same year, Atwood interrogates some of her own critical assumptions in *Surfacing*. Her work does not by any means offer a simplified recipe for cultural sovereignty; instead, the concept is shown to be complex, fraught with contradictions, and dependent upon competing narratives of the nation that overlap and, at times, interrupt each other. David Miller emphasizes the performative aspects of such narrative forms and the way in which they are ultimately shown to be artificial and prone to "discontinuity" (35). Those critical of the overtly political aspects of Atwood's writing sometimes read her work as blinkered or closed off to this possibility. However, close study of her fiction reveals that her writing, even in this early period (which coincided with Atwood's emergence as a cultural nationalist), is highly attuned to the artificiality and "discontinuity" that characterizes the narration of the nation. Moreover, it is exactly this "discontinuity" that finds sympathy with the processes of fracturing and decentring characteristic of Atwood's Bildungsroman.

The Narration of Self and Nation in *The Nature Hut* and *Surfacing*

The Nature Hut and *Surfacing*, first and foremost, express an overriding need to reject those misreadings of Canada that are detrimental to Canadian culture, although there is no assumption that these are easily replaced by culturally comfortable alternatives. In the draft typescript of *The Nature Hut* the main character, Sue, finds herself on the brink of adulthood at a Summer Camp on the edge of a lake in the Canadian wilderness – not unlike the scene set in *Surfacing*. The novel opens with the owner and manager of the camp imagining a gentrified scene that is the epitome of English refinement, afternoon tea on the lawn, comprising "frosted cakes and little cucumber sandwiches, only slightly dry around the edges, reposing on the broad arms, their flowing summer draperies disposed with propriety about their limbs, their wide hats flowering like discreet pastel sneezes against the natural air" (MS Coll. 200:17:6:1). He acknowledges that such a manicured scene is, in fact, impossible, particularly when confronted with his wild untamed surroundings, the visual impressions of which are taken straight from a Group of Seven wilderness painting: "There was his view, authentic as a print on a bank president's wall or a commemoration stamp: islands, blue lake, rocky shores, distant jack pines bent picturesquely" (MS Coll. 200:17:6:2). This is not the only time in the novel when the attempt to impose an inappropriate or clumsy reading of Canada fails. *The Nature Hut* of the title is the headquarters of a new camp initiative, which attempts to educate the camp-goers about life in the Canadian wilderness and how to endure it. This comes about when the camp organizer realizes he is out of step with his competitors, who have already started to offer this distinctively Canadian education. This selling of "native" Canadian culture is developed at a camp meeting where the camp counsellors discuss how they might pitch it to the children: "Laurie looked bored. 'A Nature Song. A contest with some kind of prize. Dressing up in funny costumes, leaves or something. You know, the kind of gimmicks we always have around camp'" (MS Coll. 200:17:6:20). Thus, the whole enterprise is acknowledged as a gimmick and the initiative quickly collapses into parody when the display at the Nature Hut turns out to be made up of a few "hysterical toads" in economy size apple sauce jars and "a Mississauga rattlesnake" (MS Coll. 200:17:6:20–1).

A scene where Sue is confronted by two of the American counsellors at the camp is worth reproducing in full, if only because of the way it dramatizes the need for the question "Where is here?" at this formative moment in Atwood's writing career. Sue is put under pressure to defend and justify Canada in the face of dismissive assumptions about Canadian sovereignty. When challenged to explain "this excuse for a country" she is faced with a multi-levelled dilemma, one that is both intentionally personal and of national significance:

> "What would you like to know?" she asked politely. "Oh, History, culture, famous wars, famous writers and artists," Sam said. The things that make a country great. Was that the principle city we passed through on our way to this godforsaken place? It looked like Cleveland Ohio. Sue pondered; she knew they were just getting back at her but at the same time it occurred to her that either nobody had told her about the famous wars and the writers or there weren't any. All that came to mind were a few lines – "Make me over, Mother Nature," in the Grade Ten poetry reader which everyone else had laughed at, though she couldn't see it was that much funnier than a lot of the other poems; and "on the brow of the hill, for all to see, God planted a Scarlet Maple Tree", that had been a printing exercise in grade four, they had to bring maple leaves to school and iron them between sheets of waxed paper and glue them onto the top of the page. Also she had never been to Cleveland. Except for the summers she had never been anywhere except Belleville to visit one set of her grandparents. She decided she would go to England as soon as she graduated. … Sue looked around at the sky, the water, the islands, their outlines melting into one another as they receded, but they gave her no help. (MS Coll. 200:17:6:52–3)

This hostile dismissal of the one of the centres of Canadian political power (Toronto) as a regional outpost of the United States, and the direct challenge regarding Canadian cultural and literary history, leaves Sue feeling under siege and unsure of her bearings. Moreover, the fact that she has no grounds for comparison, having never been outside of Canada, makes her postcolonial anxiety all the more acute. The wilderness, for all of its sublime beauty, offers no consolation or relief from the burden of her postcolonial quandary, and, in contrast to her counterpart in *Surfacing*, she finds no redemption in the landscape. It remains a mere canvas, a backdrop against which her adolescent anxieties and insecurities are played out. In *The Nature Hut*, Sue suffers for her nation's identity crisis, something that is repeatedly explicated in Atwood's early work. *The Nature Hut*, however, offers an original statement of this problem. The camp counsellors meet to plan a festival for the children and run into difficulty when "This Land is Ours" is chosen as a theme: "'So what're we going to *do* with This Land of Ours?' Howie said. 'There's fuck-all to work with.' He was a poor loser. 'We've got three weeks,' Bernie said. 'We'll come up with something'" (MS Coll. 200:17:6:58). This initial search for a Canadian theme prefigures the search for identity in *Surfacing* and has a clear impact on narratives of personal as well as national identity in Atwood's early fiction.

In *Surfacing*, the narrator finds herself and her homeplace subject to similar misreadings, although they are in some ways less open and unqualified. Placed in the position of tour guide and unwilling ambassador, she uneasily follows the other characters' exploitative gaze as they impose their own meaning on the community from which she comes. Early on in the novel, one of the main characters, David, reveals the laziness of his politics in the way that he looks at the local characters as historical curiosities: "He's enjoying himself, he thinks this is reality: a marginal economy and grizzled elderly men, it's straight out of Depression photo essays" (24). Soon afterwards, he surveys the scene with the self-righteous and deeply inappropriate denouncement: "'Do you realize,' David says, 'that this country is founded on the bodies of dead animals? Dead fish, dead seals, and historically dead beavers, the beaver is to this country what the black man is to the United States'" (33–4). Alongside these imposed misreadings, a number of false associations recur in the early stages of the novel. As they approach the Quebecois wilderness Anna sings and hums American folk songs, "The Big Rock Candy Mountain", "House of the Rising Sun", "St Louis Blues", oblivious and indifferent to the fact that she is, geographically, wildly off the mark in her associations.

In foregrounding the processes by which the idea of the nation is conceived and maintained, the bookshelf in the narrator's childhood home offers direct access to the textual preferences of Canadian national identity. A number of books, which contribute in an important way to the narrative of the nation in the novel, are to be found on the narrator's father's bookshelf. Her father's library, resonant as it is with Canada's pioneer history, includes: "*Edible Plants and Shoots*, *Tying the Dry Fly*, *The Common Mushrooms*, *Log Cabin Construction*, *A Field Guide to the Birds*, *Exploring Your Camera*", all of which document the realities of life in the wilderness. Closer still to the wilderness motif central to Canadian culture are those texts that the narrator has assimilated and committed to memory: "I memorized survival manuals, *How to Stay Alive in the Bush*, *Animal Tracks and Signs*, *The Woods in Winter*, at the age when the ones in the city were reading True Romance magazines" (42).

Alongside of these pragmatic handbooks that gesture very explicitly towards the Canadian pioneer past – the world of one of Atwood's most troublesome and interesting literary predecessors, the nineteenth-century writer Susanna Moodie – there exists another consecrated narrative of Canadian origins. The reference to the maple leaf in the extract previously quoted from *The Nature Hut* reappears in the childhood memories of the narrator of *Surfacing*. She recalls the motto strung across the classroom of the school she attended as a child: "'On the crest of the hill for all to see, God planted a Scarlet Maple Tree' printed thirty-five times, strung out along the top of the blackboard, each page with a preserved maple leaf glued to it, ironed between sheets of wax paper" (47). This fragment from a poem by the nineteenth-century Canadian poet, Bliss Carman, draws together the Canadian literary past and Canada's most universally recognizable national symbol. However, the multiple copies, the facsimiled nature of this statement of Canadian origins, suggest that the story of any nation can only be secured through repetition and a constant restatement of its central co-ordinates.

Alongside such absolutist mantras, the narrator recalls her younger self, as she encountered an obfuscation of historical reality, one that is described in frustrated terms in the novel. The discourses of national identity are laid down collectively and the narrator recalls finding herself very much at their mercy:

> That's how it was in high school, they taught it neutrally, a long list of wars and treaties and alliances, people taking and losing power over other people; but nobody would ever go into the motives, why they wanted it, whether it was good or bad. They used words like "demarcation" and "sovereignty", they wouldn't say what they meant and you couldn't ask. (91)

She responds with an instinctive irreverence to these grand narratives and official histories that she is expected to accept without further inquiry: "In the margins around the Treaty of Versailles I drew ornaments, plants with scrolled branches, hearts and stars instead of flowers" (92). Her subjective and incongruous amendments to the Treaty of Versailles hints at a refutation of official histories. This is also suggested in the film that the men in her party, Joe and David, seek to make in the course of their stay in the wilderness. "Random Samples" is a collection of images of local curiosities, including the inevitable family of stuffed moose, placed in no specific order. In *Surfacing*, this random, disordered collection of images might be read as displacing, or at least foregrounding, the artificial notion that the official histories that underlie any given national consciousness are seamless and reliable. Far from offering an uncomplicated formula for cultural sovereignty by a single-minded cultural nationalist, the novels offer a delicate exposition of the different and competing readings of Canada. A poem called "At the Tourist Centre in Boston" from one of Atwood's early collections *The Animals in that Country* (1968) also sees Canada "under glass" in much the same way as a number of characters imagine it in *The Nature Hut* and *Surfacing*: "Whose dream is this, I would like to know:/is this a manufactured/hallucination, a cynical fiction, a lure/ for export only?" (*Eating Fire: Selected Poetry 1965–1995* 33). These cultural misreadings are as likely to be perpetuated by Canadians in Atwood's writing as anyone else and this is shown vividly in an unpublished story dating to the 1960s, "Late Bus to Montreal". In this story a young woman travelling back from the United States to her home in Montreal engages in an imaginary dialogue with the French Catholic priest, who sits down next to her:

> Do priests eat lifesavers, or is it a sin? *Voulez-vous un lifesaver*? But lifesaver is an English word; I wouldn't want to offend him. *Voulez-vous un saveur de vie*? No, he might think I'm a Jehovah's Witness. By this time I know I won't be able to have a lifesaver myself without offering him one first, and offering him one at all is clearly impossible. (MS Coll. 200:40:3:2)

The narrator speculates as to his religious and cultural prejudices while also revealing her own naïveté and shows the "two solitudes" of French and Anglo-Canadian experience as she fails to look beyond her received impressions of the Quebecois.

Symbolism and Subjectivity in *The Nature Hut* and *Surfacing*

The identification of national symbols is, as suggested in the example of the maple leaf, shown to be similarly subject to challenge in *The Nature Hut* and *Surfacing*. Smith describes how national symbols serve a key function in maintaining a promise of cultural history and cohesiveness:

> These concepts – autonomy, identity, national genius, authenticity, unity and fraternity – form an interrelated language or discourse that has its expressive ceremonials and symbols. These symbols and ceremonies are so much part of the world we live in that we take them, for the most part, for granted. They include the obvious attributes of nations – flags, anthems, parades, coinage, capital cities, oaths, folk costumes, museums of folklore, war memorials, ceremonies of remembrance for the national dead, passports, frontiers – as well as more hidden aspects, such as national recreations, the countryside, popular heroes and heroines, fairy tales, forms of etiquette, styles of architecture, arts and crafts, modes of town planning, legal procedures, educational practices and military codes – all those distinctive customs, mores, styles and ways of acting and feeling that are shared by the members of a community of historical culture. (77)

The shared experience of any community is, then, affected by the overt or discreet manifestation of such symbols.

In *Imagined Communities: Reflections on the Origin and Spread of Nationalism* (1983), Benedict Anderson explores a number of novels where "we see the 'national imagination' at work in the movement of a solitary hero through a sociological landscape of a fixity that fuses the world inside the novel with the world outside" (30). Atwood modifies this reading as in her early work it is women who go in search of and interrogate Canada's symbols of choice in the course of their own coming to consciousness.

The opening chapters of *Surfacing* bombard the reader with a stream of references to just such national symbolism. In the opening pages, the narrator notes how Joe looks "like the buffalo on the U.S. nickel" (2). They arrive at their destination only to find a confusion of "signs saying GATEWAY TO THE NORTH, at least four towns claim to be that" (3). Another road sign, the ultimate statement of Canada's bifurcated identity, is damaged and shows symptoms of being under siege: "There's nothing I can remember till we reach the border, marked by the sign that says BIENVENUE on one side and WELCOME on the other. The sign has bullet holes in it, rusting red around the edges" (5). This is quickly followed by an acknowledgement of the narrator's uneasiness at being "Anglais" in Quebec: "Now we're on my home ground, foreign territory" (5). Local graffiti offers a cross-sectional view of simmering tensions, both regional and global: "Québec Libre, Fuck You, Buvez Coca Cola Glacé, Jesus Saves, mélange of demands and languages, an x-ray of it would be the district's entire history" (9). All of these signs are corrupted in some way and prove to be self-contradicting, and the roadside view of the narrator's Canada defiantly suggests the absence of any single, representative national symbol; significantly, even geographical demarcations of the Canadian North are open to contest. Those symbols that are available are less than adequate or are wheeled out for the benefit of visitors, as is the case with the cushion embroidered with an emblem of Niagara Falls at Madame's house, which is reserved exclusively for the comfort of guests (14). This troubled symbolism, which fails effectively to communicate its meaning, extends to architecture in various forms as the narrator recognizes the bar that they stop at as "an imitation of other places, more southern ones, which are themselves imitations, the original someone's distorted memory of a nineteenth century English gentleman's shooting lodge …" (21). There are times when Atwood, in this early period, seems to regret the way in which Canadian literary culture lacks easily-identifiable cultural motifs, but, as the latter reference seems to suggest, her explication of symbols in *Surfacing* also indicates a wariness of national symbols; they prove to be mere simulations derived from sources which, in some cases, are themselves simulations. The artificial and forced quality of such symbolism is acted out with particular effect in *The Nature Hut*, when the camp leader in charge of this microcosm of the Canadian wilderness is pushed to humiliating lengths to endorse it:

> He was wearing nothing but a bathing suit and was painted bright green; a vine was wound about his waist and his beard and naturally-shaggy hair were stuck full of large floppy leaves. On his back was a sign which said "Visit the Nature Hut." In his right hand, which had on a gardener's glove, was a rattlesnake, its body spiralled around his arm. (MS Coll. 200:17:6:40–1)

Although given comic treatment here, the real dangers of the allure of such symbolism emerge in Joe's delusional (borderline psychotic) fantasies that he is a pioneer hero, one who will inherit the wilderness after the inevitable destruction of urban civilization:

> He himself thinks there's no point in teaching these kids any of this. You don't learn things unless you need to know them, and those kids will never need to know how to light a fire, what kind of wood to use, where to find things to eat. They will live in cities and be well taken care of, their heat arriving by wires, their food in packages, already caught, killed and chewed. They will grow up and get married and have jobs and be healthy until the moment the bomb's dropped, and after that they won't need to know anything at all. (MS Coll. 200:17:6:44–5)

Joe quietly bides his time, waiting for the restoration of the wilderness and the death of the city, ever ready for the moment of reckoning: "He carried his knife always with him, and some matches in a waterproof container" (MS Coll. 200: 17:6:45).

Indeed, the lack of crystallized, historically grounded symbols is something that Atwood actually comes to reappraise in more positive terms – the modesty of her choice of survival as the key theme of Canadian culture is, accordingly, not necessarily a sign of perverse self-deprecation, but is a productive alternative to the more obvious route of national self-aggrandizement. This is where Atwood's environmentalism takes on a new fervour, as, not for the last time, the apparent limits of the idea of survival takes on a positive value in comparison to the colonialist values of the American Frontier, "a line that is always expanding, taking in or 'conquering' ever-fresh virgin territory" (*Survival* 31).

Smith describes the importance of reaching back to history to any conception of cultural nationalism:

> The purposes of nationalist educator-intellectuals are social and political, not academic; they aim to purify and activate the people. To do so, moral exemplars from the ethnic past are needed, as are vivid recreations of the glorious past of the community. Hence the return to that past through a series of myths: myths of origins and descent, of liberation and migration, of the golden age and its heroes and sages, perhaps of the chosen people now to be reborn after its long sleep of decay and/or exile. Together, these myth-motifs can be formed into a composite nationalist mythology and salvation drama. (66)

Atwood's cultural nationalism in this period did not have access to, nor was it necessarily interested in, such a "salvation drama". Atwood as an "educator-intellectual", particularly in *Survival*, is emphatically forward looking and aware of the limitations of her project. Those most critical of Atwood's "thematic" approach to Canadian literature objected in the main to what seemed to be its dangerous commitment to a grand narrative of Canadian survivalism. However, *Surfacing* holds a mirror up to Canadian culture in ways that emphasize the different and multiple strands of Canadian history and the inherent unreliability of apparently stable national histories and symbols.

This is vividly shown in the way that another set of conflicting symbols emerges in the juxtaposition of the narrator's artwork with her father's catalogue of Native Canadian cave drawings. In the middle of working on illustrations for a collection of Quebec Folk Tales – a Disneyfied version of local tales and stories – she discovers her father's drawings: "More hands, then a stiff childish figure, faceless and minus the hands and feet, and on the next page a similar creature with two things like tree branches or antlers protruding from its head" (53). She assumes that these drawings are a sign of madness – something that would explain her father's sudden disappearance. In fact, they turn out to be reproductions of native art, worlds away from the sanitized images of her illustrations of heavily edited Quebecois folklore. In keeping with this, *The Nature Hut* parodies the summer camp culture and its infantile reduction of the Canadian North to small animals in oversized jam jars and childish attempt at a performance of Canadian culture. While this earlier Atwood text shows a lively awareness of the danger of colonizing the Canadian wilderness for the benefit of Anglo-Canadian self-image, *Surfacing* finds a new meaningful engagement with the wilderness.

At the same time those national motifs and symbols that are most readily recognized as Canadian, although they have a significant place in the popular consciousness, are not rejected out of hand but are continually tested and reworked by Atwood. In a speech addressing the Parliamentary Committee on Free Trade in 1987, Atwood expresses an ongoing concern for the future of Canadian sovereignty: "Our national animal is the beaver, noted for its industry and its co-operative spirit. In medieval bestiaries it is also noted for its habit, when frightened, of biting off its own testicles and offering them to its pursuer. I hope we are not succumbing to some form of that impulse" (MS Coll. 200:97:10:9). This particularly rueful Atwoodian metaphor sees a jaded symbol self-consciously rewritten for a charged political purpose.

The Nature Hut, like *Surfacing*, contains a dialogue between national and individual experience, one that is very aware of the challenges and anxieties involved in writing the female Bildungsroman (particularly in a Canadian context). In this regard, the main character of *The Nature Hut* seems like a near relative, a younger and more precocious version, of the unnamed narrator in *Surfacing*. The female and feminist quest for a meaningful identity in the wilderness of Atwood's novel is something that has been explored in detail elsewhere and preoccupied many early feminist readings of *Surfacing*. In her suggestively entitled book, *Diving Deep and Surfacing: Women Writers on Spiritual Quest*, Carol P. Christ's reading of the novel leads her to conclude that "women must positively name the power that resides in their bodies and their sense of closeness to nature and use this new naming to transform the pervasive cultural and religious devaluation of nature and the body" (53) and this is representative of the critical discourse that sees Atwood rewriting the wilderness from a woman-centred point of view. It would seem, in the light of material relating to Atwood's PhD thesis, that the self-conscious aspect of Atwood's engagement with the idea of the wilderness is informed by her early academic interests as well as her creative interest in the relationship between women and nature. In a chapter on "The Power of Nature: The Victorian Motherworld" in a draft of her thesis, "Nature and Power in the

English Metaphysical Romance of the Nineteenth and Twentieth Centuries", she examines the Romantic cult of nature, drawing the conclusion: "One of the often-investigated features of this literature is its interest in Nature: not Nature as decorative landscape or source of emblems for moral homilies, but Nature as a mystical, even sentient source of wisdom and symbol of revelation and the regeneration of the imagination" (MS Coll. 200:50:7:9). By this definition, *Surfacing* is not without its Romantic influences as it enables exactly such regeneration in the main character, the "multilingual water" (172) of the lake becoming a healing balm for her worldly unhappiness. Atwood goes on, in the same chapter of her dissertation, to look at the more problematic Romantic reading of women and nature and identifies a spectrum of Wordsworthian types:

> They may be Nature's Darlings like Lucy, dewy maidens who however lack the eternal strength of Nature herself. According to both Wordsworth and later fiction, such magic virgins must either die and be resumed into the Nature that sent them forth, have "natural" children and turn into Mad Mothers, images of Nature in her wilder moments, or marry, become domesticated, and lose their charismatic nature-maiden status. (MS Coll. 200:50:7:10)

The protagonist of *Surfacing*, a character conceived while Atwood's academic meditations on Romantic Nature were still fresh in her mind, is an explicit refutation of the Wordsworthian archetype and while she may dwell "amongst untrodden ways", her communion with nature marks a new departure in the feminist appropriation of an historically problematic association between women and nature.

The Nature Hut is fundamentally a novel about the choices or lack thereof of a young woman on the brink of adulthood in Canada in the late 1950s. The main character Sue wants every aspect of her life to be chosen, self-directed and driven exclusively by her own desires and ambitions: "Most of the people she knew, older ones especially, were the result of a string of accidents, coincidences and mistakes … . Her mother said 'And then I married your father' as though she was saying, 'And then I fell off a wall.' Sue wanted everything in her life to be chosen" (MS Coll. 200:17:6:7). At the same time, she expresses frustration that "there had to be something to choose" (MS Coll. 200:17:6:7), the choices available to her in small-town Canada being limited. Canada's apparently marginalized position in the world affects her personally as she realizes: "There were things seriously wrong with the world but none of them were visible except in magazines: the trouble spots were all in other countries. More and more, she had come to feel like an audience, despite the work she had done for the Powdered Eggs for India Fund and the time she had put in sorting and tidying up bundles of used clothing in the Unitarian church basement" (MS Coll. 200:17:6:8). Her feeling of being sidelined, of coming from a place where nothing happens, partly explains the desperate and fetishized interpretation of Canada that is manifest in the "nature hut" and in the peculiar activities of the camp. Sue's determination to make her own choices marks the beginning of a long and varied investigation into life-choices in Atwood's fiction as within the next decade Atwood's fiction would confront the reality that, for women, desiring their own Bildungsroman is not enough. Sue offers an early incarnation of Atwood's coming-of-age plot and she believes most sincerely that her life is in her own hands to be ordered and managed as she sees fit, and well within her control. While the unfinished manuscript of *The Nature Hut* doesn't reveal how successful Sue is in this project, *Surfacing* provides a different kind of answer in its formula for selfhood, acknowledging as it does the unconscious fears and desires that determine the protagonist of the novel's interior journey.

In *Surfacing*, the narrator's voyage is, like so many manifestations of the female Bildungsroman in the 1960s and 70s, solitary and not without danger. In a review of Adrienne Rich's collection *Diving into the Wreck: Poems 1971–1972*, Atwood writes: "her book is not a manifesto, though it subsumes manifestoes; nor is it a proclamation, though it makes proclamations. It is instead a book of explorations, of travels. The wreck she is diving into, in the very strong title poem, is the wreck of obsolete myths, particularly myths about men and women" (280). This could also be a description of *Surfacing*. The title poem of Rich's collection, "Diving into the Wreck", charts a descent into history in search of "a book of myths in which our names do not appear" (55). Given the salient concern with interrogating language and literary convention in Atwood's writing, Rich's poem makes for an appropriate companion text to *Surfacing*, particularly with its commitment to diving as a metaphor for the retrieval of a lost history, and the restoration of a sense of self. Rich wrestles with and comes to her own solution with regard to the perennial problem of patriarchal language and the problematic gendering of language, literary language in particular, through an endorsement of androgyny. Towards the end of Rich's poem, in a play with pronouns, the diver encompasses male and female forms: "I am she: I am he" (55). *Surfacing* poses a similar challenge to language and, towards the end of the text, words are detached from their meaning in the hope of engendering new meanings, meanings that can accommodate the experience of women as well as men. The narrator identifies a problem with language and, at first, seeks to evade it: "it was that language again. I couldn't use it because it wasn't mine" (100). The "rudimentary language" of nature (35), the pre-lapsarian world of the wilderness promises an escape from this, as is most vividly seen in the later sections of the novel, as the narrator repossesses language on new terms. The narrator, like a twentieth-century version of the pioneering Susanna Moodie, arrives in the wilderness, unsure of what she will find there. Unlike Moodie, she is not concerned with overcoming the harsh realities of inhospitable nature but rather becomes part of it:

> The forest leaps upward, enormous, the way it was before they cut it, columns of sunlight frozen; the boulders float, melt, everything is made of water, even the rocks. In one of the languages there are no nouns, only verbs held for a longer moment. The animals have no need for speech, why

> talk when you are a word
> I lean against a tree, I am a tree leaning.
> I break out again into the bright sun and crumple, head against the ground
> I am not an animal or a tree, I am a thing in which the trees and animals move and grow, I am a place (175)

Here, nature is restored to its original state and the narrator retreats from the order of language. There is a deliberate omission of the full stop after "word", "ground", and "place" as the distance between experience and the words used to describe it begins to fade. This image of a world outside the order of language recurs in "The Animals Reject their Names" in *The Tent* (2006), a fantasy in which "the dictionaries began to untwist" (79): "because the page darkens and ripples/ because it is liquid and unbroken" (83). "The Animals Reject their Names" returns to the water imagery of *Surfacing*, with its reference to the "ripples" of page and the image of a language that is "liquid and unbroken". The natural landscape of *Surfacing* is all the more important because the question "Who am I?" and "Where is here?" come to have an identical meaning in a suggestive conflation of personal and national identity.

At the end of Chapter 12, the narrator looks back over her own life in the family photo album. Photography is treated as suspect throughout the novel, represented both in the cannibalizing of the Canadian landscape in "Random Samples" and in the predatory voyeuristic assault on Anna by the dock (128). The narrator looks back at her younger self – a footnote in the extended history of the family recorded in the albums – and finds the impressions less than adequate:

> I watched myself grow larger. Mother and father in alternate shots, building the house, walls and then the roof, planting the garden. Around them were borders of blank paper, at each corner a hinge, they were like small grey and white windows opening into a place I could no longer reach. I was in most of the pictures, shut in behind the paper; or not me but the missing part of me. (102)

Cut off from the "missing part" of herself, the future is equally inscrutable: "The last pages of the album were blank, with some loose prints stuck in between the black leaves as though my mother hadn't wanted to finish" (102). Her life story, her Bildungsroman, as represented in the photo album is incomplete; like the story of her lover and their lost child, there is no hope of or particular desire for a definitive version of the same.

There is agonizing uncertainty at the end of the novel: the protagonist can hear the voices of her companions calling her, and remains unsure, though she previously accepted that "the word games, the winning and losing games are finished; at the moment there are no others but they will have to be invented, withdrawing is no longer possible and the alternative is death" (185). Atwood's novels generally show a similar lack of faith in resolution. Atwood's endings often have a distinctly Beckettian aspect to them. The well-known ending of Beckett's *The Unnameable* (1958) speaks to the predicament of Atwood's characters in revealing ways: "I can't go on, you must go on, I'll go on, you must say words, as long as there are any … I'll never know, in the silence you don't know, you must go on, I can't go on, I'll go on" (418). This is an intractable dilemma that Atwood's characters often find themselves in and the protagonist of *Surfacing* is a prime example. The promise of resolution and harmonious closure, where the protagonist and the world he inhabits are reconciled, is a key interest in the early Bildungsroman. While *The Nature Hut*, as an unfinished manuscript, can't hope to offer an ending, *Surfacing,* in the full knowledge of the dangerous complacency of such endings, actively refuses to. Like the blank pages of the photo album, the undocumented chapters of the protagonist's life, we are edited out of her life history as deftly and swiftly as we were invited in.

Chapter 4
Digesting the Female Bildungsroman: Consuming Fictions in *The Edible Woman* and *Lady Oracle*

At a remove from the harmonious, interactive formation chronicled in the classic Bildungsroman, Atwood's *The Edible Woman* and *Lady Oracle* very explicitly explore an emerging multiplicity in the protagonists' selfhood. Perhaps more dramatically than in *Surfacing*, this development is unstable and fragmented, void of the measured rhythm of the Bildungsheld's linear progress. When studied against Rita Felski's useful definition of the female Bildungsroman as biographical, dialectical, historical, and teleological (*Beyond Feminist Aesthetics* 135), *The Edible Woman* makes a radical contribution to the tradition, a contribution that is at odds with many contemporaneous practitioners and critics of the genre. Atwood's subversive rendering of the genre may be read in two ways. It might be regarded as a carefully executed revenge on the Bildungsroman, as Atwood's infiltration and re-working of the genre exposes the exclusively masculine ideals embodied in its conventions. Equally, it questions the idea of appropriating the genre as a medium for nurturing the aspirations generated by the apparent feminist liberation of the 1960s and 1970s. In her fiction, Atwood recasts the established structures of the Bildungsroman, resulting in a carefully controlled implosion of the traditional model. Yet the nature and course of development manifest by her characters, though inscribing a common dynamic towards plurality, multiplicity, dissemination, and even disintegration, find very different modes of expression.

Marian MacAlpin's development in *The Edible Woman* is characterized by the repudiation of the options of "a young woman, even a young educated woman, in Canada in the early sixties" (*The Edible Woman*, introduction), a process by which her subjectivity is increasingly threatened by the social and cultural snares that entrap and almost destroy her. If the classic Bildungsroman presents a weave of experience and intrinsic potential, and the female Bildungsroman, particularly in the nineteenth century, inevitably wreaks disaster upon the aspiring heroine, Atwood introduces a new dimension to the structure: the subversion or inversion of *Bildung* based on the premise of divided selfhood and unravelling subjectivity. Linda Hutcheon writes, specifically in relation to *The Edible Woman*, that "both Atwood's feminist and postmodernist impulses work to question the very nature of selfhood as it is defined in our culture: that is, as coherent, unified, rational" (*The Canadian Postmodern* 144). This chapter is primarily concerned with such destabilizing strategies in both *The Edible Woman* and *Lady Oracle* and is particularly interested in the relationship between food and fiction, and writing and eating, in the delineation of the main characters' growth and development. The epigraph to *The Edible Woman* is taken from *The Joy of Cooking*, which is appropriate, given that the novel offers a recipe for survival or self-preservation not commonly associated with the Bildungsroman tradition. Early drafts of *The Edible Woman*, and unpublished work dating to the period in which it was written, shed new light on the symbolism of food in the novel. Moreover, the novel contains a very subtle dialogue between the feminist and postcolonial elements in the text, one that has much to say to the interactions between feminism and nationalism in *Surfacing*. To date, most discussions of the novels have focused on food and power politics and the representation of the woman writer, taking them as separate issues. This chapter seeks to offer a new perspective that brings food and fiction together. It will argue that the fictions that proliferate in these novels are figured as eminently consumable and, in the case of *Lady Oracle*, are consumed with considerable relish.

Growing Pains and Unusual Cravings in *The Edible Woman* and *Lady Oracle*

In *The Edible Woman*, Marian's quest for an autonomous identity is based on a process of negation, of rejecting the pre-set feminine roles offered by society. Her development is, then, a systematic revolt against the dismal choices open to her, as opposed to a positive striving towards the dangling carrot of maturity offered by the Bildungsroman. In describing *The Edible Woman* as a "comedy of resistance" (*Margaret Atwood* 43), Coral Ann Howells foregrounds a key aspect of Marian's progression or regression in the novel, a private resistance literalized in her growing aversion to food. The character's relationship with food is the most crucial element in the charting of her self-discovery and development in the novel, as Marian takes her place in a tradition of starving women in literature.

Before examining the significance of food as an indicator of the state of female subjectivity, it is important to acknowledge another recurring motif in the complex pattern of images of distortion and disintegration in *The Edible Woman*. While this is clearly evident in the published version of the novel, earlier drafts of *The Edible Woman* found in the Atwood Collection shed further light on the recurring references to loss of control and dissipation, images that are vital in conveying the precarious state of Marian's self-image in the novel. The loss of control realized in Marian's eating disorder is prefigured in Part One in a series of episodes where she finds her body going beyond herself – what she gravely identifies as "my sub-conscious getting ahead of my conscious self" (101). An early draft typescript of the novel places a more exaggerated emphasis on this abnegation of control and agency:

> But instead I heard a soft flannelly voice I barely recognized, saying, "I'd rather have you decide that. I'd rather leave the big decisions up to you." I was

> astounded at myself. I'd never said anything remotely like that to him before. He put his hand under my chin and turned my head on the pivot of my neck so he could look at me. I let myself be manipulated, passive as a marionette on strings. He was gazing down at me with a peculiar mixture of delight, fascination, and horror. (MS Coll. 200:18:23:90)

However, these more explicit references to Marian's acquiescence are toned down in the final version, where the somewhat didactic image of Marian as a puppet on a string is edited out.

The first draft typescript of Chapter 1 of *The Edible Woman* immediately introduces Marian as a split subject, who projects her emotions and thought processes onto a childhood doll and figures herself as a detached observer of her responses and reactions: "she doesn't like being blackmailed in that particular way; I could sense her whole body scowling, but I only said meekly, 'I'm all right'" (MS Coll. 200:18:2:4). The finished product, however, is a far more subtle examination of bifurcated subjectivity. Marian's fear of losing control over her body and her life is fully realized in a series of discreet images – the warped reflection on the back of a spoon, the water taps of her bath, and even in her fiancé's eyes – as she seems on course for disastrous metamorphosis into Mrs Peter Wollander.

In her introduction to the novel, Atwood describes how early inspiration for *The Edible Woman* came from pondering the seemingly consumable figures of the bride and groom frequently placed on top of wedding cakes. This image first features in her unpublished novel, *Up in the Air so Blue* (1964): "She walked past the next few stores; then there was a confectionary shop with a cardboard and plaster-of-Paris wedding-cake in the window. She stopped to examine the miniature bride and groom perched on the top tier beneath a flowery paper archway" (MS Coll. 200:16:3:48–9). The cannibalistic overtones of this interest in food and symbolism in Atwood's work are more fully realized in *The Edible Woman* where food takes on a new resonance in the feminist and postcolonial discourses of Atwood's fiction. The processes of formation and transformation that the protagonist undergoes in the novel are at every turn intertwined with consumption and consumerism, as the protagonist's relationship with food, and in particular her increasingly diminished appetite, serve as indicators of the unstable state of her self-image and subjectivity.

Food is recognized as an all-important metaphor for the identity crisis of the main character, Marian MacAlpin. Much like Kafka's Hunger Artist in his short story of the same name, her refusal of food is an act of resistance. While the feminist elements of the novel are most vividly expressed in the representation of food in the text, and have been the focus of most of the critical attention paid to the novel since its publication, the references to Canada in the novel serve as an important reminder that the power relations explored are relevant to the forging of a national as well as a female identity; the novel presents a recipe for self-preservation in national as well as individual terms, and lays the foundation for the more developed exploration of the precariousness of Canadian identity and survival as a key symbol of Canadian culture in Atwood's later novels, perhaps most famously *Surfacing*. The novel marks a crucial moment in Atwood's development as a feminist and postcolonial thinker; a key aspect of the novel to which critics have not paid due attention in previous discussions of the text is that the corollary between feminist and postcolonial narratives, which is so striking in Atwood's later work, is also evident in *The Edible Woman*.

The diagnosis of Marian's eating disorder as a rejection of an exploitative, predatory consumer culture (Rigney 33) is representative of the approach taken by critics who view the novel as an exposé of female objectification. This finds resonance with Maud Ellmann's work on women and hunger in *The Hunger Artists: Starving, Writing and Imprisonment* (1993) and the emphasis she places on how "the starving body is itself a text, the living dossier of its discontents, for the injustices of power are encoded in the savage hieroglyphics of its sufferings" (16). Atwood's suggestion that "Marian's difficulty is that she comes to identify with the objects the society is consuming, especially food. And because she's making that identification and seeing herself as the consumed rather than the consumer, she stops eating" (*Conversations* 28) would seem to validate this line of thinking. In the first full draft of the novel (held in the Atwood Collection), the character of Duncan draws exactly the same conclusion in relation to Marian's plight, though this is also edited out in the published version:

> "I know it isn't just Peter. I start feeling smothered by things and then I'm afraid of dissolving, but then at other times I seem to be afraid of something opposite, getting stuck, not being able to move. But most of all it's this food thing." She felt a pang of hunger as she spoke. "I'm afraid of eating, most of the time I seem to have lost my appetite completely, but I'm afraid of not eating too." Funny, she thought, how detached I'm being. "You're a mess, all right," Duncan said pleasantly. "They tell me that these days it's fashionable to regard the fear of doing something as very close to the fear of having it done to you, I wonder what that means, if anything?" (MS Coll. 200:18:32:257–8)

Again, the decision to modify Duncan's frank assessment of Marian's eating disorder ensures that the novel does not provide too emphatic a diagnosis of the character and allows for the ambiguous ending so characteristic of Atwood's early novels.

The character's revulsion towards food develops in distinct phases, as the different food groups seem to take on a life of their own. The same phenomenon, and further evidence of Atwood's long-term concern with the politics of eating, is first introduced in an unpublished short story, "Oyster Stew", written in the early 1960s. In this story, the relationship with food is reversed as the female character relishes every bite, while her male counterpart looks on, appalled by her appetite:

> He forced himself to look away, to pick up his knife and fork. He jabbed at an oyster and fished it to the surface. It was huge, pale pink, with round blunted ends

> and involuted ruffles. Where did these mute things grow? Who knew … Some people ate them while they were still alive. The idea that the oyster might still be alive … he watched it as it quivered at the end of his fork, and realized that his hands were shaking, had been shaking for some time. (MS Coll. 200:40:2:6)

This revulsion is rewritten and extended in Marian's loss of appetite as, working her way through the food groups, she is unable to override her body's refusal to eat: "She was becoming more and more irritated by her body's decision to reject certain foods. She had tried to reason with it, and accused it of having frivolous whims, had coaxed it and tempted it, but it was adamant; and if she used force it rebelled" (177–8). In spite of the fact that "she had been brought up to eat whatever was on the plate" (204), both in terms of food and female socialization, her body systematically refuses food as a gesture of protest.

In introductory notes on "Power Politics", found amongst drafts of a preface to her collection of poetry of same name, Atwood concludes:

> Power is our environment. We live surrounded by it; it pervades everything we are and do, invisible and soundless, like air. We notice it only when there is a break in the current, a conflict, when the balance of power is upset. The rest of the time things flow smoothly, each in its appointed place in the power structure, and we along with them. (MS Coll. 200:56:9)

This idea, echoed throughout Atwood's critical prose and vividly dramatized in her fiction, comes close to being an endorsement of a Foucauldian view of power relations. Marian's loss of appetite or refusal to eat represents exactly one such "break in the current" identified by Atwood – a political act of resistance. In Atwood's early writing this anxiety about power politics is visible in the Canadian nationalist as well as the feminist elements of her work; this is a preoccupation most explicitly propounded in *Surfacing*, and sustained in different forms throughout her writing career.

Marian MacAlpin's identification with food is closely linked to the more general theme of consumerism in the novel. In her work as a market researcher, managing research surveys in towns and cities dotted across the map of Canada that hangs on the wall of the Seymour Surveys office, she is accomplice to, as well as victim of the mass consumerism that she later identifies as defining her relationship with her fiancé, Peter. The character's relationship with food and her struggle towards self-determination are, then, played out against a determinedly Canadian backdrop as are, it might be argued, Atwood's nascent concerns about the survival of the country's cultural autonomy.

Sarah Sceats applies Foucault's theory of power (in particular the idea that power is exercised discreetly in everyday social processes) in identifying the complex politics underlying food and eating and its representation in literature: "feeding is established psychologically as the locus of love, aggression, pleasure, anxiety, frustration and desire for control. Precisely, in other words, the ingredients of power relations" ("Eating the Evidence: Women, Power and Food" 118). Atwood shows a similarly keen awareness of the politics of food as the earliest expression of subjectivity: "Eating is our earliest metaphor, preceding our consciousness of gender difference, race, nationality and language. We eat before we talk" (Atwood, "The CanLit Food Book" 53). Atwood's use of food as metaphor goes beyond the dramatic conceit of the "edible woman". It is, for example, no accident that one of the products being researched by Seymour Surveys in the novel is "Moose Beer", which is suggestive of the Canadian tourist-industry clichés of which Atwood is aware and interrogates throughout her oeuvre. The mapping of Canada by Seymour Surveys is also revealing in the way that tensions between different regional identities are exposed in the attitudes of the company's Toronto-based employees. A disconcertingly comic example of this can be seen in the discussion of a planned survey of laxative products in Quebec: "'I guess people are just more constipated there. Don't they eat a lot of potatoes?' … 'It can't only be the potatoes,' Ainsley pronounced. 'It must be their collective guilt-complex. Or maybe the strain of the language problem; they must be horribly repressed'" (23). Thus, the motif of consumerism in the novel shows that the commercial and marital marketplace have much in common, and, at the same time, effectively draws attention to distinctively Canadian pressure points.

In her introduction to "The CanLit Food Book", Atwood comments on the prevalence of cannibalism – metaphorical and actual – in Canadian literature (55); with this in mind, it seems all the more important to place *The Edible Woman* in the context of this darker tradition of Canadian writing. Even though the novel is interested in the effect of consumer culture on its female protagonist, the nationalist concerns more fully expressed in Atwood's later writing, most directly and extensively in *Survival: A Thematic Guide to Canadian Literature*, can be identified as an important subtext.

Sarah Sceats observes that the interpretation of the significance of food and eating patterns and rituals and the ways in which they are invested with social, political, and psychological meaning is most relevant to reading twentieth-century women's writing: "Because of the close cultural association between women and food, or because of feminism's politicization of the domestic, or because of the advance of material culture, the work of women writers in the latter half of the twentieth century is particularly fruitful for an examination of the relations between power and food" ("Eating the Evidence: Women, Power and Food" 117). Atwood's novel is one of the most dramatic examples of this relationship, both in the main character's refusal to eat and in the ironic "politicisation of the domestic" involved in her decision to bake a cake as a sacrificial effigy of herself.

The edible woman in the shape of a cake acts as a punch line to Atwood's extended food metaphor in the novel, representing as it does Marian's exposure of the threat posed by Peter to her autonomy and her reclamation of agency. However, this result is also complicated by Peter's refusal to eat the cake in the shape of a woman. It is Marian who cannibalizes the edible woman, helped rather ominously by Duncan, the solipsistic misfit whom she befriends when carrying out door-to-door market research surveys. For Sarah Sceats, this is the main complication of the ending of the novel: "Marian has learned assertiveness, that sexual politics means 'eat or be eaten', but although it has the desired effects of frightening Peter away and returning Marian's appetite, it does not address the conundrum of how she can live without either being consumed or becoming a predator" (*Food, Consumption and the Body in Contemporary Women's Fiction* 99). This concern with the predatory nature of gender politics – something that is vividly illustrated by Marian's fiancé being repeatedly imagined as a hunter in the novel – marks another point of contact between Atwood's early feminism and the Canadian wilderness. The untamed aspects of gender politics and of the Canadian landscape were, I would argue, crucial and interlinked dimensions of Atwood's literary imagination even before the appearance of *Surfacing*.

In *The Edible Woman*, Atwood's interest in survival as a Canadian theme is, then, already being explored in the unexpected context of modern, urban Toronto. In the tradition of hunger and starvation in literature, Marian is ultimately compatible with Kafka's original hunger artist. His plaintive explanation of a life devoted to the spectacle of starvation is simply, "weil ich nicht die Speise finden konnte, die mir schmeckt" (257) [because I could never find the food I wanted to eat]. It is ultimately upon the same premise that food functions as such a vivid and complex metaphor in *The Edible Woman*, marking a new departure in the feminist impetus of Atwood's work, but also sowing the seeds of Atwood's preoccupation with the relationship between feminist and nationalist discourses of power.

In both *The Edible Woman* and *Lady Oracle* development often coincides with weight loss and shrinkage. While critics of the female Bildungsroman have identified eighteenth- and nineteenth-century examples of the genre as providing models for "growing down" (Pratt and White 14), it is curious that Atwood's novels represent shrinkage as revealing of change, self development, and a growing self-awareness. It is immediately apparent that Joan's relationship with food in the early part of *Lady Oracle* is the absolute reverse of Marian's eating disorder. If Marian's antipathy to food may be read as a feminist hunger-strike, then Joan's protest is based on strategic overindulgence in a silent war against her mother: "I rose like dough, my body advanced inch by inch towards her across the dining-room table, in this at least I was undefeated" (70). If Marian's refusal of food is a declaration that she is not an object for consumption, Joan's overeating is a declaration of her existence in the face of her mother's rejection. Joan's relationship with food is at every mark affected by her mother, from her mother's wheedling and plotting to get Joan to lose weight to her later attempts to sabotage her daughter's diet. Food is a weapon in the war against her mother and Joan asserts this power by overeating and by exaggerating her size in spite of her mother.

The politics of food in Margaret Atwood's novels has attracted the necessary attention of many feminist critics and it serves, as far as the development of Joan Foster is concerned, as a complex metaphor for the issue of female subjectivity. Overeating and starvation in turn are used as a means of protest against Joan's mother. As a result of her dramatic weight loss in the second part of the novel,

Joan is forced to adjust to life without the body that served as a protective barrier to the world but also denied her access to the coming-of-age rituals of Braeside Highschool. As will become clear, Joan compensates (and perhaps even overcompensates) for this loss, or rather denial, by inventing her own alternative, and ultimately more flamboyant and exciting, Bildungsroman.

Literary Consumption in *The Edible Woman* and *Lady Oracle*

In *The CanLit Foodbook* Atwood shows a particular interest in the recurrence of cannibalism as a theme in Canadian literature. Due attention has also been paid to the intertextuality of *Lady Oracle*, a novel in which literary references to Tennyson and Charlotte Brontë are given similar treatment to references to fairytales and Hollywood cinema. For example, John Thieme's reading of *Lady Oracle* in "'A Female Houdini': Popular Culture in Margaret Atwood's *Lady Oracle*" considers the importance of parody to the function and effect of such references in the novel. Indeed, *Lady Oracle* is a novel that bulges at the seams with literary and cultural references. If Atwood's literary interest in cannibalistic motifs surfaces in the image of the edible woman in her first novel, then Joan Foster in *Lady Oracle* is more preoccupied with voraciously consuming the textual narratives available to her as a writer. Moreover, the novel's reliance upon fantastical and mythical intertexts as a medium for representing or even parodying the course of development of a character further removes Atwood's early Bildungsromane from the rationalist tradition of the genre's Enlightenment origins.

Even though Joan Foster's life narrative at times seems to relish, even gorge on, other literary sources, there are a number of revealing references to writing in *The Edible Woman* that prefigure Joan's adventures in textuality. In Chapter 1, Marian details the requirements of her job: "I'm supposed to spend my time revising the questionnaires, turning the convoluted and overly-subtle prose of the psychologists who write them into simple questionnaires which can be understood by the people who ask them as well as the people who answer them" (19). That Marian is employed to translate the style and register of the questionnaires might seem to be an unremarkable detail, but when considered alongside the dramatic translation and rewriting of texts that occurs throughout Atwood's novels, this mundane act of interpretation can be read as prefiguring other more audacious literary experiments. As will be apparent in the discussion of *Lady Oracle* to follow, Joan Foster is perpetually caught up in translating her own life according to the conventions of the fictions that she reads and with rewriting her life though, more often than not, the end result complicates rather than simplifies her relationships with other people.

In addition to this early example of what would become a career-long concern with narrative translations and interpolations – literary and cultural – there is a moment in *The Edible Woman* which speaks to the image of the transgressive writing hand that, as will be explored in more detail in Chapter 6, emerges as a key motif in Atwood's later novels. As is vividly portrayed in *Lady Oracle*, the female artist and author in Atwood's novels often find that the fictions that they produce threaten to escape their control and Marian encounters a version of this when working through the questionnaire on Moose Beer with Duncan in Chapter 6 of the novel. In spite of the ridiculous digressions in his answers to her simplified market research questions, she finds herself "scribbling madly to get it all down" (54), while thinking all the time "of what would happen to the I.B.M. machine if they ever tried to run this thing through it" (53).

That Duncan should instigate this instance of Marian's text running away with her ("The notes I had made of his answers were almost indecipherable in the glare of the sunlight; all I could see on the page was a blur of grey scribbling" (55)) is most appropriate given that his life is consumed by the production of directionless texts. As a graduate student of English desperately searching for an original idea, Duncan's life, like that of his fellow graduate students, Trevor and Fish, and much like his paper-crammed apartment, is overwhelmed by the literary texts that he reads and the critical texts that he attempts to produce: "All exposed surfaces of the room were littered with loose papers, notebooks, books opened face-down and other books bristling with pencils and torn slips of paper stuck in them as markers" (50).

The textual production in which Marian and Duncan engage is closely aligned with the processes of consumer culture so threatening to Marian's subjectivity elsewhere in the novel. In Marian's case, her writing is bound up in the mechanics of market research and the capitalist enterprise it represents while Duncan comes to see himself and his fellow students as victims of the "paper-mines" (97) of graduate school, compulsively producing texts to meet the market demand of his course requirements: "Poor old Fischer is writing his thesis now, he wanted to do it on Womb Symbols in D.H. Lawrence but they all told him that it had been done. So now he's got some impossible theory that gets more and more incoherent as he goes along" (97).

Lady Oracle is a less restrained experiment in such textual exercises as Joan Foster constructs her own life and the literary texts that she produces out of the possibilities offered by a diverse range of genres and conventions. This can also be seen in the textual relationships that emerge in Atwood's play with the idea of "the novel within the novel". As will become apparent, *Lady Oracle* and *The Blind Assassin* are the most striking examples of this device at work. While the actual "edible woman" of Atwood's first novel – appealing directly to the title as it does – is consumable in an immediate and literal way, Joan Foster's literary output in *Lady Oracle* is also consumed, or rather devoured, by publishers and the reading public alike.

Most readings of the novel have focused on the intertextual nature of Joan's competing life narratives and the complexities of her writing life. Ann Parsons in her article "Women who Lie and Pose in the Fiction of Margaret Atwood" and Kim Worthington in her analysis of *Lady Oracle* in *Self as Narrative: Subjectivity and Community in Contemporary Fiction*, although the focus of their arguments differ, share a common interest in the potential for reading *Lady Oracle* as a novel that sets out to rewrite a pejorative image of female neuroses and charge it with positive meaning. Worthington's analysis of the novel, in particular, stresses how Joan seems to successfully reconnect with reality and secure control over her own life story.

It is, however, also possible to read the novel as an extravagant experiment in life-writing – in writing the female Bildungsroman. Joan's powers of storytelling lie in her ability to take on and discard different subjective costumes according to her needs. From the outset, Joan does not show a great deal of commitment to the authentic, progressive self of the classic Bildungsroman. *Lady Oracle* is a classic Barthesian "tissue of quotations drawn from the innumerable centres of culture" (146) and Joan Foster as a writer and narrator paves the way for the mutually-dependent literary selves that proliferate throughout Atwood's fiction. True to the Barthesian prophecy, Joan is more than happy to imagine her role as an author as a filter for language (most dramatically illustrated in the way that her critically-acclaimed poetry is the product of an experiment in automatic writing), which resonates with Barthes' notion that "a text is not a line of words releasing a single 'theological' meaning (the 'message' of the Author-God) but a multi-dimensional space in which a variety of writings, none of them original, blend and clash" (146). Joan's last word on this is that, in life and in literature: "hidden depths should remain hidden, facades were at least as truthful" (197). This is, of course, not just Joan's position, but also a distinctively postmodern one, one that comes to have a defining influence on Joan's personal Bildungsroman.

In a draft of a letter to Marge Piercy, dated August 1973, Atwood responds to Piercy's review of *Surfacing* in the following way:

> I felt you had in the review yr fingers on a lot of the important pressure points … espec. the question of what then? what next? Obviously one can work out personal solutions or semi-solutions; social ones are much more difficult not only to bring about but to imagine. Marian's life will be circular (one more time around) rather than spiral partly because I could see in 1965 (when book written; publisher lost ms for 2 years) no "out" for her provided by the society. Woman in *Surfacing* is left at the edge … all we know is that it will be different but we don't know how. (Because I don't.) Next novel won't resolve that, I don't feel (novels seem always about 2 years behind what I think when writing them) but the one after that will either have to or die. (MS Coll. 200:2:4)

In spite of her concern that resolution was not in sight, *Lady Oracle* does present a creative solution to the victim status of Atwood's previous protagonists and at the end of the novel it is made clear that Joan will live to write another day.

While most discussions of the novel focus on the fictions that Joan writes and interpret the fictions that come to define her own life as nets of entrapment or a necessary duplicitous alternative for the woman writer, it is also possible to read Joan's engagement with other narratives, whether that of Tennyson's "Lady of Shalott" or her costume gothics, as a series of textual choices – rather than being a victim of those fictions, Joan effectively exploits them for her purpose and the appearance of victimhood serves as a useful disguise in the process. In the opening lines of the novel, Joan ponders:

> I planned my death carefully; unlike my life, which meandered along from one thing to another, despite my feeble attempts to control it. My life had a tendency to spread, to get flabby, to scroll and festoon like the frame of a baroque mirror, which came from following the line of least resistance. I wanted my death, by contrast, to be neat and simple, understated, even a little severe, like a Quaker church or the basic black dress with a single strand of pearls much praised by fashion magazines when I was fifteen. (7)

That Joan thinks of her life fictions as "flabby" is very suggestive as it makes a direct link between the two modes of consumption that influence her development as a woman and, more particularly, as a woman writer. This acutely self-conscious retrospective glance back at her life history and, more particularly, the attention drawn to the scrolling, festooning fictions that make up her life narrative has a Dickensian ring to it, particularly because of the way it draws attention to the meta-commentary on writing a life offered in the course of Joan Foster's literary adventures.

In spite of Joan's claim to helplessness, those very fictions that on the surface seem to threaten her autonomy as she switches from one fabricated alias to the next are, in fact, ultimately chosen by Joan, and are crucial turns in the literary and textual maze of the novel. Moreover, her desire for an uncomplicated death turns out to be somewhat disingenuous as she fakes her own death in the most dramatic and spectacular way possible, by implicating herself in a faux terrorist plot, thus ensuring attention of the most public kind. The choices that she makes in the course of writing her own Bildungsroman and the identities that she creates are, in fact, very much self-determined by her textual preferences. She makes extravagant choices as she occupies the role of a whole spectrum of literary and fairytale characters including, to name a few, The Lady of Shalott, Rapunzel, Hans Christian Andersen's "The Little Mermaid", as well as the victimized heroine of the gothic romances that she writes. She succeeds more often than not in rewriting these roles on her own terms and, as John Thieme stresses, she proves more than capable of becoming her own rescuer, as she adjusts the plot for her own purpose (79–80). This ongoing modification of generic expectations is hinted at from the outset of the novel where Joan's reality collides with one of her many romantic fantasies:

> I'd always been fond of balconies. I felt that if I could only manage to stand on one long enough, the right one, wearing a long white trailing gown, preferably during the first quarter of the moon, something would happen: music would sound, a shape would appear below, sinuous and dark, and climb towards me, while I leaned fearfully, hopefully, gracefully, against the wrought-iron railing and quivered. But this wasn't a very romantic balcony. It had a geometric railing

> like those on middle-income apartment buildings of the fifties, and the floor was poured concrete, already beginning to erode. (7–8)

True to a near relative with an active imagination in the gothic tradition, Catherine Morland in Jane Austen's *Northanger Abbey* (1818), the conventions of Joan's romances, as seen here, are frequently interrupted or reined in by reality and so Rapunzel's balcony is reimagined as modern, concrete, and inhospitable to the rescue fantasies that she is exposed to and nurtures from a young age.

If, as I suggested earlier, food and fiction in Atwood's work are subject to similar processes of ingestion and digestion, references to writing in *The Edible Woman* hint at these processes while *Lady Oracle* acknowledges the corollary very explicitly. As in *The Edible Woman*, eating and processes of consumption reflect Joan's consumption of the fictions that she encounters and consumes from a young age in her fantasy-making, but also in the fiction that she produces to satisfy the needs of her hungry reading public. It is very revealing that it is directly after Joan undergoes her bodily transformation and ceases trying to feel secure in the world by overeating that she begins to write. This marks the beginning of a new chapter in her life narrative as writing displaces eating, and fiction takes the place of food as a source of consolation and compensation. Like Marian, Joan (aka Louisa K. Delacourt, author of romantic fiction) writes to a set formula, or indeed recipe, for commercial success: "As the whores say, why the hell should I be a waitress?" (36). This latter acknowledgement of the extent of her literary ambitions is especially resonant as she happily prostitutes herself as a writer of gothic romances and her products are packaged and sold to the public in much the same way as the consumer goods surveyed by Marian in *The Edible Woman*; her novels are described as being "available at the corner drugstore, neatly packaged like the other painkillers" (34), just down the aisle from the products tested by the market researchers in *The Edible Woman*. The foregrounding of the literary text as a consumable, even disposable, object has considerable implications for the representation of the woman writer in *Lady Oracle*, one that runs contra to, and demystifies, the expectation of the male-centred portrait of the artist discussed in Chapter 2.

In 1980, Atwood writes in a draft of a "Letter from Canada" to *The Washington Post*:

> One out of every four books bought in the country is a Harlequin Romance (Harlequin, it should be said, is a Canadian company), and writers of thrillers, disaster novels and sexcapades burst forth each season. Publishers are not deploring this trend, but writers are feeling squeezed. Soon, they think, there may no longer be a place for the well-written, thoughtful criticism of society we have come to think of as the modern novel. (MS Coll. 200:56:53:2)

It is appropriate that this statistic should have prompted Atwood to make a defence of the modern novel, given that a version of the Harlequin romance – an apparently domestic product and export – features so prominently in *Lady Oracle*. As a writer with one keen eye on developments in the Canadian literary market, Atwood's novel offers a critique of the functions, processes, and products of publishing and shows a particular wariness towards the packaging, marketing, and public consumption of the woman writer.

Joan's performance as a writer also pays homage to her nineteenth-century predecessors – she takes a pseudonym to protect herself from public notoriety and goes to great lengths to keep her writing secret. It should perhaps come as no surprise that Atwood requested a copy of *Jane Eyre* in the process of writing *Lady Oracle* (MS Coll. 200:27:1) – Elizabeth Gaskell's account of Charlotte Brontë's struggle to protect her identity in her literary biography *The Life of Charlotte Brontë* (1857) being one of the best-known chronicles of the fear of public infamy that plagued the Victorian woman writer. More than this, true to the playful intertextuality evident throughout *Lady Oracle*, there is a discreetly-placed reference to one of the most famous twentieth-century engagements with *Jane Eyre* that reinvents and, to some degree, rehabilitates Brontë's novel: Jean Rhys's *Wide Sargasso Sea* (1966). In Joan's description of married life with Arthur, she describes how, due to the economy of doing the washing up in the bath: "we would often be surprised by the odd noodle or pea, floating in the soap scum like an escaped fragment of Sargasso Sea" (208–9). Atwood's own novel contains more than a fragment of Rhys's *Wide Sargasso Sea* as it shows a lively (and at times irreverent) awareness of the nineteenth-century literary tradition. As a footnote to this, Joan hides her manuscripts from her husband in a folder marked "recipes", again drawing attention to the domestic context of women's writing in the nineteenth century. Thus, Joan gestures at the covert strategies adopted by the women writers who came before her, both in the process of writing as well as in the content of what she writes. With regard to the latter, Joan ensures that the boundaries of her genre of choice remain permeable; late in the novel, the villainess of her gothic narrative *Stalked by Love*, Felica, is turned into a neglected suburban housewife:

> *Tonight he was later than usual. Felicia snuffled, wiping the tears with the back of her free hand. She was too distraught to bother with the niceties of a handkerchief. ... All she wanted was happiness with the man she loved. It was this one impossible wish that had ruined her life; she ought to have settled for contentment, for the usual lies*. (319, italics in original)

In her private life as well as in her fiction, Joan refuses to see generic categories as distinct and impermeable and, in this way, shows signs of the "suspicion of genre borders" identified by Linda Hutcheon as a key feature of Canadian literature and, more generally, Canada's "firm suspicion of centralizing tendencies" (*The Canadian Postmodern* 3).

In *Lady Oracle*, Joan Foster discovers that the literary marketplace has much in common with the marital marketplace and indeed the consumer marketplace depicted in *The Edible Woman*. While Joan enjoys relative anonymity as Louisa K. Delacourt – though this is threatened by the predatory literary detective, Fraser Buchanan – she discovers that her literary persona as Joan Foster author of "Lady Oracle" very quickly becomes public property. Her publishers imagine packaging her as "a sort of female Leonard Cohen" (225). Joan's editor is called Colin Harper – a very Atwoodian play on the publishing might of Harper Collins – and she very quickly finds herself swept away by other people's agenda. The gnawing public demand for details of her private life takes on a darker edge after her fake death as she opens a Canadian newspaper to find that "every necrophiliac in the country was rushing to buy a copy. I'd been shoved into the ranks of those other unhappy ladies, scores of them apparently, who'd been killed by a surfeit of words" (313). In *Negotiating with the Dead*, Atwood looks back on her own encounter with such literary necrophilia as she recalls the grim careers of some of the most influential women writers of the nineteenth and twentieth centuries and apprehensively queries: "Is that where the priestess of the imagination was fated to end up – as a red puddle on the floor?" (89). Thus, both in the weft and weave of her fictions, personal and literary, and in the public reception of her work, Joan Foster encounters and overcomes longstanding obstacles to the woman writer and arrives at a powerful position of irreverence towards the literary past.

The conclusion drawn by Kim Worthington casts a much-needed positive light on Joan's position at the end of the novel: "Rather than escape, she chooses to exercise her contestational voice in the activity of partial self-authorization; she has gained the power to speak/write (for) herself" (300).Worthington sees Joan as gaining control of "the story that others will know her by" (301) and, in effect, gaining control over her Bildungsroman, and yet, right at the end of the final chapter, we learn that Joan has abandoned the costume gothic to take up science fiction. The fact that years later *The Blind Assassin* presents an author of science fiction just as involved in literary game playing as Joan Foster suggests that *Lady Oracle* does not necessarily end with an absolute promise of definitive control over her own narrative but marks the beginning of a new set of textual choices for the figure of the female author, both in telling the story of her own life and in rewriting stories from the literary past. In spite of her previous concern about the state of Canadian publishing, Atwood muses in a review of Margaret Ann Jenson's *Love's Sweet Return: The Harlequin Story* (1984) that Harlequin Romances, a near relative of Joan's costume gothics, are "among other things, how-to books on the fantasy level, for women who experience daily their own lack of power" (MS Coll. 200:90:32:10). The formula of the costume gothics can be read, on these terms, as a set of choices with Joan ultimately in charge of the script.

While I have previously tried to navigate a pathway through opposing theories of selfhood and their reception in early feminist and woman-centred fiction and criticism, there remains the question of how *The Edible Woman* and *Lady Oracle* hold up against the most important definitions of the female Bildungsroman. To some degree the novels encompass Susan Rosowski's notion of the Novel of Awakening and Rita Felski's definition of a woman-centred Bildungsroman.

They describe, in part, an awakening to the limitations of feminine roles available to women and women writers in the 1960s and 70s while also including the elements of biography, dialecticism, history, and teleology outlined by Felski. Felski's definition, however, implies linearity and coherence in the course of this development and does not allow for the splitting and unravelling of identity apparent in *The Edible Woman* or the playful juxtaposition of multiple identities present in *Lady Oracle*. As emphasized in the early chapters, such working definitions are most useful if they incorporate the possibility of inversions and subversions of, and disruptions and interruptions to, these processes. Felski suggests that biography always implies "the existence of a coherent individual identity which constitutes the focal point of the narrative" (*Beyond Feminist Aesthetics* 135). *The Edible Woman* and *Lady Oracle* dramatically challenge that assumption. According to the same definition, development must be dialectical: "defining identity as the result of a complex interplay between psychological and social forces" (*Beyond Feminist Aesthetics* 135). In *The Edible Woman*, this is not so much an interplay of forces but a process of resistance and protest on the part of the individual. History and teleology in the novel are similarly troubled, as the course and realization of Marian's self-knowledge runs contrary to the expectations of the genre.

In *Lady Oracle*, the positive potential of imagining the self as comprised of different narrative strands is literalized in the way that Joan Foster's performed identities foreground the divided, multiple nature of her subjectivity. Atwood's early work might, then, be read retrospectively as representative of a new direction in women's writing, one that does not rely either on the straightforward appropriation of male-centred forms, or on the formula for emancipation put forward by the literature of the women's movement. Rather, her work, much like so many of her characters, in Annette Kolodny's terms, "dances through the minefield" of choices available to the woman writer in the second half of the twentieth century.

PART 3
Towards Maturity: Atwood's Later Novels

Chapter 5
Canadian Afterlives: The Power and Pleasure of Storytelling in *The Robber Bride* and *Alias Grace*

The fairytale tower looms large in Atwood's fictional oeuvre. Early references to imprisonment in Rapunzel's tower appear in *Survival* (209–10) and, just a few years later, *Lady Oracle* engages very explicitly with the Rapunzel motif and, more subtly, with Tennyson's "The Lady of Shalott". The tower represents a problematic symbol of the imprisonment of the woman writer by a male-centred literary tradition and this motif of imprisonment and escape finds a powerful new expression in Atwood's later novels. This chapter will focus on how, in Atwood's later writing, the tower is reconstructed for a new and different purpose and, as is often the case in Atwood's work, the relationship between prisoner, prison guard, and rescuer is not as stable as it might seem. Zenia in *The Robber Bride* is a conduit for all of the Bildungsromane that women might write about their own lives, and she also proves adept at filling in the gaps of other characters' life stories. Her wilfully misleading and deceptive narrative strategies refute any last vestige of faith in the teleology prized by earlier versions of the Bildungsroman. In the shadow of her malevolent power, Rapunzel's tower is turned into a retreat, a fortress against Zenia's manipulation, where a defence against Zenia is executed with military strategy.

In the case of *Alias Grac*e, Grace Marks overturns the relationship between prisoner and prison guard and, as her story is told, the novel resembles an empowered rewriting of the "Lady of Shalott". In weaving her life story for her unsuspecting patron, Simon Jordan, she holds him in thrall so that he comes to crave her narrative. In this case, Tennyson's mirror reflects not life but the delicate embroidery of Grace's storytelling. In *Lady Oracle*, in another formulation of "The Lady of Shalott" (or the "Lady of Small Onion" as the novel sometimes prefers), Joan Foster discovers her borrowed fictions to be an inadequate means of engaging with the world as they often seem to conspire against her: "There I was, on the bottom of the death barge where I'd once longed to be, my name on the prow, winding my way down the river. … Maybe they were right, you could stay in the tower for years, weaving away, looking in the mirror, but one glance out the window at real life and that was that" (313). In contrast, Grace Marks offers a new reading of Tennyson's poem, one that refuses the fatal ending of "The Lady of Shalott". As she sits quietly sewing, Grace's own narratives, the crafting of her own Bildungsroman, prove far more compelling than anything a second-hand reflection of the world might have to offer. Grace is a progenitor of texts, both in the stories that she tells and in the stories that are told about her. Like Zenia, she is an empowered muse, capable of adding footnotes and corrections to the narrative of her life.

In both novels, these powerful, Arachne-like narrators disseminate complex narratives about the lives of women, but such narratives also very directly engage with Canadian history. Far removed from the necessary cultural nationalism of her early work, and the pursuit of a cohesive narrative of Canadianness, in *Alias Grace* Atwood returns to the scene of colonial Canada (and the scene of Grace's alleged crime) and looks at the divisions and fractures that make up the tangled origins of the Anglo-Canadian community. In sympathy with this, *The Robber Bride* shows a concern with bringing to the surface the tensions and complications of Canadian identity in the late twentieth century.

Writing the Self: Weaving and Deceiving in *The Robber Bride* and *Alias Grace*

Both Zenia in *The Robber Bride* and Grace in *Alias Grace* have much to say to a recurrent critical interest in the liberation available through storytelling. In *Honey-Mad Women: Emancipatory Strategies in Women's Writing*, Patricia Yaeger assesses the differences between American and French feminism and identifies the importance of play to each feminist approach. According to Yaeger's assessment, French feminists exult in a utopian vision of an alternative female language, with the female body as the primary site for this new mode of expression, removed from the restrictions of patriarchal language and what they identify as the inadequacy of the existing feminist tradition to emancipate itself. Anglo-American feminists, on the other hand, have been more concerned with identifying existing strategies in women's writing in their reformation of the canon and their reformulation of critical approaches to writing by and about women (17–20). For Yaeger, the ideal approach is a combination of these methods (20). Atwood clearly numbers amongst the women writers who "have shattered male plots, have successfully called upon verbal resources that are unavailable to their male contemporaries" (29). *The Robber Bride* and *Alias Grace* offer a particularly dramatic illustration of this shattering of plots, literary and historical. This concept of the woman writer at play would seem to be an invaluable resource in cultural revision, from the euphoria evoked in French feminist texts to the more cunning plot subversions found throughout Atwood's work. Atwood's particular brand of play is very often politically driven but, at times, deliberately undercuts itself, never fixing complacently on a single point of view. This is, in part, because Atwood's brand of feminism is self-interrogating as she is cautious of investing in any single feminist ideology. It is for this reason that Atwood's novels resist not only the expectations of the Bildungsroman but also the assumptions of many contemporary feminist writers and critics. It is for the same reason that *The Robber Bride* and *Alias Grace* show a particular sensitivity to the relationship between power and storytelling. The novels demonstrate how narrative can be exploited as a dangerous and divisive force or, alternatively, how it can unleash the emancipatory pleasure that Yaeger insists is to be found in a space between the French and Anglo-American feminist imagination.

In these novels, storytelling, as we have come to expect from Atwood's fiction, is, at every turn, bound up with the progress and development of the self. While Zenia exults in the power and pleasure of storytelling, *The Robber Bride* also draws attention to its inherent dangers and hazards. Tony, the military historian in the novel, is especially aware of this and she finds an innovative means of protecting herself against Zenia's narrative machinations and, with her expansive knowledge of human warfare, has the capability to go behind enemy lines in order to gain a better understanding of her nemesis. In this way, the novel presents a playful parody of the idea of "the battle of the sexes", but it quickly becomes apparent that alliances are uncertain.

In an undated note found in the Atwood archive at the University of Toronto, Margaret Atwood queries the source of the following quotation or song lyric: "Ask a woman where she's going and she'll tell you who she's been" (MS Coll. 200:27:1). It is clear to see why this quotation would have struck a chord with Atwood as it illuminates a very Atwoodian tactic in writing a woman's life. It highlights the importance of play as a strategy in the fashioning of female identity in Atwood's fiction, perhaps most noticeably in *The Robber Bride* where Zenia's flair for storytelling privileges simultaneous, invented identities over any pretence of a commitment to cohesive subjectivity.

In *Concepts of the Self*, Anthony Elliott, in keeping with this interest in plural subjectivity, concludes that with the advent of postmodernism in the 1980s: "questions concerning the individual's capabilities for autonomous thought, independent reflection and transformative social practices emerged as politically important. In the face of these changes, another terminological shift occurred, one from the analysis of subjectivity and individual subjection to the study of the creative dimensions of the self" (13). In narrating the various versions of her life story, Zenia explores exactly such "creative dimensions" and artfully alters her history to meet the needs of the other characters in the novel – Charis, Roz, and Tony. The narrative structure of the novel is shaped around the way in which Zenia taps into each character's uncertainties and anxieties about their personal origins and promises to provide the missing pieces in their individual life stories. In telling the stories that they want or need to hear, Zenia insidiously manipulates her way into other characters' life narratives. As will be seen, Grace Marks's stories have a similar effect, though in Grace's storytelling it is fashioned to seem more accidental than deliberate.

It is her role as a cunning interloper that renders Zenia such a potent and portentous figure and this is most evident in the relationship that she forges with the character of Tony in the novel. Tony, who imagines herself to be a twin, "the other half of which had died" (137), comes to view Zenia as the crucial missing element in her life history, a soul-mate in the twinning suggested in Tony's ambidexterity: "Tony will be Zenia's right hand, because Zenia is certainly Tony's left one" (169). This preoccupation with left-handedness is something that clearly interested Atwood from the early stages of research for the novel. The Atwood archive contains photocopied extracts from Stanley Coren's *The Left-Hander Syndrome: The Causes and Consequences of Left-Handedness* (1992) (MS Coll. 200:166:15). In part a historical survey of meanings attributed to left-handedness, the book focuses on prejudiced interpretations of the same. In a passage that seems particularly resonant with *The Robber Bride*, Coren describes the meaning of the left hand in witchcraft:

> It was the left hand that was used to harm or curse another person. To effect a curse, witches were instructed to silently touch the recipient with the left hand. Through it the curse, already prepared through ritual and incantation, would be directly conveyed to the victim. (14)

Zenia's "rituals and incantations" take the form of the irresistible lies that she peddles to each character in turn.

Zenia makes Tony over and fundamentally changes her relationship with the events of the past. Tony considers that "she has hardly gone in for self-revelation, in her previous life" (134), but Zenia irreversibly changes that. Zenia holds up a sympathetic mirror to the characters' lives only to spoil any chance of a happy ending. This relationship proves to be particularly harmful to Tony as it allows Zenia the power to destroy Tony's life from the inside out. At the same time, as is vividly illustrated throughout Atwood's work, happy endings come at a price, something that the female Bildungsroman foregrounds repeatedly throughout its history. The next chapter will more fully explore Atwood's interest in this twinning and doubling as it is restated more vigorously in *Cat's Eye* and *The Blind Assassin* as an expected, even necessary, feature and function of Atwood's Künstlerroman.

Crucial to this concern with the divided identity of the female artist is a restatement of Atwood's interest in the role of language and narrative in the construction of identity. Tony, whose professional life is dedicated to the study of conflict, considers history to be a synonym for narrative, and in one of her lectures cited early in the novel she warns her students of its inherent dangers: "History is a construct, she tells her students. Any point of entry is possible and all choices are arbitrary" (4). Later in the novel, Tony revisits this idea in concluding that, "War is what happens when language fails" (39), and insists that "words are so often like window curtains, a decorative screen put up to keep the neighbours at a distance" (62). This can be read as another expression of the narrator's wariness of the vicissitudes of language in Atwood's earlier novel, *Surfacing*: "Language divides us into fragments, I wanted to be whole" (140). A similar dynamic can be observed in Atwood's short story 'Giving Birth' (1977), in which a fraught relationship with language is implied from the opening paragraph in the immediate challenge posed to the title of the story: "Certainly it doesn't feel like giving, which implies a flow, a gentle handing over, no coercion" (225). Here, Atwood draws attention to this idea of identity as fixed by, and in, language but elsewhere she responds to this crisis in a way that promises a new rendering of language and, by association, of the cultural and aesthetic model under investigation here: the female Bildungsroman.

That "the story of Zenia is insubstantial, ownerless, a rumour only" (461) is ultimately what makes Zenia so treacherous to the other characters in *The Robber Bride* (and, as will become apparent, it is exactly the same undecidability that empowers Grace's storytelling in *Alias Grace*). Tony sounds a warning note about the textual unreliability of history on more than one occasion in the novel. She goes so far as to create for herself a protective fortress against Zenia's insidious gift for storytelling and, more than any other character in the novel, is capable of critically analysing Zenia's methodologies and recognizing that Zenia sympathizes with the other characters only to take advantage of the vulnerabilities of their individual histories. As an historian, Tony is especially alert to the dangers of "the pleasures of narration" (371).

Zenia is an acutely self-conscious storyteller: she revels in narrative invention and at the same time audaciously references the sources that inspire her fictions. In telling Tony about her life as a child prostitute in Paris, she says of her mother: "She was sick a lot of the time. Coughing, just like an opera! … What a corny death!" (165). She proves particularly talented at recreating the scenes of her own invented histories, staging them anew for any available audience, as can be seen in the way that she depicts her return visit to Germany, where as a baby she had supposedly been rescued from the Nazis by Roz's father: "I went in and up the stairs, just as my parents must have done hundreds of times. I touched the same banister, I turned the same corners. I knocked at the door, and when it opened I said some relatives of mine had once lived there and could I look around. … I think my parents became real to me for the first time. Everything, all of it became real. Before that it was just a bad story" (359). There is a suggestive ambiguity in Zenia's reference to the "bad story" of her life in this case. As with all of Zenia's narratives, it raises the question as to whether the "bad story" of her past is a reference to the tragic circumstances or to the borrowed clichés that constitute the different versions of her life. Thus, Zenia not only relishes the fictions of her life histories, but she slyly draws her audience's attention to their inherent deceitfulness. The "bad" story with its suggestion of infection is an appropriate description for the contaminated texts that Zenia perpetuates in the novel. Brought together as they are by their uneasy alliance against Zenia, it is no coincidence that the women hold a regular council of war at a café called The Toxique, the place where Zenia makes her first appearance. Moreover, Zenia's power over Tony is exerted via another infected text, the essay that she blackmails Tony into writing that hangs perpetually over Tony's academic credibility.

There is, however, alongside this discourse of decentred "ownerless" versions of Zenia, a knowing reference to an alternative model for the subject in literature (one more traditionally associated with the Bildungsroman). Roz responds to the version of her life that Zenia fabricates for her with considerable editorial enthusiasm and imagines it having a place in her magazine *WiseWomanWorld*: "A story about overcoming fears and obstacles, about facing up to yourself and becoming a whole person" (364–5). Roz's description of her meetings with her psychiatrist is suggestive of how for feminism, the allure of the "whole person", is, up to a point, a powerful one:

> Together the two of them labour over Roz's life as if it's a jigsaw puzzle, a mystery story with a solution at the end. They arrange and rearrange the pieces, trying to get them to come out better. They are hopeful: if Roz can figure out what story she's in, then they will be able to spot the erroneous turns she took, they can retrace her steps, they can change the ending. They work out a tentative plot. (382–3)

The emphasis placed here on the significance of "plotting" a life serves as an appropriate figure for the relationship with language and identity explored throughout Atwood's oeuvre. While her work exhibits a wariness of such plots, it also suggests that they might be irresistible and even inevitable, however knotted or tangled they become.

Atwood makes a persuasive defence of Zenia in a draft of an introduction to the novel, and enumerates her "virtues" as follows: "For one thing, she makes it clear that there are more plots available than the one about the fleeing, virtuous maiden pursued by evil barons. If women are human beings, they too make moral choices; and not all of them choose to be nice. … So we shouldn't be too hard on Zenia; for isn't she striving for what every novelist hopes to achieve – the willing suspension of disbelief?" (MS Coll. 200:169:3:3–4). That Atwood should draw an explicit corollary between Zenia's storytelling and authorship implies that the stories told in day-to-day living are closely aligned with and affected by those explored in literary narratives. As in *Lady Oracle*, literary authorship is demystified and democratized as ordinary women are seen to claim their own stories – to write their own Bildungsroman. One example of the "virtuous maiden" under threat described by Atwood comes from the fairytale "The Robber Bridegroom", read by Roz to her twins as a bedtime story: "The beautiful maiden, the search for a husband, the arrival of the rich and handsome stranger who lures innocent girls to his stronghold in the woods and then chops them up and eats them" (294). Hence, from the very title of the novel, there is a clear intention to move away from such images of victimized female innocence. Atwood's defence also calls to mind the value of the "she-devil" figure in contemporary women's fiction more generally. As demonstrated by characters as different as Fay Weldon's Ruth Patchett in *The Life and Loves of a She-Devil* (1984) and Toni Morrison's eponymous Sula (1973) who embrace and exult in the role of pariah, and Angela Carter's celebration of *Wayward Girls and Wicked Women* (1986) in her edited collection of stories of the same name, Atwood is not alone in turning a myth of the sinister feminine into something powerful and compelling.

However, Tony is, initially at least, less convinced of this, and her defence against Zenia is carried out with military precision. The independence afforded by her buying her own home is described in terms of military strategy as are many of her life choices. As Atwood insists in notes on fairytale motifs in the Atwood Collection: "Over our own lives we have a little more control. We can play roles, strike poses, co-operate with the poses of others. The knight in shining armour is of course incomplete without a maiden to rescue. Being rescued has also its price" (MS Coll. 200:56:9). Tony refuses the rescue motif, embracing instead the fantasy of the medieval warrioress. Tony's home, and indeed Tony herself, with her boyish figure, gender ambiguous name, and short hair – a shorn Rapunzel – present a radical adjustment to the tower motif as it appears in Atwood's earlier work. Early in the novel, Tony muses: "She has never seen the point of lawns. Given the choice she'd prefer a moat, with a drawbridge, and crocodiles optional" (18). The moat surrounding the fairytale castle is designed to keep Zenia and her stories out, rather than securing a prison. Tony chooses the house that she and West live in to serve exactly this purpose: "A solid house, reassuring; a fort, a bastion, a keep. Inside it is West, creating aural mayhem, safe from harm" (18–19). Tony buys the house after Zenia has appropriated West and she describes it as a convent, "a nunnery" (190); her isolation is chosen rather than enforced. This unravelling of the meanings associated with the fairytale tower is particularly evident in the way that Tony's "turret room" also serves as a fortress lookout: "From the street her room must look like a lighthouse, a beacon. Warm and cheerful and safe. But towers have other uses. She could empty boiling oil out the left-hand window, get a dead hit on anyone standing at the front door" (189). Tony's character is less concerned with weaving the means of her own rescue, as is the case in *Lady Oracle*, but rather she invades the fairytale tower and renovates it as a refuge complete with its own defence strategy. Perhaps here Atwood fully realizes another possibility for a Canadian and feminist version of Rapunzel: one that reinvents the "garrison mentality" discussed previously. The novel's interest in military history is illuminated by the extent of Atwood's research for the novel. Articles on everything from the death of Dr Gerald Bull, inventor of the Supergun (Zenia hints to Tony that she was involved in his assassination (412)), to copious references to the history of warfare and its minutiae are referenced in the Atwood papers (MS Coll. 200:166:14).

The Robber Bride provides an appropriate analogy for Atwood's own relationship with language as a writer as, from the beginning of her career, she was always most interested in the emancipatory potential of multiple identities, particularly from a feminist and postcolonialist perspective. It is apt that *The Robber Bride* ends with the promise of more stories, as the former victims of Zenia finally claim the power of storytelling: "That's what they will do increasingly in their lives: tell stories. Tonight their stories will be about Zenia" (470). Just as they pay their respects at Zenia's grave at the beginning of the novel, they will tend to Zenia in the writing of their own stories. Jeanette Winterson provides a telling metaphor for history and narrative in *Oranges are not the Only Fruit* (1985) (another novel that breaks new ground in the writing of the female Bildungsroman):

> Some people say there are true things to be found, some people say all kinds of things can be proved. I don't believe them. The only thing for certain is how complicated it all is, like string full of knots. It's all there but hard to find the beginning and impossible to fathom the end. The best you can do is admire the cat's cradle, and maybe knot it up a bit more. History should be a hammock for swinging and a game for playing, the way cats play. Claw it, chew it, rearrange it and at bedtime it's still a ball of string full of knots. (91)

In *The Robber Bride*, as in Winterson's description, there is no tying up of loose ends as promised by the Bildungsroman in its original form. The women are free to claim Zenia's control over the stories that infiltrated their lives: an explicit acknowledgement that their relationship with Zenia was based on envy and desire, as well as fear of her treacherous narratives. *The Robber Bride* explores the postmodern potential of an identity that is decentred and multiple: an unreliable story, "drifting from mouth to mouth and changing as it goes" (461). It is perhaps, then, all the more appropriate that Atwood should have pondered the line: "Ask a woman where she's going and she'll tell you who she's been", as the origins of Zenia's identity remain elusive to the end and leave the reader, much like the other characters in *The Robber Bride*, in a state of uncertainty.

"Pick any strand and snip, and history comes unravelled" (3) insists Tony in *The Robber Bride*. The sewing metaphor is all the more appropriate in the light of a feminist interest in sewing, embroidery, and quilting as metaphor described by Jeannette Batz Cooperman: "Quilting is one of the most frequent feminist symbols, and it works especially well for literature. Quilts are discontinuous in process, as women's writing has had to be, creating a whole from fragments and working one bit at a time" (56). This has a powerful resonance with the character of Grace Marks in *Alias Grace*; she proves peculiarly sensitive to the unravelling of history as she is confronted with multiple and various reading of herself. Gazing at herself in the mirror in the opening chapter of the novel, she marvels at the different versions of Grace Marks that proliferate in the public sphere and asks in genuine wonder: "How can I be all of these different things at once?" (25). These competing narratives expand within the novel but are also woven into the text via Atwood's carefully chosen epigraphs to each chapter. Susanna Moodie's contemporary reports of Grace Marks's alleged crime are the most striking of these though, as will be seen, Atwood's narrative, in contributing another fiction to the sensationalist myth of Grace Marks, the "celebrated murderess", gives Grace the means to write back to Mrs Moodie. Others include references to the Victorian discourses that informed and fashioned the different public images of Grace, such as Coventry Patmore's prescription of feminine purity in his poem "The Angel in the House" (1854). Hugely popular in its own time, the title of the poem has achieved a common currency in feminist criticism as a shorthand for female compliance, virtue, and obedience. Another revealing epigraph comes from Mrs Beeton's recipe for respectable middle-class life and cure for female hysteria in *Mrs Beeton's Book of Household Management* (1861). These are representative of the cultural references that framed the image of Grace Marks in the period. The epistolary elements of the novel also contribute to this, as Grace the medical subject is put under the microscope in letters to and from Dr Simon Jordan, as does the Governor's wife's scrapbook (29), a record of reports of the murders in which Grace is implicated.

In amongst these interpretations lies Grace's own narrative (or at least another version of it) and the novel gestures at a number of Victorian influences in the way Grace comes to tell the story of her own life, told as she sits quilting in the sewing room of the Governor's house with Simon Jordan as her audience. Grace is described as "a wonderful seamstress, quite deft and accomplished" with "an eye for trimmings" (26), a description that applies as fittingly to her storytelling as to her abilities as a dressmaker. The patchwork self is something that reappears throughout Atwood's work. For example, a much earlier story "Hair Jewellery", collected in *Dancing Girls* (1977), while articulating this idea in different terms, ultimately alludes to the same process:

> That's my technique, I resurrect myself through clothes. In fact it's impossible for me to remember what I did, what happened to me, unless I can remember what I was wearing, and every time I discard a sweater or a dress I am discarding a part of my life. I shed identities like a snake, leaving them pale and shrivelled behind me, a trail of them, and if I want any memories at all I have to collect, one by one, those cotton and wool fragments, piece them together, achieving at last a patchwork self, no defence anyway against the cold. (102)

However, this process receives its most extended treatment in *Alias Grace*.

Shuli Barzilai's incisive explication of the Tennysonian subtexts in *Lady Oracle* draws the conclusion that: "*Lady Oracle* demonstrates the tensions inherent in the interpellation of a female hero into an ideological (symbolic) order that continues to construct and value women as 'lovely' to look at" (250). These subtexts take on a slightly different emphasis in *Alias Grace*, particularly in the way that the novel contributes to the meaningful architecture of women's writing. In *The Madwoman in the Attic*, Gilbert and Gubar pay careful attention to the spatialization of female experience in the nineteenth- and twentieth-century literary tradition (83–92). Virgina Woolf's image in *A Room of One's Own* of the woman writer forever displaced represents an iconic moment in this history:

> I thought of the organ booming in the chapel and of the shut doors of the library; and I thought how unpleasant it is to be locked out; and I thought how it is worse perhaps to be locked in; and, thinking of the safety and prosperity of the one sex and of the poverty and insecurity of the other and of the effect of tradition and of the lack of tradition upon the mind of a writer, I thought at last that it was time to

> roll up the crumpled skin of the day, with its arguments and its impressions and its anger and its laughter, and cast it into the hedge. (27–8)

More recent women's writing has reanimated this theme of confinement and exclusion in new ways; Doris Lessing's short story "To Room 19" (1963), in which the main character makes a daily pilgrimage to a room in a hotel in Bloomsbury in search of refuge and eventually ends her own life there, is a particularly striking contemporary descendant of Woolf's seminal text.

Alias Grace takes its place in this tradition and alters it. On the occasion of their first meeting at the penitentiary, the door is locked behind Simon Jordan, so from the beginning it is not fully clear whether he or Grace is the real prisoner of the scene. Grace, like the Lady of Shalott, is absorbed in her sewing, but her attention is not on the outside world as represented by Simon Jordan, the authorized public figure, but on the crafting of her story. Just as Zenia's storytelling is potent and seductive in *The Robber Bride*, in *Alias Grace*, Grace Marks holds the young Doctor in thrall so that he is locked into her story and irrevocably affected by its suggestiveness.

Grace alters her looks for the benefit of those present, second-guessing what is required of her as a suspected murderess: "But if I laughed out loud I might not be able to stop; and also it would spoil their romantic notion of me. Romantic people are not supposed to laugh, I know that much from looking at the pictures" (27); "I look at him stupidly. I have a good stupid look which I have practised" (43). It soon becomes clear that this applies equally to her narrative strategies: "Perhaps I will tell you lies" (46), she announces calmly to the doctor, before she has ever begun her story. There is, then, a frank acknowledgement of Simon Jordan's and the reader's dilemma. If craftiness, deceit, and duplicity frequently emerge as potentially valuable and necessary devices in the female creative process in Atwood's work, Grace pushes it to new limits. From the moment that they meet it seems "as if it were he, and not she, who was under scrutiny" (69) and so it becomes clear that their exchanges will not adhere to the conventions of the "talking cure", that Grace's compliance is not to be fully trusted.

When Grace is ready to begin her story – in effect, her Bildungsroman – the attention paid to the commencement of the narrative has a definite Dickensian flavour to it, recalling as it does the opening lines of *David Copperfield*:

> And he says, Let us begin at the beginning.
> And I say, The beginning of what, Sir?
> And he says, The beginning of your life
> I was born, Sir, like anyone else, I say, still annoyed with him. (116)

The opening lines of *David Copperfield* read: "Whether I shall turn out to be the hero of my own life, or whether that station will be held by anybody else, these pages must show. To begin my life with the beginning of my life, I record that I was born (as I have been informed and believe) on a Friday, at twelve o'clock at night"

(49). "To begin my life, with the beginning of my life", immediately foregrounds the fraught relationship between "real life" and its rendering in narrative.

"Sometimes I just bite the thread off with my teeth" (71) says Grace of her sewing technique and there are a number of similar breaks in the narrative of the novel. In Chapter 25 in response to an indelicate question from Jordan, she seems to reply: "I hoisted my skirts and sat down above the buzzing flies, on the same seat everyone in the house sat on, lady or lady's maid, they both piss and it smells the same" (251), but immediately retracts it, reassuring the reader: "But I do not say any of this to Dr. Jordan. And so forth, I say firmly because And so forth is all he is entitled to" (251). This is another reminder of how Grace's narrative digressions and elisions are to her own liking, her own enjoyment even.

In speculating about what Simon Jordan might be "entitled to" she hints at the sexual frisson in their relationship: "he does not understand much of what I say, although I try to put things as clearly as I can. It's as if he is deaf, and has not yet learnt to read lips. But at other times he appears to understand quite well, although like most gentlemen he often wants a thing to mean more than it does" (282). Passages such as this vividly illustrate that *Alias Grace* is, as Atwood reminds her editor, in a letter dated 11 March 1996, "partly about miscommunication and the misreading (and misleading) of others" (MS Coll. 335:10:2:7).

Grace is, at other times, happy to comply with the Doctor's needs: "Dr. Jordan is writing eagerly, as if his hand can scarcely keep up, and I have never seen him so animated before. It does my heart good to feel I can bring a little pleasure into a fellow-being's life; and I think to myself, I wonder what he will make of all that" (328). Further to this, there are times when she confides in the reader: "What should I tell him, when he comes back? He will want to know about the arrest, and the trial, and what was said. Some of it is all jumbled in my mind, but I could pick out this or that for him, some bits of whole cloth you might say, as when you go through the rag bag looking for something that will do, to supply a touch of colour. I could say this:" (410). The loaded colon at the end of this speculation, the conditional mode, and the reference to the "patchwork" of her story are reminiscent of moments in nineteenth-century fiction where the realist narrator pauses to consider their responsibilities and commitments, moments "in which the story pauses a little", as a key chapter (one that ponders the nature of literary realism) in George Eliot's *Adam Bede* would have it.

As her story progresses, the relationship between the narrator and narratee alters subtly as he becomes dependant on her plots and starts to suffer the effects of "an overheated brain" (69). In Chapter 21, Jordan's departure from Grace is likened to a release from prison: "Simon takes his hat and stick from the Governor's wife's maid, and staggers out into the sunlight. It's too bright for him, too harsh, as if he's been closed up in a dark room for a long time, although the sewing room is far from dark. It's Grace's story that is dark; he feels as if he's just come from an abattoir" (215). Indeed, Dr Jordan's symptoms echo Mrs Beeton's description of female hysterics in *Mrs Beeton's Book of Household Management*: "The fits themselves are mostly preceded by great depression of spirits, shedding of tears, sickness, palpitation of the heart, &c" (538). Still in a feverish state, Simon returns to Richmond Hill in search of clues that might corroborate Grace's story, only to realize that his search for absolute truth is meaningless. Simon Jordan's erratic behaviour does not end there, however, as he forms an unlikely erotic attachment to his landlady, in which Grace's story comes to have an aphrodisiacal effect. Towards the end of the novel, Grace reveals of her husband Jamie Walsh: "He listens to all of that like a child listening to a fairy tale, as if it is something wonderful, and then he begs me to tell him yet more" (530) and details how his attention to her narrative is frequently accompanied by other desires (531).

In a speech on writing historical fiction, "In Search of *Alias Grace*: On Writing Canadian Historical Fiction" (first delivered in Ottawa in 1996), Atwood writes: "In my fiction, Grace too – whatever else she is – is a story-teller, with strong motives to narrate, but also strong motives to withhold; the only power left to her as a convicted and imprisoned criminal comes from a blend of these two motives. … In a Victorian novel, Grace would say, 'Now it all comes back to me'; but as *Alias Grace* is not a Victorian novel, she does not say that; and if she did, would we – any longer – believe her?" (174). In looking back on her relationship with Simon Jordan, Grace's tone takes on a curious inflection, one that brings her even closer to Atwood's assessment of her. She is affectionate and also takes clear pleasure in his prone state:

> I could tell when your interest was slacking, as your gaze would wander; but it gave me joy every time I managed to come up with something that would interest you. Your cheeks would flush and you would smile like the sun on the parlour clock, and if you'd had ears like a dog they would have been pricked forward, with your eyes shining and your tongue hanging out, as if you'd found a grouse in a bush. It did make me feel as if I was of some use in this world, although I never quite saw what you were aiming at in all of it. (531)

This false modesty is misleading in its pretence of self-effacement as Grace has shown herself to be adept at second-guessing Jordan's needs. As Grace's last word on the matter it is very revealing of the ambiguous pleasure to be enjoyed by women in telling the story of their own lives, one that is less excessive and more restrained than Zenia in its methods, but is ultimately as stealthy and potentially powerful.

Who Do You Think You Are? The Tangle of Origins in *The Robber Bride* and *Alias Grace*

Who Do You Think You Are? with its accusatory undertones, is a question raised in Alice Munro's short story sequence of the same name, published in 1978, and is one that has long troubled the Canadian writer. Coral Ann Howells argues that *The Robber Bride* is concerned with interrogating the idea of Canadian identity at a specific historical moment: "The novel primarily addresses English Canadian anxieties about changing representations of national identity, focused at a precise point in time and space: Toronto in 1990–1991" ("*The Robber Bride*; or, Who is a True Canadian?" 89). According to Howells, the novel is largely concerned with challenging myths of Anglo-Canadian authenticity:

> If we look at *The Robber Bride* from these postcolonial perspectives, we begin to notice that Atwood is peering beneath the surface of English Canadian narratives of identity as she looks into the life stories of three white Canadian women born during World War II, growing up and still living in Toronto in the 1990s. And what does she see? She sees hidden histories of immigrancy and cultural displacement, split subjects, dislocated identities, reinventions and renamings, a pervasive sense of otherness and not belonging. To read *The Robber Bride* in postcolonial terms reveals how the white subject fractures under this analysis too. This is in no way meant to trivialize or minimize the experience of nonwhite subjects in Canada, nor the painful experiences of "negative othering," but rather to highlight how Atwood's fictional representations of subjectivity reveal the nonfixity of identity, and how her narrative strategies uncover secrets hidden in the past as she deconstructs myths of white English Canadian authenticity, showing how difference is a crucial factor in any identity construction. ("*The Robber Bride*; or, Who is a True Canadian?" 90)

Atwood's interest in freeze-framing a moment in the social history of Canada is reflected in the newspaper articles and research notes in the Atwood papers. These range from articles on the reception of American draft dodgers in Toronto to planning developments on the Toronto islands in the same period (MS Coll. 200:166:15–16). *The Robber Bride* is a novel that is very tuned in to the detail of events in Toronto in the 1990s, as Howells makes clear. In keeping with this, Atwood turns a cool revisionist eye on the cultural nationalism that characterized her early work. Zenia's power in the novel lies, in part, in her lack of origins; she is, as Tony tells us in the opening pages, from somewhere "bruised, and very tangled" (3).

The novel is full of reminders of the divergent histories that constitute an apparently cohesive white Canadian identity. Listening to Tony talk about European warfare, colliding European histories, Charis shrugs: "I guess that's how we ended up here" (65). Roz, who suffers more than most from the dislocation identified by Howells, muses: "Maybe that's what people mean by a national identity. The hired help in outfits. The backdrops. The props" (88), in a restatement of the idea of national identity as performed or staged explored in *The Nature Hut* and *Surfacing*. Roz, with her Irish mother and Jewish, Eastern European grandfather, acknowledges that "there are many boats in her ancestral past, as far as she can tell. Everyone she's descended from got kicked out of somewhere else, for being too poor or too politically uncouth or for having the wrong profile or accent or hair colour" (305). Intimidated by her husband's apparently impeccable

WASP credentials, she feels herself to be a perpetually Displaced Person and her "coming of age" is marked by the assumption of different cultural identities according to her family's circumstances. As Howells observes, Atwood explicitly avoids equating this feeling of displacement directly with the experience of non-white Canadians (90). If, as discussed previously, some critics have expressed concern that Atwood's work does not comprehensively address the multifaceted and difficult question "Is Canada Postcolonial?" (something explored in detail in Laura Moss's collection of the same name), then the character of Shanita invites consideration of how Atwood is, in fact, sensitive to the complex and seemingly contradictory nature of Canadian postcolonialism. The character of Shanita is also, in many respects, an interesting corollary to Zenia in the novel. Shanita offers a positive version of Zenia's model of self-creation. She even resembles her in looks with her hair "black, neither curly nor frizzy but wavy, thick and shining and luscious, like pulled taffy or lava. Like hot black glass. Shanita coils it, and winds it here and there on her head: sometimes on top, sometimes on one side" (56). However, Shanita's stories of her origins are generated in an attempt to secure herself against the painful, casual racism that she encounters daily:

> People coming into the store frequently ask Shanita where she's from. "Right here," she says, smiling her ultra-bright smile. "I was born right here in this very city!" She's nice about it to their faces, but it's a question that bothers her a lot. "I think they mean, where are your parents from," says Charis, because that's what Canadians usually mean when they ask that question. "That's not what they mean," says Shanita. "What they mean is, when am I leaving." (57)

In spite of Charis's conciliatory, perhaps naïve, attitude, Shanita draws attention to the tensions beneath the Canadian cultural mosaic. At the same time, her refusal to identify with any place of origin other than Toronto, the place in which she lives, closely aligns her with Atwood's other self-creating heroines: "Shanita has more grandmothers than anyone she knows. … She can be whatever she feels like, because who can tell?" (57). This is, on another level, a sign of her business acumen; she transforms her store in order to fit the needs of a changing market. Avoiding the excesses of Zenia, Shanita's different versions of herself provide a positive countertext, which draws attention to the value of such creative licence.

At the same time, Toronto takes on a new importance in the novel. In "Answers to Frequently Asked Questions" (1982) (MS Coll. 200:74:1:4), Atwood responds to the question "Are your novels autobiographical?" as follows: "My books are certainly autogeographical, so far at any rate. That is, they are set in places that really exist, and in which I've spent some time". The University campus at St George, Queen St, Spadina Avenue, Chinatown, Kensington Market, Charis's home on the Toronto islands, and the CN Tower are marked out as the characters go about their business in the novel. This seems to me to be another Joycean move in Atwood's writing career. Joyce wrote *Ulysses* with the kind of "autogeographical" commitment that would ensure that if the city of Dublin were burnt to the ground it might be reconstructed from the encyclopaedic detail of his work. Atwood does not perhaps have quite the same purpose in mind, but the Toronto of this novel is far removed from the anonymous backdrop of *The Edible Woman*. Looking back, in an article for the *New York Times* entitled "Toronto: The City Rediscovered", in 1982, Atwood recalls how "The notion of anyone actually *visiting* Toronto, for any purpose other than to attend the sickbed of a moribund relative, was alien to me. I set my first published novel in Toronto (where else was I to set it?) but was so embarrassed by the location that I never actually named the city and disguised the streetnames as best I could. Everyone knew that real novels were not set in Toronto" (MS Coll. 200:90:14). The article goes on to chart the radical changes and change in attitudes to the city, something that finds its apotheosis in *The Robber Bride*. If "Where is here?" is the question that runs throughout Atwood's earlier work, then this is the novel which offers a definitive answer. Towards the end of the novel, Tony displaces the military scenes on her games room table with a map of the city; a move read by most critics as a restatement of the importance of the need to write Canada into literary history. This final strategic turn on Tony's part also serves another purpose as it displaces obvious military tactics with a more cunning and discreet strategy of defence; one executed on the doorstep of her suburban home.

The figure of Susanna Moodie haunts Atwood's work, something that is most evident in her poem cycle *The Journals of Susanna Moodie*, but is as apparent in *Alias Grace*. Over a hundred years on from Mrs Moodie's arrival in Canada, characters in *The Robber Bride* still suffer under the cool, judgemental gaze of Mrs Moodie. As previously mentioned, growing up, Roz is painfully aware that she is "outside the pale" – out of synch with the white Anglo-Saxon Protestant co-ordinates of her husband's experience. Mrs Moodie's middle-class Victorian sensibility finds subtle expression in Tony's mother in the novel. Tony's mother is a discreet twentieth-century incarnation of Mrs Moodie:

> She was forced, she was coerced, she was carried off by that crude thieving lout, Tony's father, to this too-cramped, two-storey, fake Tudor, half-timbered, half-baked house, in this tedious neighbourhood, in this narrow-minded provincial city, in this too-large, too-small, too-cold, too-hot country that she hates with a strange, entrapped, and baffled fury. *Don't talk like that!* she hisses at Tony. She means the accent. Flat, she calls it. But how can Tony talk the same way her mother does? Like the radio, at noon. The kids at school would laugh. (145)

Her mother's mounting hysteria and "strange, entrapped, and baffled fury" is an echo of her pioneer predecessor Susanna Moodie during her more frustrated moments in *Roughing it in the Bush*. In *The Robber Bride*, however, Canada answers back. Nothing is left unscrutinized by Tony's mother's neuroses and Tony ponders: "Anthea says that Canadian bread is a disgrace, all air and sawdust, but it tastes fine to Tony. The bread is like many of Anthea's hatreds – Tony doesn't get the point. Why is this country too big, or too small? What would "just right" be? What's wrong with the way she talks anyways? *Anyway*" (148–9, italics in original) Tony mocks her mother's dissatisfaction by reducing her (and, by association, her historical ancestor, Mrs Moodie) to a petulant Goldilocks who is never fully satisfied.

The power of storytelling to contest and alter history is given an even greater value in *Alias Grace*. First of all, the historical figure Grace, the real life murderess, whose alleged crimes are described by Atwood in the afterword to the novel, is not just rescued from Susanna Moodie's damning account of her. The novel's relationship with Moodie's account of Grace Marks adds another frisson to Atwood's ambivalent relationship with a challenging literary foremother. Moreover, Atwood also writes back to her younger self in her conception of Grace in the novel. In "In Search of *Alias Grace*" (171) she describes how her first attempt to write Grace in a script for television for the Canadian Broadcasting Company in the early 1970s was very much determined by Mrs Moodie's reading of her.

In *Alias Grace*, Grace Marks's origins are treated with the kind of sympathy not afforded by her other biographer, Susanna Moodie. Mrs Moodie's account of Grace after her prison visit is challenged by Simon Jordan (221–3) and Reverend Verringer posits Dickens as a possible influence on the tone and style of Moodie's description of Grace. Another plausible influence, to my mind, is Bertha Mason in *Jane Eyre* – the archetypal Victorian madwoman. In *The Female Malady: Women, Madness, and English Culture, 1830–1980* Elaine Showalter describes how Brontë's madwoman influenced medical reporting on female hysteria and madness in the same period (68). It would seem that Mrs Moodie is another writer who does not escape this influence, as her description of Grace Marks and her fellow inmates at the lunatic asylum in Toronto in *Life in the Clearings Versus the Bush* contains echoes of Bertha Mason's animalism:

> There was one woman in this ward, with raven hair and eyes, and a sallow, unhealthy complexion, whom the sight of us transported into a paroxysm of ungovernable rage. She rushed to the door, and doubled her fists at us, and began cursing and swearing at a furious rate, and then she laughed – such a laugh as one might fancy Satan uttered when he recounted, in full conclave, his triumph over the credulity of our first mother. … She lay kicking and foaming, and uttering words too dreadful for human ears to listen to; and Grace Marks came out of her hiding-place, and performed a thousand mad gambols round her. (272)

Moodie's reading of Grace is keen to establish her at the monstrous end of Gilbert and Gubar's well-known Angel-Monster dichotomy explicated in the opening chapter of *The Madwoman in the Attic* (17): "Moodie portrays Grace as the driving engine of the affair – a scowling, sullen, teenage temptress – with the comurderer, the manservant James McDermott, shown as a mere dupe, driven by his own lust for Grace as well as by her taunts and blandishments" ("In Search of *Alias Grace*" 171). Official histories, medical, legal, literary, and anecdotal are questioned in *Alias Grace* and Mrs Moodie is held up for particular scrutiny in this regard.

Grace Marks's Irishness is given a very particular kind of attention in Atwood's text. In *The Robber Bride*, Roz recalls her family history on her mother's side:

> Tony, who is more interested in these details than Roz is, once showed Roz an old picture – the men standing in metal washtubs, to protect their legs from their own axes. Low comedy for the English middle classes, back home, living off the avails. Stupid bogtrotters! The Irish were always good for a smirk or two, then. (305)

This cartoon image of the Irish in the style of *Punch* magazine caricatures is one that affects Grace in a more profound way. Reverend Verringer acknowledges this in his description of how a jeering public have mistaken the part for the whole:

> There is still a widespread feeling against Grace Marks; and this is a most partisan country. The Tories appear to have confused Grace with the Irish Question, although she is a Protestant; and to consider the murder of a single Tory gentleman – however worthy the gentleman, and however regrettable the murder – to be the same thing as the insurrection of an entire race. (91)

Atwood draws attention to how Grace's Irishness, her difference, affects accounts of her alleged crime. Grace plaintively focuses the reader's attention on this early on in the novel:

> What it says at the beginning of my Confession is true enough. I did indeed come from the North of Ireland; though I thought it very unjust when they wrote down that *both of the accused were from Ireland by their own admission*. That made it sound like a crime, and I don't know that being from Ireland is a crime; although I have often seen it treated as such. (118, italics in original)

The opening chapter of *Roughing it in the Bush* offers an insight into exactly what Atwood was up against in responding to Mrs Moodie. In the first chapter entitled "A Visit to Grosse Isle" (24), Mrs Moodie, all but waving *Mrs Beeton's Book of Household Management* at the scene, is deeply offended by the sight of her cultural Other swarming over the New World:

> Never shall I forget the extraordinary spectacle that met our sight the moment we passed the low range of bushes which formed a screen in front of the river. A crowd of many hundred Irish emigrants had been landed during the present and former day and all this motley crew – men, women, and children, who were not confined by sickness to the sheds (which greatly resembled cattle-pens) – were employed in washing clothes or spreading them out on the rocks and bushes to dry. … The confusion of babel was among them. All talkers and no hearers – each shouting and yelling in his or her uncouth dialect, and all accompanying their vociferations with violent and extraordinary gestures, quite incomprehensible to

> the uninitiated. We were literally stunned by the strike of tongues. I shrank, with feelings almost akin to fear, from the hard-featured, sunburnt women as they elbowed rudely past me. (24–5)

Moodie's description might have been lifted straight from the pages of W.M. Thackeray's *The Irish Sketchbook*, an account of his travels through Ireland on the eve of the famine, the same historical moment in which Grace Marks's family departed from Ireland for Canada. Like Mrs Moodie, Thackeray is, at times, shocked by what he presents as the unruly lack of civilisation of the natives and their curious looks. He is, on more than one occasion, torn between the idea of melancholy Celt and the apparent savagery of the natives, and makes note of the "two sorts of physiognomies which are common; the pleasing and somewhat melancholy one before mentioned, and a square high-cheeked flatnosed physiognomy, not uncommonly accompanied by a hideous staring of head of dry, red hair" (146). Grace, although aware that her Protestant identity distances her somewhat from these stereotypes, is nevertheless subject to a similar unapologetic prejudice in the novel. Atwood's novel, and in particular the description of Grace's progress and the journey to the New World, has a humanizing influence that deliberately tempers Mrs Moodie's prejudices.

In a scene very similar to the one recreated by Moodie, the Marks family arrive in Canada, bedraggled and mourning the death of their mother:

> We were required to stop at an island and to undergo an inspection for cholera, as many before us had brought it into the country on the ships; but as the dead people on our ship had died of other things – four besides my mother, two from consumption and one from apoplexy, and one jumped overboard – we were allowed to proceed. I did have the chance to give the children a good scrubbing-off in the river water, although it was very cold – at least their faces and arms, which they were very much in need of. (142)

Here, we see not the barely civilized "motley crew" of Moodie's vision, but a frightened, famished young girl, ill-equipped to take over the role of her dead mother.

Atwood affords Grace the opportunity to get her own back on Moodie, in describing her as "a beetle": "Round and fat and dressed in black, and a quick and scuttling sort of walk; and black, shiny eyes too. I do not mean it as an insult, Sir, I added for he'd given one of his short laughs. It was just the way she looked in my opinion" (417). Mrs Moodie is identified by Reverend Verringer as a literary woman who liked "to embroider" (223), and Grace replies in kind, demonstrating that she too has a penchant for theatrical description.

The Robber Bride and *Alias Grace* are novels that in different but related ways address serious narrative elisions in Canadian cultural history and remind the reader of lost or missing narrative strands in the story of Canada. Combined with this historical interest is a continued interest in the narration of selfhood, and the writing of the Bildungsroman under culturally-specific pressures. Atwood's fiction continues to work within established literary and historical models, exerting pressure from the inside out and the Bildungsroman, in its distinctively Canadian version, is the most radically re-worked form of all.

Chapter 6

Keeping Secrets, Telling Lies: Fictions of the Artist and Author in *Cat's Eye* and *The Blind Assassin*

From an early stage in her writing career, Margaret Atwood shows a striking interest in the fate of the female artist and author in Canada. While evidence of this can be found throughout her work, her later fiction, most particularly *Cat's Eye* (1988) and *The Blind Assassin* (2000), revisits and reformulates this interest in images of the female artist in especially innovative ways. A comparative reading of the novels proves particularly fruitful because both novels explore the distinctive aspects of female creativity and question myths of the female artist; both also present painting, writing, or telling a life story as a crucial medium of reading and rewriting the past. The novels share an interest in the challenges and paradoxes of "writing a life" and draw attention to the processes of evasion, subversion, and illusion that are at work in all narratives of selfhood, but are perhaps, necessarily, most dramatically manifested in narratives that are self-consciously committed to writing women's lives. In this way, the artistically mature Atwood makes her most profound exploration of issues with which she and many other contemporary women writers have been perennially preoccupied.

In identifying the ways to "write a woman's life" (1), Carolyn Heilbrun establishes autobiography, biography, and autobiographical fiction as three equally powerful statements of female subjectivity. Other theorists of women's life writing, such as Leigh Gilmore and Linda Anderson, have pursued this theme, positing that the act of writing her life is, for a woman, a deeply political gesture and an important public announcement of selfhood. In *Subjectivity, Identity and the Body: Women's Autobiographical Practices in the Twentieth Century*, Sidonie Smith expands on this line of thinking in establishing a series of vital questions regarding female appropriation of autobiography:

> at the scene of writing, each woman struggles with inherited autobiographical narratives constitutive of the official histories of the subject. When does she take up the sanctities of official narratives and when set them aside? How far does she accommodate inherited forms, the official and officious calls to a specific subjectivity, and how far does she stretch the form to fill her own needs and desires? What are the pressure points she puts on traditional autobiography as it presses her into a specific kind of autobiographical subject? Where exactly does she find the narrative elasticities and subversive possibilities of the genre?

> What narrative counterpractices does she import into the text? What formal experiments or out-law practices does she pursue? And how do those experiments enable her to evade narrative fixture in official scripts of the universal subject or the embodied subject? (23)

These key questions, with their emphasis on the woman writer's need to renegotiate the paradigms of autobiographical models such as the Bildungsroman and Künstlerroman are highly relevant to the construction of a narrative of selfhood as performed in *Cat's Eye* and *The Blind Assassin*. As discussed in Chapter 1, an interesting complication in Atwood's relationship with woman-centred autobiographical fiction emerges on consideration of her relationship with the Künstlerroman or Novel of the Artist, as interpreted in the criticism of Jerome Buckley, and these later novels explore new models for female authorship and creativity.

Margaret Atwood's Ventriloquists: Alternate Subjectivities in Atwood's Künstlerromane

Like Joan Foster's self-construction in Atwood's early Künstlerroman, *Lady Oracle* (1976), Elaine Risley's narrative of her early life in *Cat's Eye* relies on two equally unreliable sources: her memory and the visual record provided by her abstract paintings. Like her fictional predecessor, she juggles different versions of her self, both in her private and artistic life. The first-person narrative of the novel shifts from Elaine's traumatic experiences at the hands of her school-friend Cordelia to her emerging artistic potential as a young woman and her return to her home town of Toronto for a retrospective of her life's work. Judith McCombs summarizes the novel as "a *bildungsroman* portrait of the artist that incorporates transmuted autobiography; and its contrarily re-membering seer-narrator is Atwood's most elaborate representation of the human self as complexly layered, with fluid and sometimes buried layers" (9). This complexity of the construction of the self is acknowledged early on in the novel: "There is no one I would ever tell this to, except Cordelia. But which Cordelia? The one I have conjured up, the one with the roll-top boots and the turned-up collar, or the one before, or the one after? There is never only one, of anyone" (6). This applies not just to Cordelia, but to Elaine herself as different versions of Elaine are fashioned as her life narrative develops. Elaine's "mean mouth" is a typical illustration of Atwood's rendering of the subject as ventriloquist (234) and might be read as a preface to the more elaborate role-playing explored in Atwood's later novel, *The Robber Bride* (1993).

Indeed, more generally, Cordelia is frequently read as a literary precursor to the character of Zenia in *The Robber Bride*. Cordelia emerges not only as a catalyst but also as a threat in the way that she dominates Elaine's formative years. Her power lies in a similar promise of inclusion and affirmation to that practised so deftly by Zenia. Cordelia promises access to a secret sorority – "This time her voice is confiding, as if she's talking about something intimate that only she and I know about and agree on. She creates a circle of two, takes me in" (71) – one based on a cult of femininity complete with exacting rules and expectations. Cordelia uses this unspoken social code to persecute Elaine: "The white socks, the Mary Janes, the always-inadequate birthday present swathed in tissue paper, and the little girls with their assessing eyes, their slippery deceitful smiles, tartaned up like Lady Macbeth" (113). The power and danger of Cordelia, the "tartaned up" little girl is only a short imaginative leap away from her "tarted up" adult version: Zenia. This Shakespearean formulation, drawing together apparently contradictory notions of femininity in its invocation of Cordelia and Lady Macbeth, has an impact on all of Elaine's future relationships with other people, other women in particular. Also, she finds herself bound to her childhood nemesis by the same combination of fear and desire that keeps Roz, Charis, and Tony in thrall to Zenia in *The Robber Bride*.

Elaine's childhood traumas are reconstructed in all of her subsequent relationships with women, such as in her relationship with her rival for Josef's affections, fellow painter Susie, who, in a later dream sequence, is cast as another tormentor, another Cordelia (323). Thus, *Cat's Eye* presents a female Künstlerroman that is a collage of selfhood compatible with Atwood's earlier work. The main difference is that while a novel like *Lady Oracle* explores multiple, competing selves, Elaine Risley's artistic and personal retrospective is captured in a frequently-cited passage in the opening pages of the novel as "like a series of liquid transparencies, one laid on top of the other" (3).

One of the most revealing Shakespearean references in the novel centres on the comic performance of *Macbeth*, during which the power relations between Cordelia and Elaine begin to shift and Elaine develops a "mean mouth". Shakespearean performance has a particular place in the history of the Bildungsroman and performances of *Hamlet* recur in both *Wilhelm Meister* and *Great Expectations*. The production of *Macbeth* in *Cat's Eye*, then, finds resonance with the Bildungsroman's apparent interest in performing Shakespeare, and indeed this performance – as with its precedents – marks a pivotal moment, in this case in Elaine's relationship with her nemesis. The tables of power turn and Elaine finds herself indulging in behaviour that was once the sole privilege of her tormentor. She takes particular relish in watching Cordelia's dismay as the prop for which she is responsible – Macbeth's head fashioned out of a cabbage – bounces comically across the stage (245). The complex intertextuality of Atwood's engagement with Shakespeare in *Cat's Eye*, then, reveals her further engagement with – and rejection of – the incarnation of the Bildungsroman intent on singular personal development; Shakespeare might be seen as providing some powerful alternative templates, even if they are only a shadowy presence in Atwood's works.

The image of "the mean mouth" and the "series of liquid transparencies" invoked at the beginning of the novel adds an important emancipatory dimension to this multiplicity and "choices" of self-construction in Atwood's fiction and this is foregrounded early on in *Cat's Eye* where Elaine says of the old ladies that she sees on the bus:

> This is the kind we like best. They have a certain gaiety to them, a power of invention, they don't care what people think. They have escaped, though what it is they have escaped from isn't clear to us. We think that their bizarre costumes, their verbal tics are chosen, and that when the time comes we also will be free to choose. (5)

These choices take on even more significance in Atwood's later novel *The Blind Assassin*.

Spanning the first and second world wars, *The Blind Assassin* chronicles the experience of two sisters, Iris and Laura Chase, their shared passion for a socialist agitator, and their unhappiness at the hands of Iris's industrialist husband. In an early discussion of the novel, J. Brooks Bouson describes it as "at once an intricately designed literary puzzle featuring a classic Atwoodian narrator – the elderly memoirist Iris Chase-Griffen, who is a master storyteller and illusionist – and an unsettling cautionary tale that, like Atwood's other novels, focuses attention on the power politics of gender relations" (251). Bouson goes on to focus on the "literary puzzle" of the novel as revealing a "fictional documentation of the ways in which gender and class expectations shaped and confined women's lives in the first half of the twentieth century" (252). While there is certainly an explicit social critique at work in Iris Chase-Griffen's narrative, the novel also presents a "puzzle" of self as narrative in the way that it offers a number of versions of the life of Iris and her sister Laura, none of which are complete in themselves but which interact with other, official and unauthorized narratives. The recurring motif of mutually dependent literary selves is a crucial feature of Atwood's fictional oeuvre – and a defining feature of the Atwoodian Bildungsroman – but also emerges as a recurring preoccupation in her non-fictional writing, something that has yet to receive due critical attention.

The framing narrative of *The Blind Assassin*, written by a frail and elderly Iris Chase-Griffen, is both a life's retrospective and a confessional. As with *Lady Oracle*, this is interrupted by interpolated sections from the novel within the novel, which is also called *The Blind Assassin*, as well as newspaper death notices, social announcements, and extracts from gossip columns that tie in with and illuminate the primary narrative. If *Cat's Eye* presents the development of the self as a collage of reconstructed memories, *The Blind Assassin* offers a scrapbook version of the self. Iris's memoir is interrupted by the official, public version of events, which is revealed to be wildly at odds with the private reality of the Chase-Griffen family. Yet this "reality" is at every point mediated through Iris, a highly self-conscious, intrusive and audaciously unreliable narrator. Furthermore, the main characters of the novel within the novel are preoccupied with yet another narrative: a science fiction fantasy, which makes up a considerable part of the work. At the end of *Lady Oracle*, the main character toys with the idea of switching from costume gothics to science fiction, and *The Blind Assassin* actually includes a writer of science fiction, Alex Thomas. It also depicts a woman writer (Iris Chase-Griffen) just as caught up in stealthy manipulations of a literary persona as her precursor, Joan Foster. This emphasis on the controlled and indeed artificial nature of life narratives finds early expression in a draft in progress dated to 1964–65, foundational material for *Cat's Eye*. A short story called "Cut-Out" describes three young girls at play, cutting out a "Lady" complete with domestic accoutrements from a homeware catalogue. The lovingly made paper women suffers a sinister fate, as soon as the project is complete:

> The third girl gathered up the pairs of scissors. She started to close the scrap-book. The Lady, bland, doll-like, perfect, simpered up at her from the center of the page. She took the sharp-pointed sewing scissors and carefully snipped out the pink oval of the face, leaving the long hair around the edges. She was smiling: they would be surprised, later. They would think the boys had done it. Anyway, she thought, closing the book, it looked better with no face. (MS Coll. 200:99:5:5)

The removal of the woman's face – the only part of her that stops her from being an accumulation of cut-out parts – is suggestive of an early interest, on Atwood's part, in an image of subjectivity that dramatizes the idea of the postmodern self as made up of different surfaces or veneers.

As a Bildungsroman, *The Blind Assassin* bears fruitful comparison to *Cat's Eye*, concerned as it is with a life reconstructed through Art. Just as Elaine Risley reconstructs the traumas of her early life through her paintings, Iris's life can be read as a fusion of the interpolated fictions in the novel. The three narrative layers are not mutually exclusive but contain valuable textual clues essential to the development of each narrative strand, presenting a "series of liquid transparencies" not unlike that described at the beginning of *Cat's Eye* (3). As indicated by J. Brooks Bouson, the science fiction narrative offers an "intratextual commentary" (260) on the primary narrative, and so the rape, sacrifice, and trauma described in the science fiction story of *The Blind Assassin* contains echoes of Laura's and Iris's suffering at the hands of Richard Griffen. In fact, the former might be read as a more extreme, explicit dramatization of the latter; Laura and Iris are sacrificial victims on the same spectrum as the brutalized figures who inhabit the science fiction fantasy. As a further example of this, the current-time narrative hints at the true nature of Iris's relationship with Alex Thomas long before it is officially disclosed: "We preferred – or I preferred, and Laura tagged along – those with stories about other lands or even other planets. Spaceships from the future, where women would wear very short skirts made of shiny fabric and everything would gleam" (152). In the same way, Ovid's *Metamorphoses* is an important feature of Iris's Latin studies under the instruction of the misogynous Mr Erskine and is later evoked in the interpolated novel in exchanges between the characters based on herself and her lover, the aforementioned socialist agitator, Alex Thomas. In the early stages of the novel within the novel, the narrator pauses to consider the fate of sacrificial children in the dystopian Sakiel-Norn. A graphic description of the ritual of cutting out the tongues of young girls in advance of their being sacrificed is followed by a meditation on how "tongueless, and swollen with words she could never again pronounce, each girl would be led in procession to the sound of solemn music, wrapped in veils and garlanded with flowers, up the winding steps to the city's ninth door. Nowadays you might say she looked like a pampered society bride" (29). The very direct link drawn between the ritualized violence inflicted upon the sacrificial virgins and Iris's own experience as one such society bride is a further illustration of how the fictional narrative in progress replicates key events in the main narrative.

The Blind Assassin reveals much about Atwood's critical take on the nature of writing and contains a meta-commentary on Atwood's critical interpretation of ideas of the author and of authorship. The novel is fundamentally concerned with the idea of selfhood as a narrative construction or invention. Iris's daughter, Aimee, reads her aunt's (in fact her mother's) novel as an exposé of a family scandal, particularly in relation to her own origins (she imagines herself to be the daughter of Laura and Alex, who are identified as the fictional lovers), and this knowledge ultimately leads her to her death. On the other hand, Iris makes clear that the manuscript in progress is intended as a redemptive message for her granddaughter Sabrina, which reveals the unknown origins of her biological grandfather (a refugee orphan from Eastern Europe), thus freeing her from the tainted legacy of the Griffen industrial empire and leaving her at liberty to make up her own life story: "Rich man, poor man, beggar-man, saint, a score of countries of origin, a dozen cancelled maps, a hundred levelled villages – take your pick. Your legacy from him is the realm of infinite speculation. You're free to invent yourself at will" (513). Much like Roz's experience in *The Robber Bride*, Eastern European origins are invoked to undermine the bourgeois suburb of Rosedale's aspirations to an Anglo-Canadian identity, one validated by a conviction of the anglocentric nature of a true Canadian identity. Here, the liberation of invention and reinvention through storytelling and narrative is restated, though as suggested in the violent imagery of Iris's promise, the same processes are not entirely without trauma. Nevertheless, the redemptive and positive possibilities of self-construction and reconstruction explored elsewhere in Atwood's fiction are given a new endorsement in the novel.

Negotiations with the Dead: Writing the Female Artist in Atwood's Fiction

Elaine Risley's cultivation of different private and artistic personae finds resonance in other Atwood characters, most strikingly Joan Foster in *Lady Oracle* and Zenia in *The Robber Bride*. For example, there are two versions of Elaine the artist: the Art and Archaeology student and the serious artist who studies life-drawing outside of college hours. From the outset, Elaine plays with the expectations of the female artist in the same way that she responds to critical misconstructions of her work. Thus, to Josef, her Hungarian mentor and lover, she becomes a pre-Raphaelite fantasy while to her first husband Jon, she takes on the guise of a disconsolate existentialist. As in *Lady Oracle*, these disguises are easily assumed and discarded according to circumstance.

Cat's Eye is the novel most explicitly interested in, to borrow Atwood's phrase, the "paradoxes and dilemmas" of being a Canadian woman artist. Early on in the novel, Elaine Risley confesses that, "The word *artist* embarrasses me; I prefer *painter*, because it's more like a valid job. An artist is a tawdry, lazy sort of thing to be, as most people in this country will tell you" (15, italics in original). In spite of showing an awareness of the occupational hazards of being an artist – "If I cut off my ear, would the market value go up? Better still, stick my head in the oven, blow out my brains. What rich art collectors like to buy, among other things, is a little vicarious craziness" (86) – Elaine achieves notable success. Yet, throughout the novel, she is subject to various imposed views of her work as a female artist, views that seem removed from her idea of herself as a "painter". Atwood's own critical musings on her experience of being a young writer are most carefully documented in Chapter 1 of *Negotiating with the Dead: A Writer on Writing*:

> When I was an aspiring female poet, in the late 1950s, the notion of required sacrifice was simply accepted. The same was true for any sort of career for a woman, but Art was worse, because the sacrifice required was more complete. You couldn't be a wife and mother and also an artist, because each one of those things required total dedication. As nine-year-olds we'd all been trotted off to see the film *The Red Shoes* as a birthday-party treat: we remembered Moira Shearer, torn between Art and love, squashing herself under a train. (85)

Atwood's comments on her early writing career have real resonance for reading novels like *Lady Oracle* and *Cat's Eye* as investigations of a spectrum of myths of the female artist and for understanding the need for women writers to subvert the ideologies which underlie such myths by telling their own stories. Yet, throughout the novel, she is subject to various imposed views of her work as a female artist, views which seem removed from her idea of herself as a "painter". Feminist representations of the trials of being a woman writer in the 1960s and 70s might stand accused of taking on a constructed enemy and yet there is plenty of evidence to suggest that there were powerful obstacles to the aspiring woman writer at this time. The reader reports from McClelland and Stewart on the submission of Atwood's first draft of *The Edible Woman*, her first novel, is quite telling in this regard. One of the reports suggests that "WOMAN [sic] isn't quite a novel as much as it is a diary-like record of experience and impressions during the first year of a student of literature out of university – a year of indirection and indecision" (MS Coll. 200:95:5) before going on to recommend that the novel be referred to a "female reader" at the publishing house. Yet, another moment of clarity in Atwood's own development as a writer reveals a different complication for the female artist: "When Betty Friedan and Simone de Beauvoir came my way, like shorebirds heralding land, I read them with much interest. They got a lot right, for me, but there was one thing they got wrong. They were assuring me that I didn't have to get married and have children. But what I wanted was someone to tell me I could" ("Great Unexpectations" xvi). In *Cat's Eye*, Elaine Risley's experience as a middle-aged woman in a powder-blue sweatsuit, "my disguise as a non-artist", resonates very strongly with this as she is made painfully aware of a need to dress the part: "Powder-blue is lightweight. I should've worn nun black, Dracula black, like all proper female painters" (87). Thus, as an Atwoodian costume, Elaine's tracksuit and the life that it represents becomes the bolder statement as it is one part of her refusal to conform to imposed expectations. This defiance is most apparent in her encounter with politicized readings of her life as an artist, in particular, in an interview with a young journalist in advance of the exhibition opening:

> What I have to say is not altogether what she wants to hear. She'd prefer stories of outrage, although she'd be unlikely to tell them about herself, she's too young. Still, people my age are supposed to have stories of outrage; at least insult, at least putdown. Male art teachers pinching your bum, calling you *baby*, asking you why there are no great female painters, that sort of thing. She would like me to be furious, and quaint. (90)

Her painting plays a crucial role in her development in the novel. Elaine's early life is recorded in her artwork: the portraits from early on in her career depict the women who most influenced her formative years in domestic situations characterized by surreal, carnival elements, or rendered in caricature. Elaine puts the fragments of her life together in a new order as intimated in her brother's scientific theories: "'When we gaze at the night sky,' he says, 'We are looking at fragments of the past'" (331–2). Elaine's paintings are just such fragments of her past and play a major role in the way that they bear meaning in relation to the present. Thus her evangelist tormentor Mrs Smeath comes to have a serious impact on her artistic imagination, as do the more minor details of her childhood. For example, the silver paper from cigarette boxes that she faithfully collects as a child finds its way into one of the key paintings in her first exhibition (348). Also, as with Atwood's other artists, Elaine finds ways of engaging with tradition and convention so that it is meaningful to her as a Canadian woman artist in the twentieth century. Hence, the mirror in Van Eyck's portrait "The Arnolfini Marriage" is transformed into Elaine's childhood talisman, the cat's eye marble, and the inscription on the painting becomes graffiti from a spray can (327).

In *Cat's Eye* and *The Blind Assassin*, as in her early career, Atwood's fiction and critical commentary overlap and are mutually illuminating. Thus, Atwood's meditation on writing in *Negotiating with the Dead: A Writer on Writing* makes a most revealing companion text to *The Blind Assassin*. *Negotiating with the Dead* is the published version of a series of lectures given by Atwood in 2000, which coincided with the writing of *The Blind Assassin*. As with the inevitable and fruitful pairing of *Surfacing* and *Survival*, the novel shows signs of an acute awareness of the critical issues in Atwood's essays, particularly those essays on the female writer and writing, and many of her critical comments are highly relevant when thinking about the challenges of writing a woman's life, or telling a woman's story.

As an author and narrator, Iris Chase-Griffen is most interested in disrupting and challenging official histories and is especially adept at exploiting the "narrative elasticities" and "subversive possibilities" identified by Sidonie Smith as crucial elements of autobiographical fiction as a genre. Iris pursues various narrative "outlaw practices" and may be read as another illustration of an idea developed by Ann Parsons in "The Self-Inventing Self: Women Who Lie and Pose in the Fiction of Margaret Atwood" of how woman as artist is very close to woman as "con-artist" in Atwood's fiction (105). This is something that Atwood herself acknowledges directly in an unpublished speech (first delivered to the Cheltenham Literary Festival in October 1993): "Mercury is one of the patrons of art, and all writers are – among other things – con-artists" (MS Coll. 335:33:5:7).

Atwood returns to complex issues of female creativity throughout her critical writings and most comprehensively in her recent study of the role and characteristics of the writer as a character in literature in *Negotiating with the Dead*. Much of her critical writing suggests a consciousness of the act of writing at both a political and personal level and *The Blind Assassin*, like *Lady Oracle*, seems to be a fictional outlet for many of her thoughts and conclusions about writers and writing. Long before the appearance of *The Blind Assassin*, in an unpublished address (undated ca. 1960–81) to a conference in Washington on "Writing and Craft", Atwood lays the groundwork for what would become a defining motif in her work. On thinking about the association of craft and creativity, Atwood surmises:

> The first thing that came to my mind was those Thornton W. Burgess stories, the ones with Old Mother West Wind and Jolly Round Red Mr. Sun in them. Reddy Fox was *crafty*. What did that mean? He concealed his intentions. He went the long way around so as to lie in ambush for Peter Rabbit when Peter Rabbit wasn't looking. He was sly. He was tricky. He prowled. (MS Coll. 200:56:2, italics in original)

From this morality tale comes a crucial paradigm for writing, one that is most fully explicated in Atwood's *Negotiating with the Dead*. In this, her most elaborate meditation on the craft of writing, Atwood asserts that there is an essential duplicity in the writer and the writing process:

> What is the relationship between the two entities we lump under one name, that of "the writer"? The particular writer. By *two*, I mean the person who exists when no writing is going forward – the one who walks the dog, eats bran for regularity, takes the car in to be washed, and so forth – and that other, more shadowy and altogether more equivocal personage who shares the same body

> and who, when no one is looking, takes it over and uses it to commit the actual writing. (35, italics in original)

Chapter 2 of *Negotiating With the Dead*, entitled "Duplicity: The Jekyll Hand, The Hyde Hand and the Slippery Double", is concerned with questions of authorship and authorial intention, and the critical model of the writer that emerges is based on splitting and division: "As for the artists who are also writers, they are doubles twice times over, for the mere act of writing splits the self into two" (32). In *The Blind Assassin* such doubling is not the result of self-division but of Iris's and Laura's literary twinning:

> You see how quickly we have begun talking about hands – two of them. Dexter and sinister. There has been a widespread suspicion among writers – widespread over at least the past century and a half – that there are two of him sharing the same body, with a hard-to-predict and difficult-to-pinpoint moment during which the one turns into the other. (*Negotiating With the Dead* 37)

The model of the author outlined here is certainly illuminating in studying Atwood's own work. As an author who has had a high profile as a critic and a journalist, the moment during which "the one turns into the other" is something that has preoccupied and frustrated many critics, particularly readers of the seemingly semi-autobiographical *Cat's Eye*. A key image in the opening chapter of the novel within the novel in *The Blind Assassin* is of a photograph showing "a hand, cut by the margin, scissored off at the wrist, resting on the grass as if discarded. Left to its own devices" (5). This can be positioned on the same schema by which Atwood imagines the writing process in her critical prose. A recent real-life complication of this idea of the detached writing hand has appeared in the form of Atwood's invention of the "LongPen" a device which transmits a real autograph via the internet. Atwood's invention caused a certain amount of controversy, as it was interpreted by some critics as an attempt to keep her reading public at bay. Though this invention has perhaps added to Atwood's mystique, as a writer she has, from the early stages of her career, been remarkably forthcoming and generous in discussions of her writing in numerous interviews and in lecture series such as the Clarendon Lectures (1991) and Empson Lectures (2000). It is worth paying careful attention to Atwood's writing in the mode of cultural critic as, while she steers clear of offering any definitive readings of her work, her writing in this category is always illuminating when read as a companion text to her contemporaneous fiction. With this in mind, I would argue that Atwood's fiction and her critical prose, with its playful irreverence in relation to established literary discourses, occupies a mid-ground between traditional Anglo-American and French feminist models of women's writing. Atwood is a writer most concerned with infiltrating traditionally male-centred literary genres and conventions and productively renegotiating the terms that define them. She represents the Anglo-American commitment to engaging with patriarchal discourses in a way that also finds sympathy with the French feminist idea of Écriture Féminine. Indeed, in a 1988 article called "Two Countries of Writing: Theater and Poetical Fiction", Hélène Cixous develops a very similar metaphor that complements the double-handedness invoked by Atwood in a discussion of the differences between writing poetical fiction and writing for theatre:

> I have been writing for a long time with my right hand and now I am writing with two hands. … It's a metaphor. I write with my right hand. But it's my right-left hand that I use. That is, I use a hand that is very awkward. … It's not really contradictory; in a way, it's a complement. However, it makes me travel all the time between two countries and remark again on differences. (191–2)

A further example of this interest in splitting and twinning can be found in an essay entitled "The Thieves of Language: Women Poets and Revisionist Mythmaking" by Alicia Ostriker. In a discussion of a range of twentieth-century women poets, Ostriker draws on a motif of division that is similar to that employed by Cixous: "Insofar as the subject of the poem is always the 'I' of the poet, her divided voices evoke divided selves: the rational and the passionate, the active and the suffering, the conscious life and the dream life, animus and anima, analyst and analysand" (331). Atwood's descriptions of the writer at work, and more significantly the models by which her female artists work, has much to say to this dual reality. As ever, the intensely personal also finds an application to national discourses in Atwood's work. In an introduction to an anthology on Canadian Studies, she writes:

> *Ambivalence* is a most appropriate title for a collection of essays about Canadian Literature, implying as it does the qualities of contradiction and doubleness, but also of those of weighing and balance. It's been said of one of our earlier Prime Ministers that "he never let his on the one hand know what his on the other hand was doing" (F.R. Scott); the same could be said of Canada as a country, and of the literature that country has produced. (MS Coll. 200:147:10:1)

The symbiosis of literary selves is most fully realized in the form of Laura's and Iris's literary doubling in *The Blind Assassin*. Like *Lady Oracle* and *The Robber Bride*, the novel opens with yet another dramatic death: Laura Chase's suicide. Laura is sacrificed by the text in order to provide the writing persona that Iris needs in order to publish her work. While the true author of the notorious novel is not revealed until towards the end of *The Blind Assassin*, a series of clues are provided. Laura is described early on as "A tabula rasa, not waiting to write, but to be written on" (46). At the same time, at the moment at which the true identity of the author of the novel within the novel is revealed, Iris explains that "Laura was my left hand, and I was hers. We wrote the book together. It's a left-handed book. That's why one of us is always out of sight, whichever way you look at it" (513) and, thus, Laura's iconic literary persona serves as Iris's "slippery double". Iris, the true author of *The Blind Assassin* (the novel within the novel), hides behind the persona of her dead sister; the novel is published posthumously as the work of a gifted but troubled young woman. Iris comes to think of herself as "Laura's odd, extra hand, attached to no body – the hand that passed her on, to the world, to them" (287). This provides Iris with a release on two fronts as she manages both to execute a risqué literary coup and at the same time make a bold statement of her contravention of social expectations. The stereotype of the tormented, suicidal woman writer in Laura Chase is evoked perhaps as an ironic footnote to Atwood's own critical interrogation of received stereotypes of the woman writer and artist discussed previously. Iris, the actual author of the cult classic *The Blind Assassin*, hides behind a fabricated persona, all the better to serve that persona. The most striking example of this is in the way that she positions herself as executor of Laura's estate and curator of Laura's memory: the guardian of Laura's Künstlerroman. The hostility of her response to queries and requests from academics and readers interested in further researching the life and writing of Laura Chase is further evidence of her need to exert full control over her sister's legacy. On her reply to an academic seeking access to her sister's manuscripts, she writes: "I have no wish to satisfy your lust for phials of dried blood and the severed fingers of saints. Laura Chase is not your 'project'. She was my sister. She would not have wished to be pawed over after her death, whatever that pawing over might euphemistically be termed" (287). This careful preservation of a literary mask or persona might be read as a postmodern innovation, but also as the continuation of a long tradition of subterfuge on the part of the woman writer. Ellis, Acton, and Currer Bell, and George Eliot can be thought of as literary precursors to Iris Chase-Griffen, whose literary alter ego is also borne out of necessity, but who turns it to her advantage by indulging in elaborate narrative game playing.

The Blind Assassin shows a similar awareness of the danger of a commitment to words to that explored in *Negotiating with the Dead*; in one of her many self-conscious narrative intrusions, Iris warns, "Anyone intending to meddle with words needs such blessing, such warning" (41), and later ponders that "Things written down can cause a great deal of harm. All too often, people don't consider that" (287). These sentiments are echoed in *Negotiating with the Dead* in Atwood's discussion of the "anxiety of authorship": "No wonder St. Matthew looks so apprehensive in Caravaggio's painting of him, clutching his pen while a rather thuggish angel dictates to him what he must write down: the act of writing comes weighted with a burden of anxieties. The written word is so much like evidence – like something that can be used against you later" (47–8). Yet, in spite of Iris's apprehension and anxiety, she shows herself to be capable of narrative trickery on two fronts – she is the secret author of *The Blind Assassin* and manages to sustain this secrecy throughout her current-time memoir. At the same time, she sees herself as being controlled and overpowered by her writing hand:

> To the task at hand. *At hand* is appropriate: sometimes it seems to me that it's only my hand writing, not the rest of me; that my hand has taken on a life of its

> own, and will keep going even if severed from the rest of me …. Certainly it's been writing down a number of things it wouldn't be allowed to if subject to my better judgement. (373, italics in original)

A valuable coda to Atwood's explication of "the writing hand" in *Negotiating with the Dead*, is the way in which Iris draws a similarly Barthesian conclusion about the fate of the text: "That's what happens a set number of years after the death of the author: you lose control. The thing is out there in the world, replicating itself in God knows how many forms, without any say-so from me" (283). In the same way that in *The Robber Bride*, "the story of Zenia is insubstantial, ownerless, a rumour only, drifting from mouth to mouth and changing as it goes" (461), in *The Blind Assassin*, literary narrative is fluid, changing, and far removed from the control of the author. In fact, the author is similarly "ownerless", a myth that is both fabricated yet carefully preserved.

Cat's Eye and *The Blind Assassin* present a critical subtext that raises urgent questions closely related to those in Atwood's non-fiction writing, and such questions define another phase in Atwood's oeuvre as an author and literary critic. In the course of her writing career, Atwood has been regarded as one of Canada's most important literary ambassadors as well as a stellar figure in the constellation of Canadian literature. Perhaps as significant, as we have seen, is the way in which, in her fiction and critical prose, she provides an ongoing commentary on the life of the writer and artist that establishes her as an author who is fundamentally concerned with the complications, complexities, and hazards faced by "anyone intending to meddle with words" (*The Blind Assassin* 41).

Chapter 7

Full Circle: The Chaos of Living in *Moral Disorder*

From the "assemblage of lies and alibis" invoked in *Lady Oracle* (211) to the "series of liquid transparencies, one laid on top of the other" of *Cat's Eye* (3), it has been clearly established that Atwood's work consistently offers vivid metaphors for writing the female Bildungsroman. However, her most recent work, *Moral Disorder*, seems to mark a new departure in Atwood's imaginative engagement with writing women's lives. In discussions of her work, Atwood frequently uses spatial metaphors to illustrate the shape of a text's narrative – the circle of *The Edible Woman* and the spiral of *Surfacing* described by Atwood in a letter to Marge Piercy in 1973 are typically explicit examples of this (MS Coll. 200:2:4). Decades later, *Moral Disorder* brings something new to the dramatization of growing up female and Canadian in Atwood's fiction and, in terms of its spatialization of experience, it offers a kaleidoscopic reflection of female coming of age.

With a seemingly casual but, in fact, carefully managed haphazardness, the narrative moves backwards and forwards over the life of the main character, Nell, refusing any straightforward chronology. It alternates between the first person and the third person (the narrator of the different episodes is not always named so there are times when it is not fully certain that the main character in a single episode is, in fact, Nell) and blends different narrative strands. As with so much of Atwood's other work, literary texts have the potential to offer models for living, though the results are sometimes enhancing, sometimes misleading. With its sensitivity to the literary past, to both Atwood's own work and a range of other literary traditions, *Moral Disorder* presents another example of Atwood "talking back" both within and outside her own literary oeuvre. With this in mind, the "Full Circle" of the title of this chapter is not intended to suggest that this text represents a moment of completion in Atwood's work, but rather that it is a text that looks to the past for inspiration while pushing the experimental aspects of Atwood's work to new levels.

This chapter will focus on three aspects of *Moral Disorder* that have a particular resonance with the Atwoodian Bildungsroman. It will look at how it offers a mature perspective on Atwood's oeuvre to date, returning to familiar territory, but juxtaposing Atwoodian motifs in ways that render them new. *Moral Disorder* in many ways represents a confluence of the preoccupations, interests, and commitments that readers have come to associate with Atwood's work, but here they take different shapes and forms. As a writer, Atwood is quite recuperative in the way that she sometimes revisits her younger writing self and modifies and adjusts the assumptions of her early work (for example, in the way her treatment of the Canadian North in her collection *Wilderness Tips* seems to write back to *Surfacing*) and *Moral Disorder* shows signs of a similar connectedness to Atwood's earlier novels. This chapter will also focus on how the novel presents a new departure in Atwood's treatment of time and progress; of particular interest is the complex form and structure of the text. Finally, it will consider the importance of the intertextual references that come to the fore at key transitional moments in the main character's life and have a unifying effect in the text, one that holds the episodes in the collection together, but also draws attention to the complex and rich relationship between life and literariness.

Reading the Past in *Moral Disorder*

Moral Disorder presents a new kind of collage of selfhood in Atwood's treatment of the female Bildungsroman, one that takes a sidelong glance at Atwood's previous work. Indeed, it is very frank in acknowledging material that has been previously published and its reliance upon other sources. This is something that the acknowledgements at the end of the book make clear, where it is also noted that the title, *Moral Disorder*, is taken from an unfinished novel by Atwood's partner, Graeme Gibson. This is, then, a text that is very direct in drawing attention to the previously existing sources upon which it relies, adding a new layer of meaning to Atwood's longstanding interest in literary translation and transformation. While so many of the coming-of-age narratives of her other novels are built on interwoven, competing narrative strands, or a retrospective engagement with the past that inevitably alters or rewrites it, *Moral Disorder* seems to look back on the body of work that came before and reshape it, presenting the reader with a retrospective of a different kind to Atwood's other female Bildungsromane.

Moral Disorder opens with "The Bad News" and a glimpse of the main character in later life. Nell fears the indignities of age and is acutely aware of the trap of the present and the relative uncertainty of the future tense as she becomes painfully aware that she is near the end of her life: "These are the tenses that define us now: past tense, *back then*; future tense, *not yet*. We live in a small window between them, the space we've only recently come to think of as *still*, and really it's no smaller than anyone else's window" (4, italics in original). Representative of the blending, shading, and merging of narratives that takes place in the text is the way in which, midway through the first episode, the story suddenly and unexpectedly breaks into an alternative narrative. It begins with the couple eating toast for breakfast in their kitchen as they muse on the horrors of violence taking place in far away places; without warning the narrator abandons the scene and shifts into a classical fantasy in which she imagines she is in a Roman garrison under attack from barbarians. While this shift from domestic realism to fantasy is not new to Atwood's fiction, what is curious is the abruptness of the change in direction. In novels such as *Lady Oracle*, *The Robber Bride*, and *The Blind*

Assassin, private and public histories are intertwined with literary and fantastical intertexts in ways that prove to be mutually revealing. Here, the text jumps from twentieth-century suburbia to ancient Rome, mapping the former experience onto the latter, so that time becomes a palimpsest; life is shown to be exactly the same in ancient Rome as twentieth-century Canada, the difference being marked only by alternative points of reference and inflections.

The intratextual elements of *Moral Disorder* offer a fragmented account of the Atwoodian canon and more specifically the Atwood novels that are fundamentally concerned with writing lives. Fragments, echoes, and reflections of Atwood's earlier work resurface in the deliberately "disordered" narrative structure of the text. Up until this point, Atwood's best known Bildungsromane relied upon a dual narrative structure, with the mature, knowing self of the current-time narrator looking back and reconnecting with and reconstructing the past. The opening episode of *Moral Disorder* seems suggestive of this, but quickly breaks free from it and moves towards a more experimental structure. At the same time, there are many aspects and features of the text that are immediately familiar and reach back to the very beginning of Atwood's work. The form of the novel poses an immediate challenge, one that is acknowledged on the flyleaf, which reassures the reader that *Moral Disorder* "could be seen as a collection of eleven stories that is almost a novel … or a novel broken up into eleven stories". This undecidability, the situation of the text somewhere between the short story sequence and the novel, reconnects Atwood with two previously discussed influences: James Joyce and Alice Munro. Munro's *Lives of Girls and Women* and *Who Do You Think You Are?*, both of which present a portrait of the artist with distinctly Joycean inflections, might be thought of as literary precursors to *Moral Disorder*. Atwood's text reads like an homage to Munro's short story sequence and it pays considerable attention to many of the same Victorian intertexts that are so important to Munro's work. Atwood has often been thought of as painting in broad brushstrokes, being concerned with the national rather than regional expression of Canadian literary identity, but *Moral Disorder* brings her closer to Munro's finely written appreciation of the minutiae of lives lived in "deep caves paved with kitchen linoleum" (*Lives of Girls and Women* 249).

At the same time, this new experiment with form and structure might be read as Atwood's most elaborate renovation of the Bildungsroman yet, one that self-consciously engages with her own writing past. The references to survival manuals in the episode entitled "The Art of Cooking and Serving", the return to the pioneer experience in the wilderness in "The Boys at the Lab", and the story of "The Labrador Fiasco" take us back to a preoccupation perennially associated with Atwood and the representation of the wilderness in her work. In "The Labrador Fiasco", this relationship with the wilderness is reframed and given a new meaning; the narrator's father battles against infirmity as he recalls a disastrous expedition in Labrador, and his own agonizing struggle towards death is conflated with the failed expedition.

"The Bad News" is followed by a flashback to the narrator's childhood, "The Art of Cooking and Serving", which begins with the narrator knitting baby clothes for her sister. Knitting, sewing, and weaving are by now established metaphors for writing in Atwood's work, as seen in the repeated references to "The Lady of Shalott" in *Lady Oracle* and Grace's quilting in *Alias Grace*. Nell's admission that "my style of knitting required total concentration and caused my arms to ache, and irritated me a lot" (11) says a lot to the effort of Atwood's narrators, writers, and artists. In "Monopoly", Nell actually knits a patchwork quilt that becomes a means of silently expressing her anxiety about her relationship with her partner Tig: "She would knit it in long strips, a red square, a purple one, a blue one, and then she would sew the strips together. It would take some planning to make it come out right, with the squares creating the bold checkerboard effect she had in mind" (122–3). Knitting and quilting are once again presented as important and intensely private modes of expression for women and are seen to reflect the historically private, sometimes secret, endeavour of the woman writer.

In "The Art of Cooking and Serving", young Nell further braces herself against change and insecurity by immersing herself in a conduct manual, *The Art of Cooking and Serving* (19). The apparent security of the rules and regulations in the book is misleading as she discovers the tyranny behind the class divisions laid down in the manual: "Was I to be the kind homemaker, or the formerly untidy maid?" (21). Domestic conduct manuals prove to be significant elsewhere in Atwood's fiction: *The Joy of Cooking* makes an appearance in *The Edible Woman* and *The Robber Bride*, and *Mrs Beeton's Book of Household Management* has an important place in *Alias Grace*, in setting Grace's story against the Victorian values of Grace's nemesis, Susanna Moodie. Pondering an illustration of a maid in the book (one that matches the cover illustration of Atwood's book), the narrator longs to live in the "future tense": "All the same, I envied her. She was already transformed, and had no more decisions to make" (21). Young Nell, like Mrs Moodie, works hard to meet the exacting demands of the manual in spite of the vicissitudes of summer time in the Bush (the same landscape that is central to the childhood episodes of *Cat's Eye*). Her efforts are stymied in ways that find sympathy with Mrs Moodie's frustration at the impossibility of importing middle-class bourgeois values to the New World: "The charm of my centerpiece would not however cancel out the shabbiness of our paper napkins: my mother insisted they be used at least twice, to avoid waste, and she wrote our initials on them in pencil. I could imagine what Mrs. Splint would think of this grubby practice" (22). In this way, *Moral Disorder* offers a filter for many of the motifs and characteristics of Atwood's own work, but also reaches back to the nineteenth century to other influential histories.

Another episode which represents a moment of apotheosis in relation to a recurring Atwoodian motif is "The Other Place". Atwood's novels contain an ongoing tension between the opposing alternatives of engagement and escape, in particular when confronted by limits imposed by patriarchy. There has been considerable critical attention paid to the "Other Side" of *Lady Oracle*, as a reference to what Kim Worthington reads as the temptation of excommunication

(289). But Atwood's other novels also frequently convey a conflict between a retreat from those social forces that are damaging or engagement with those forces in order to agitate for change. "The Other Place" in *Moral Disorder* is empty and removed from social exchange. In this episode, the character's younger, rootless self haunts and challenges the stability of life in the present:

> But my dreaming self refuses to be consoled. It continues to wander, aimless, homeless, alone. It cannot be convinced of its safety by any evidence drawn from my waking life. I know this because I continue to have the same dream, over and over. I'm in the other place, a place that's very familiar to me, although I've never lived in it or even seen it except in this dream. … I'll have to be all by myself, forever. (101)

Thus, its promise of safety from the constant change of life proves less than satisfactory as it comes to represent isolation rather than security.

Aside from this existential dilemma, another feature of characterization that is very closely associated with the representation of female subjectivity and development in Atwood's work is the way in which life and the milestones of growing up are seen to have a literary quality and are best understood as literary devices. In "The Boys at the Lab", Nell describes the young men who accompanied her entomologist father on his research trips into the forest as "characters from a novel, a novel I've never read" (242–3). Her mother's recollection of memories of that period of their lives are susceptible to the same complexities as literary narratives. In spite the fact that her mother seems incapable of lying, she admits: "But there are some stories with no endings, or none I've been told, and when I come across them in the invisible file of stories I haul around with me and produce during my visits, my curiosity gets the better of me and I pester her because I want to know what happened. She holds out, though. She's not telling" (246). Towards the end of the same episode her mother's decline is described in similar terms: "She's no longer voluble, she can't carry a plot, not all by herself, but she knows what's happening, or what happened once, and she can manage a sentence or two" (238). The ability to "carry a plot" is something that all of Atwood's protagonists have in common, some more audaciously than others, but in *Moral Disorder* it is granted a different kind of positive value. In relation to her father's loss of memory and loss of identity, she muses "stories are no good, not even short ones, because by the time you get to the second page he's forgotten the beginning. Where are we without our plots?" (229) thus reasserting the relationship identified by Atwood and Northrop Frye between the questions "Who am I?" and "Where is here?".

Stories, as suggested in Atwood's other Bildungsromane, have the capacity to trap, mislead and disappoint, and yet they take on a talismanic value in "The Labrador Fiasco"; in this text, telling the story of endurance in the Bush is what keeps the narrator's father alive. While previous Atwood characters suffered the trials of being "hooked on plots" (*Lady Oracle* 310), in this case there is a definite suggestion that literary plots are also capable of providing a secure point of reference amidst life's disorder.

The guide to surviving the wilderness and the modern self-help manual are only a short imaginative leap away from each other in Atwood's work. Guidance for living (rather than staying alive) is offered in the form of Mrs Splint's *The Art of Cooking and Serving*, Dr Spock's *Baby and Child Care* and Oona's guide for discerning modern women, *Femagician*, in "Monopoly". These are texts that lodge in the narrator's consciousness only to resurface unexpectedly in later life. However, Nell discovers that more meaningful guidance and direction is to be found in literary texts and literary plots. The interaction of literary narratives and life narratives in *Moral Disorder* allows different ways of organizing reality to be tested and challenged.

The Literariness of Life in *Moral Disorder*

"In the end, we'll all become stories" (213) promises the final episode of *Moral Disorder*. Genre fiction, detective stories, historical fiction, and melodrama are all cited as formative influences at one point or another and the collision and interaction of forms and literary registers is central to Atwood's writing. The self-conscious appreciation of literary influences is given new expression in "My Last Duchess", particularly in the way that Nell's critical analysis of Browning is informed by her penchant for popular fiction: "I'd picked up *bumped off* from the detective stories I was in the habit of reading as a way of evading my homework, or at least delaying it" (60, italics in original). That Browning's dramatic monologue should be central to a moment of transition in the young narrator's life is suggestive as the dramatic monologue is associated with a rebellion against the Romantic cult of "self-expression", an idea that is at the heart of the original Bildungsroman. The dramatic monologue is most concerned with entering into dramatic situations and adopting different personae (something that resonates strongly with the role-playing and performance of identities explored in previous chapters).

The different interpretive possibilities entertained by Nell as to how the Duchess might have died are clearly influenced by her reading outside school hours. Literary criticism becomes a kind of speculative detective work as different possibilities borrowed from literary sources are put forward and attributed to the misogynous Duke:

> Nor had he buried her in the cellar and covered up the grave with wet cement, or cut her up into pieces and heaved the pieces into the lake or dropped them down a well or left them in a park, like the husbands in some of the more grisly narratives I had encountered. (61)

While many characters in Atwood's fiction read their own lives in literature and are susceptible to being influenced by literary plots, *Moral Disorder* presents a more intrusive meta-commentary on critical analysis as the process is put under the microscope.

A key moment in the narrator's development is when she breaks from the line of her teacher's dogmatic critical practice, one that Nell is taught to reproduce verbatim. Her encounter with Browning's carefully constructed misogynous madman leads her to a moment of rather naïve but nonetheless significant feminist awakening, as Tess, Ophelia, and the Duchess of Browning's poem are described in the terms of the narrator's teenage vocabulary:

> It didn't take me very much reading and skimming to discover that Tess had serious problems – much worse than mine. The most important thing in her life had happened to her in the very first part of the book. She got taken advantage of, at night, in the woods, because she'd stupidly accepted a drive home with a jerk, and after that it was all downhill, one awful thing after another, turnips, dead babies, getting dumped by the man she loved, and then her tragic death at the end. (I peeked at the last three chapters.) Tess was evidently another of those unlucky pushovers, like the Last Duchess, and like Ophelia – we'd studied *Hamlet* earlier. These girls were all similar. They were too trusting, they found themselves in the hands of the wrong men, they weren't up to things, they let themselves drift. They smiled too much. They were too eager to please. Then they got bumped off, one way or another. (84)

Retrospectively, she comes to consider Miss Bessie's English lessons as having an educative value akin to the self-help manuals referenced copiously throughout the text.

She also comes to recognize the differences between her methods for reading and those of her male counterparts. In talking her boyfriend Bill through the poem, she realizes that he is drawn to and understands best through binary opposites, while she is more interested in the knotty potential of multiple interpretive possibilities.

The powerful impact and influence of literary styles is something that continues into the narrator's adult life. Teaching a course on the Victorian novel leads her to see her love affair through the prism of nineteenth-century fiction: "they'd be shivering under Tig's duvet, between Tig's threadbare sheets, locked in the sort of desperate embrace that reminded Nell of her Victorian novelists' description of drowning. People drowned quite a lot in such novels, especially if they'd had sex out of wedlock" (112). But Nell is equally susceptible to registers at the other end of the traditional hierarchy of high and low literary culture. Tabloid news reporting is shown to have the same effect as she imagines headlines to describe their relationship: "Runaway Hubby Gassed Near Rural Love Nest with Editorial Cutie" (112). However, Nell is not just a victim to the allure of literary influences but proves capable of contesting and rewriting earlier texts as, like so many contemporary women writers, Atwood challenges the plot of Brontë's *Jane Eyre*. In "The Entities" she revisits Brontë's "Madwoman in the Attic" in Oona, or rather Nell does, as the Victorian novels on her course hold up a mirror to her own private life. "Drudge, Fortune Hunter, Hysteric" (123), these are some of the models of femininity associated with problematic images of women in nineteenth-century fiction, and ones that Nell seeks to avoid in the way that she imagines her relationship with Tig and his ex-wife Oona.

At the same time, she can't avoid reading her own situation as a classic Victorian love triangle and even comes to explicitly identify herself with the Jane Eyre figure: "So that's who I'm supposed to be, thought Nell. I'm the governess" (129). As Tig's relationship with his first wife disintegrates and she falls into a deep depression, she is pushed towards the role of the madwoman: "She wrote some pretty vicious letters to Tig. By that time she was acting as if he'd abandoned her like some Victorian scoundrel" (200). Tig, on the other hand, like Rochester in *Jane Eyre*, is unwilling to act. His procrastination and refusal of responsibility continues even after his first wife's death as on the occasion of her exorcism: "Tig drove Nell over to the house, but stayed outside in the car. He wasn't going to have anything to do with this" (209).

In another imaginative return to *Jane Eyre*, one that adjusts the original plot, rather than allowing Oona's madwoman to languish in the attic, Nell finds her an estate agent and a new house to match her requirements. After Oona's death, Nell fends off attempts to interpret her as a lingering, spectral presence in the house: "Was Oona still in the house? Was she hindering the sale out of vengeance? Nell didn't think so. She couldn't imagine Oona doing anything so banal. But then, both of them had been guilty of equivalent banalities. The first wife, the second wife – they could have been typecast" (209). This refuses the "equivalent banalities" of clichéd plot formations and challenges typecasting in a way that aligns Atwood with writers such as Jean Rhys and Margaret Drabble, who have, in different ways, foregrounded and rehabilitated some of the more problematic aspects of Brontë's original. This process is not without a comic dimension, as Nell finds herself accompanying the clairvoyant she employs to perform the exorcism in a dance to oust the spirit of the first wife.

Towards the end of *Moral Disorder*, Nell notes how in inscriptions on photographs, her mother would, at a young age, always refer to herself, in quotation marks, as "Me": "she always refers to herself as 'me', with quotation marks around the word, as if she's citing some written opinion to the effect that she is who she is" (244). In Atwood's fiction and in *Moral Disorder* in particular, the sources of such "written opinion" range from conduct manuals and self-help guides to literary (including canonical) influences. The disorder of life and its inevitable haphazardness is embraced with a new relish, writing large a longstanding feature of Atwood's version of the female Bildungsroman. Moreover, literary sources and influences are seen to interact more intimately with life in the text. This interest in the crossover of life and literariness marks another Woolfian moment in Atwood's writing. In *Autobiography*, Linda Anderson writes: "It is not possible to separate lives from books, or identities from how they are represented, Woolf suggests, and much of what we think of as 'true' or historically given, is really an ideological construct; in other words, a fiction" (96). *Moral Disorder* is most interested in the relationship between lives and books as the suggestive power of literary vocabularies are important to almost all of the episodes in the collection. Previous novels by Atwood showed a preoccupation with the consequences of literary plots that threaten to outrun the author and are potentially dangerous. *Moral Disorder*, on the other hand, presents such plots as inextricable from life in ways that can be productive, as literary art and the art of living are seen to be intimately involved.

Postscript
New Departures: The Life and Times of the Contemporary Canadian Female Bildungsroman

Atwood's special relationship with the female Bildungsroman may be seen to have had considerable influence on a number of contemporary writers, particularly, as one might expect, on Canadian women writers. This chapter offers a survey of developments in the female Bildungsroman in Canada since the late 1970s – the decade in which, as I have suggested, Atwood herself came of age as a writer. The chapter provides an illuminating contrast and comparison between Atwood's engagement with the Bildungsroman and that of other Canadian women writers. Its main interest is in providing a largely descriptive sketch of the directions taken by women writers who draw on the female Bildungsroman as a model in their work. The range of texts surveyed includes novels by writers influenced by Atwood, and writers whose work makes for an interesting comparison to Atwood. The survey will consider a number of new Canadian literary voices, most significantly the novels of Canadian Native women writers. It will also include writers from multicultural backgrounds, who share the common goal of expressing first- and second-generation immigrant experience in Canada. I am aware that such a cursory treatment of these writers runs the risk of homogenizing their literary articulation of "hyphenated" Canadian identities. However, this is just an introductory investigation of the female Bildungsroman in Canadian literature over the past three decades and is intended to give a sense of the developments since Atwood's early writing career. Thus the chapter further consolidates the main argument of this book: that Atwood's engagement with coming-of-age narratives constitutes an especially powerful aspect of her work, one that carved out an imaginative space within which other women writers could work.

The texts under discussion have been chosen because they are most explicitly concerned with the reclamation, translation, or construction of selfhood and identity in a range of contemporary Canadian contexts. While many of these writers have received considerable attention, my purpose is to consider their individual and collective contribution to the expansion and renegotiation of the Bildungsroman as a literary concept. The conclusions drawn in Chapter 1 regarding the potential usefulness of the Bildungsroman as a generic construct are borne out here, as it is reanimated by women writers writing from diverse but related Canadian perspectives. This chapter will draw attention to relevant points of contact with Atwood's fiction and the issues discussed in the main body of the book, but it also seeks to consider new patterns that have emerged in the development of the Canadian female Bildungsroman. Many of the writers featured engage explicitly or implicitly with ideas central to Atwood's rendering of female and Canadian identity. Moreover, many of the texts discussed suggest the conflation of literary and sociological or historical processes so prevalent in Atwood's early fiction.

Anglo-Canadian Women Writers and the Female Bildungsroman

Atwood's influence on later representations of female development and progress by Canadian women writers can be seen in the way writers appropriate her slant on the Canadian wilderness, in the way they develop or engage with typically Atwoodian preoccupations, and in how they represent the Canadian woman writer or artist. In "From Housewife to Hermit: Fleeing the Feminine Mystique in Joan Barfoot's *Gaining Ground*", Heidi MacPherson notes the established link between the Canadian wilderness and Canadian women writers' novels of female development (92). Atwood's *Surfacing* might be considered a prototype in this regard, as its influence can be read in works published later that decade such as Marian Engel's *Bear* (1976) and Joan Barfoot's *Gaining Ground* (1978). *Gaining Ground* is concerned with the narrator's necessary abandonment of her role as wife and mother and associated myths of femininity in exchange for a self-sufficient life in the wilderness. The narrator draws attention to her absolute powerlessness at the mercy of these myths: "When they were not there, I was empty. I felt as if I did not exist. I had no power, no way to be known. There were months filled with that kind of emptiness, the motionlessness of a mannequin in a fairytale who only comes to life when real people appear. … 'Do I exist when there is no one here to see me existing?'" (69). She ekes out a self-sufficient existence in rural Ontario until years later her daughter comes in search of her. Atwood's influence is clear, though Barfoot places a more laboured emphasis on the strong-willed separatism of the protagonist with none of the ambivalence that characterizes *Surfacing*. In the 1980s, writers such as Barbara Gowdy began to explore further the possibility of survival as a theme in suburban Canada. In *Falling Angels* (1989), three sisters come to maturity under a sinister regime masterminded by their father. Set in Toronto in the 1960s, the novel culminates in the girls' father's decision to force his daughters underground for a two-week trial of his self-constructed nuclear bomb shelter, offering a new take on what Northrop Frye identifies as the Canadian "garrison mentality" (226). Thus, in the decades after the literary revival in which Atwood played such an important part, Canadian writing showed a keenness to engage in the critical and creative paradigms so strongly associated with Atwood in this period. Susan Swan's *The Biggest Modern Woman of the World* (1983) is a semi-biographical chronicle of the remarkable growth of Anna Swan, a nineteenth-century Nova Scotian giantess. The account of the development of the giantess, her entry into P.T. Barnum's freak-show at the American Museum in New York, and subsequent encounters with British Royalty at the court of Queen Victoria is infused with a sometimes farcical take on the typically Atwoodian paradigm of female and Canadian identity. Set in the mid to late nineteenth century, the novel conveys how Anna, the giantess, undergoes a feminist and nationalist awakening in the course of her travels in the United States. On the occasion of their first meeting, her future husband, Kentucky giant Martin Van Buren Bates, remarks in relation to his Northern neighbours:

> "Ah, our friendly neighbours in the land of snow and ice," the giant smiled knowingly. "Not evolved enough to submit to my anthropometrics." He came to the edge of the stage and stood directly before me. "Though I'd say, God willing, there is every chance that the Canadian will join us on the evolutionary tree!" (120)

In spite of this inauspicious beginning to their relationship, Anna marries the American giant and soon afterwards is forced to conclude: "I feel I am acting out America's relationship to the Canadas. Martin is the imperial ogre while I play the role of genteel mate who believes that if everyone is well-mannered, we can inhabit a peaceable kingdom. That is the national dream of the Canadas, isn't it?" (273–4).

Atwood's impact as a writer and a critic, in particular her foregrounding of Canadian themes, can be seen in all of these works. Furthermore, later representations of the artist in Canadian women's writing also make for interesting comparison. Audrey Thomas's *Intertidal Life* (1984) exhibits signs of the same interrogation of language, genre, and popular stereotypes and heterosexual romance myths so prevalent in Atwood's early fiction. Language games – in particular, play with popular songs, rhymes, word meanings, and etymologies – are a major feature of the novel. In the opening pages, Alice and her daughter lie on the beach guiltily reading Harlequin romances – a genre so carefully dismantled in *Lady Oracle*. In an insightful description of the main concern of the novel Jacqueline Buckman suggests that:

> a struggle takes place between humanist and postmodernist conventions pertaining to the representation of the subject. Representational strategies in the novel include a liberal humanist discourse that is concerned with questions of authenticity and truth, and the struggle to reinstate a coherent unified subject with Cartesian powers of agency, resistance, and control. However, formal experimentation in the novel, which includes the textual gaps, fragments, and word play of a postmodernist discourse, problematizes the stability of these humanist categories and redefines identity in terms of conflicting subject positions whose incompatibilities exert pressure on individuals to find new ways of being and seeing. (71)

In this way, the quest narrative of the novel also directly challenges the presumptions of the traditional Bildungsroman: "But one went on a true quest alone and, except for magical and divine intervention, one fought the terror of the dark wood alone. One didn't bring along three kids, a lame dog and a spiteful cat" (141). Indeed, the novel is most explicit in its questioning and subversion of the language and instruments of male imperialist conquest: "we all need new maps, new instruments to try and fix our new positions, unless we think we're competent enough to try and steer by the stars" (171). This echoes the sentiments of the narrator of *Surfacing* and draws on the same vocabulary as that of Adrienne Rich's poem "Diving into the Wreck", in the course of which the diver encounters the "half-destroyed instruments", the "water-eaten log" and the "fouled compass" of the past (55). However, as intimated by Buckman, this seemingly subversive declaration implicitly runs the risk of reinforcing the humanist idea of authenticity and essential selfhood as a conscious goal (81–2). Thomas, like Atwood, then, seems most interested in the creative possibilities of this tension between the competing impulses to conform to or subvert conventional narrative trajectories.

Thomas also presents a familiarly Atwoodian woman writer torn between art and domesticity. According to Linda Hutcheon: "*Intertidal Life* is a novel about women and woman, in the same way that *A Portrait of the Artist as a Young Man* is about men and man. This is a portrait of the artist as mother, of woman as creatrix" ("'Shape shifters': Canadian Women Novelists and the Challenge to Tradition" 220). Hutcheon goes on to make the connection between the Canadian wilderness and creativity in Canadian women's writing (specific reference is made to many of the novels previously mentioned: *Gaining Ground*, *Bear*, *Surfacing*, *The Diviners*, and *Intertidal Life*), and concludes: "Clearly, it is Susanna Moodie's experience in the bush that is the literary forebear of the lives of these women characters as they cope with the wilderness that is both outside and inside them, that is both physical nature and their human and sexual nature as women, and, often, as creatrix-figures, as well" (226).

Atwood's influence can also be seen in Claudia Caspar's more recent Künstlerroman *The Reconstruction* (1996). *The Reconstruction* examines the breakdown of personal identity set against the reconstruction of the history of human evolution. Margaret, a sculptor, works on a model of a female fossil throughout her divorce, subsequent breakdown and recovery. In reconstructing her human ancestor she also begins the reconstruction of an independent, meaningful life. The novel draws on the history of human evolution and juxtaposes it with the protagonist's modern, urban, personal crises in a way that is reminiscent of Atwood's *Life Before Man* (1979). However, unlike Atwood's development novels, Caspar's novel ends on a decisive affirmation of the narrator's newly acquired consciousness.

The other major trend noticeable in Canadian novels of female development can be seen in the importance of Canada's regional literary identities in a number of these works. While this trend can be traced back to the previous generation, in the writing of Margaret Laurence and Alice Munro, it can also be observed in more contemporary writers, such as Sandra Birdsell, Gail Anderson-Dargatz, and Ann-Marie MacDonald. Sandra Birdsell's *The Chrome Suite* (1992) investigates familiar Atwoodian preoccupations, most noticeably survival and victimhood (in fact, late in the novel the main character, Amy Barber, attends a reading group at which *Surfacing* is the novel under discussion). Perhaps more striking is how, in addition to the development narrative, the novel is most concerned with painting a detailed portrait of working-class life in small-town Manitoba in the 1950s and 1960s. Birdsell's *The Chrome Suite* is particularly interested in regional origins and the transmission of a regional landscape. The same can be said of more recent works such as Gail Anderson-Dargatz's *The Cure for Death by Lightning* and Ann-Marie MacDonald's *Fall On Your Knees*, both of which were published in 1996. True to the frequently regional character of Canadian literature, these novels double the development of an individual with the vivid illumination of distinctively British Columbian and Nova Scotian landscapes.

Canadian Native Women Writers and the Female Bildungsroman

In her essay "Aboriginal Literature: Native and Métis Literature", Penny Petrone summarizes the achievement of Canadian Native writers over the last 30 years:

> Canada's Native writers are creating a body of new writing that has an amazing versatility, vitality, and commitment. They are questioning why they should be expected to conform to the constraints of Eurocentric critical theories; they are using the language of "the enemy" to break from a colonized past, bending and stretching mainstream rules of genre, reinventing new ones, and redefining traditional notions of orality and literacy to enrich and extend Canada's literature. (15)

This is echoed by historian Howard Adams in his study *A Tortured People: The Politics of Colonization*, published in 1995, in which he writes: "The present position in the Aboriginal nation is a renaissance of self-conscious artists, authors, poets, actresses, film producers and intellectuals who hold strong national/class themes. It emerged from the nationalist movement of the 1960s and has become a successful reality within the last few years" (131). Petrone's understandable disaffection with Eurocentric literary models does not necessarily preclude the inclusion of Canadian Native women writers in this survey; as has been already established, the term "Female Bildungsroman" is most valuable precisely because of the way that it draws attention to, and deconstructs, its ideological roots. This is something that Petrone acknowledges in *Native Literature in Canada: From the Oral Tradition to the Present*, in asserting that:

> Canada's native writers have borrowed from Western traditions the forms of autobiography, fiction, drama, and the essay. Their uses, however, judged by Western literary criteria of structure, style, and aesthetics, do not always

> conform. They are different because form is only the expression of the fabric of experience, and the experience of native writers has been different. (183–4)

There are, however, a number of concerns that need to be kept in mind to avoid the misappropriation of Native literature. Lee Maracle addresses these very directly in an essay on Native women's writing and feminism in *I am Woman: A Native Perspective on Sociology and Feminism*: "I represent the future of women in North America, just as any other woman does. That white women only want to hear from me as a Native and not as a voice in the women's movement is their loss" (139). The diversity within First Nations culture and experience is highlighted by Kateri Damm who asserts that applying representative critical labels runs the risk of undermining the cultural diversity of the 52 First Nations in Canada ("Says Who: Colonialism, Identity and Defining Indigenous Literature" 12–13). Finally, there remains the reality (explored by Kimberly M. Blaeser in her essay "Native Literature: Seeking a Critical Center") that the literary works in question need to be understood as bi-cultural (56–7).

This bi-cultural tension is most apparent in fictional explorations of Canadian Native experience in modern, urban environments. This is something that Atwood addresses in detail in an article on Native Canadian writing for the *Times Literary Supplement* (16–22 March 1990). She begins by acknowledging the problem of representation:

> Non-native portrayals of first people range from outrage and condescension to Rousseauesque Noble-Savage admiration, to shock and guilt at the disease, alcoholism, high suicide rates, and cultural disintegration that have hit these communities at the point of impact with aggressive European values. But whether these people were being denounced, emulated or championed, the factual or fictional stories in which they appeared had one thing in common: they were not told by the people themselves. (MS Coll. 200:147:29:282)

In summing up the changes afoot in Native Canadian writing, she makes specific reference to Jeannette Armstrong's work chronicling Okanagan myths and the development of a new research centre and associated publisher – Theytus Books – at the En'owkin Centre at the University of Victoria. Her description of the pioneering influence of Armstrong and writers like her has much in common with Atwood's own efforts in the fostering of a writing community in the 1970s.

Autobiography, or autobiographical fiction, is a form preferred by many Native women writers. The structures common to these semi-autobiographical or fictional narratives bear comparison to the female Bildungsroman as defined in previous chapters. Individual development, progress, and awakening are very often inextricably tied to a historical or political narrative in these novels. They are concerned with deconstructing racist stereotypes of First Nations people in Canada. Such works are, then, highly politically charged and often concerned with personal or historical events. Following on from Maria Campbell's influential memoir

Halfbreed (1973), the three writers under discussion here, Beatrice Culleton, Lee Maracle, and Jeannette Armstrong, refract Native Canadian and Métis social, political, and cultural realities through individual development narratives. Their works have a political impetus in so far as they are concerned with articulating the effects of the attempted annihilation and erasure of First Nations culture in Canada and are most interested in communicating a woman-centred response to that legacy of dispossession.

Beatrice Culleton's semi-autobiographical *In Search of April Raintree* (1983) was, according to Kateri Damm, one of the first novels by a First Nations writer to "question, blur, and displace fixed delineations of genre, culture and race and assert their own space" ("Dispelling and Telling: Speaking Native Realities in Maria Campbell's *Halfbreed* and Beatrice Culleton's *In Search of April Raintree*" 95). Culleton's *In Search of April Raintree* offers an example of a twin Bildungsroman, where two development narratives intersect and complement each other. April and Cheryl Raintree relate to their Métis heritage in diametrically opposed ways. Both are subjected to the "native girl syndrome" stereotype outlined in Chapter 4 by the social worker who places them in foster care:

> It starts out with the fighting, the running away, the lies. Next come the accusations that everyone in the world is against you. There are the sullen, uncooperative silences, the feeling sorry for yourselves. And when you go on your own, you get pregnant right away, or you can't find or keep jobs. So you'll start with alcohol and drugs. From there, you get into shoplifting and prostitution, and in and out of jails. You'll live with men who abuse you. And it goes on. (62)

While April rejects her Métis heritage, her younger sister Cheryl is, from a young age, inspired by Métis history, in particular by the nineteenth-century Métis hero, Louis Riel, and becomes determined to challenge imposed stereotypes and to fight what she sees as her sister's internalized racism. Ultimately, however, Cheryl grows disillusioned with the self-fulfilling stereotypes of her people and it is April who awakens to and embraces her Métis identity. Culleton's novel is considered one of the first expositions by a Native writer of the traumas of Native struggle against racism. The "search" of the title is both an individual identity quest and a collective struggle for an existence removed from the institutionalized racism of Canadian society.

Lee Maracle introduces further complexities to the search for identity in Canadian Native women's writing in her novel of adolescence, *Sundogs* (1992). *Sundogs* explores the coming of age of Marianne in the summer of 1990 and is set against key events in First Nations history. Marianne's search for identity is affected by the pressures of her immediate family and her disaffection with life as a young Native woman in Vancouver: "At home, I am not Indian enough and at school I am much too Indian" (10). In an essay entitled "Popular Images of Nativeness", Marilyn Dumont explains how this thinking has a more general application, as the

> prevalent 19th Century notion of culture as static which is founded on the belief that there exists in the evolution of cultures, a pristine culture which if it responds to change is no longer pure, and therefore, eroding and vanishing affects our collective "self-images" as either: pure – *too Indian* or diluted – *not Indian enough*. These colonial images we have of ourselves informs me that internalized colonialism is alive and well in the art we generate and which gets transferred by media into the popular images which are supported by the art buying public (read white patrons). (47–8, italics in original)

Marianne is forced to fight this internalized colonialism on two fronts: in her relationship with her family and her relationships with Native men. Her relationship with her mother is most important in this respect. Having formerly dismissed her mother's political stridency and penchant for arguing back to politicians on television as an eccentricity to be endured or ignored, she realizes regarding her mother that: "She wants to take Canada on. She wants to be a citizen, a citizen who adds her own cultural stamp to the garden of flowers that bloom in the urban centres of the country" (105). *Sundogs* is a prime example of how personal and national narratives intersect in Canadian Native literature. The novel centres, in part, on events at the Quebec town of Oka in the summer of 1990, which drew nationwide attention to the issue of aboriginal rights and are considered a turning point in the Canadian Native campaign for autonomy, one that is ongoing and remains high on the Canadian political agenda. In his survey of Native activism, Tony Hall describes the events as:

> an extraordinary Indian summer of activism initiated in June when Elijah Harper (Cree) successfully blocked the progress of the Meech Lake accord through the Manitoba legislature. Practically overnight, Elijah became a hero for millions of Canadians opposed to Meech Lake, but particularly for Native people, who were suddenly given a champion in a system of Canadian government that until then had proven almost impervious to the direct exercise of aboriginal political will. (58)

Thus, the evolution of Marianne's self-consciousness as a young Native woman is, in part, informed by national and political paradigms.

This close relationship between the personal and the political is further developed in Jeannette Armstrong's *Whispering in Shadows* (2000). Here, Native spiritual practice finds expression through anti-capitalist, environmentalist politics. It traces the political awakening of Penny (an artist and activist) to social and economic crimes against Native peoples across Canada, the USA, Mexico, and Central and South America. This awakening is largely concentrated in the "Year of Indigenous Peoples" and takes Penny to demonstrations and conferences across North America. The novel is a chronicle of personal awakening and is more generally a treatise of political protest against injustices against Indigenous populations. The narrator makes an explicit address to Atwood on a trip to the

United States: "Oh Margaret, your *Handmaiden's Tale* may not be a fantasy. It comes, the long deep shadow just before dawn's first light" (201). Furthermore, like Atwood's artists, Penny encounters troubling assumptions about her art: "most Native American artists incorporate or reconstruct symbolism from their heritage in their works" (126) and the repeated warning from gallery owners and curators that "Art sells, not politics" (203).

Exile in the Canadian Female Bildungsroman

In Chapter 7 of *Survival*, "Failed Sacrifices: The Reluctant Immigrant", Atwood summarizes some of the key differences between the Canadian and American immigrant experience in literature. Compared to the American immigrant's need and even desire to efface all impressions of his origins and give him or herself up to the assimilation of American ideologies, the Canadian immigrant faces a very different dilemma:

> Canada does not demand a leap into the melting pot, though the immigrant may decide to attempt one anyway. Secondly, if he does wipe away his ethnic origin, there is no new "Canadian" identity ready for him to step into: he is confronted only by a nebulosity, a blank; no ready-made ideology is provided for him. And thirdly, though he has sacrificed his past and tried for success, he is much more likely to find only failure. (150)

She identifies the gloomy conclusion drawn by Brian Moore's Ginger Coffey in *The Luck of Ginger Coffey* (1960) as typical of the experience of the Canadian immigrant, as Coffey concludes: "He could not believe in this America, this land that half the world dreams of in dark front seats in cities and villages half a world away. What had it in common with his true America? For Canada was America; the difference a geographer's line. What had these Hollywood revels to do with the facts of life in a cold New World?" (170–1). Moore, as a writer of Irish origin, finds his own literary consolation and solution to this problem in James Joyce. The character of Ginger Coffey has much in common with and pays homage to Joyce's Leopold Bloom in *Ulysses*. Atwood, in contrast, remains focused, from the beginning of her writing career, on reviving a sense of the value and importance of the Canadian literary tradition on its own terms.

More recent fiction by Canadian writers who are either expatriates or exiles is less interested in exposing the lack of a distinctive Canadian identity than in exploring a fractured identity based on a divided sense of home. In some cases, home is an imagined landscape constructed from inherited stories and mythologies; in others home is a real place that has been recorded and transformed in memory. Jane Urquhart's novel *Away* (1993) is an example of how Irish identity is translated in memory through the inheritance and regeneration of the poetry, legends, myths, and songs of the old country. Set in Ireland and Canada, the main narrative shifts from the famine-stricken Irish coast of the 1840s to colonial Canada. The political is once again projected onto the personal as the development of the main character, Eileen, is inextricably fixed to the historical trauma of Ireland in the mid-nineteenth century. Her unearthly, ghostly presence pervades both the main retrospective narrative and the current-time narrative of the novel, as she emerges as a tragic symbol of Irish dispossession and loss in this most brutal period of Irish history. While the coupling of individual and collective history recurs frequently in the Bildungsroman, in this context it is problematic in that it seems to rely on what contemporary Irish poet Eavan Boland identifies as a poetic and literary tradition of women as "passive, decorative, raised to emblematic status" (134), "where the nation became a woman and the woman took on a national posture" (135). Urquhart inadvertently perpetuates this tradition of woman as emblem or myth, as the main function of Eileen as a character is to serve as a vehicle for the mourning of a lost language, culture, and identity.

Multicultural Canadian literary perspectives present a more charged challenge to the historical assumptions made regarding Canadian identity in Anglo-Canadian literature and literary criticism. Dionne Brand is one writer concerned with interrogating myths of Canadian multiculturalism and tolerance. In particular, she deconstructs the idea of Canadian identity as "something to be filled in ready-made with a flag and an anthem and no discernible or accountable past (despite colonization by the British and the French)" (*Bread out of Stone* 80). Born in Trinidad, Brand moved to Toronto when she was 17 and her semi-autobiographical novel *In Another Place, Not Here* (1996) is another twin Bildungsroman that explores two very different experiences of the pressures of assimilation in Canada. The individual development of lovers Elizette and Verlia is based respectively on a struggle to negotiate a new sense of self in the face of alienation and the striving towards a selfhood removed from the debilitating influence of nostalgia for the originary home place and reconstructed through political ideology. The emphasis in Elizette's narrative is on arrested growth – she arrives in Toronto, haunted by the recent death of her lover and by the memory of her Caribbean island home and lapses into a grief-stricken haze in the city where Verlia had lived for 13 years:

> No reason for this numbness overtaking her bit by bit or how much of her body she was giving over to the pull of Toronto days. That waking in the dark, and going home in the dark where morning and night were the same and no part of the day governed anymore by nature, no sleep that was finished, no waking complete. Truth is she hardly knew where she was. (87)

Verlia, having arrived in the city 13 years previously at the age of 17, faces a different prospect. She is sent to live with her Uncle and Aunt in the Ontario town of Sudbury and becomes increasingly frustrated by their desperation to assimilate and insistence that she do the same: "Look, it is easy – you can imagine yourself out of your skin and no one will notice" (142). The first step in Verlia's self-realization is the rejection of her Aunt and Uncle's vision of her future in Canada: "She cannot see how they think that this is love, how they think that she should live with them quietly dying in acceptance, asking permission and begging pardon, cutting herself off from any growing, solidifying when she wants to liquefy, to make fluid, grow into her Black self" (148–9). At this point in the novel, Verlia's narrative of personal development becomes political as she leaves Sudbury for Toronto and joins the Community for Revolutionary Struggle. While ultimately she returns to the Caribbean to rally the cane workers on her island home, she refuses to allow her life in Toronto and political commitment to civil rights to be undermined by any compromizing nostalgia for home: "The cell has been her life here. Holding her together like family, it's the only family she can bear. Comradeship chosen, friendship that was not chance or biology" (192).

This doubling of narratives of development that intersect or complement each other is also seen in Ukrainian-Canadian writer, Janice Kulyk Keefer's *The Green Library* (1996). The novel weaves Eva Chown's search for the truth of her family's history in the Ukraine with that of her childhood nemesis Oksanna Moroz, who, in her determination to distance herself from her Ukrainian heritage, translates her name and adopts a new identity as Susanna Frost. This inverse, dual pattern of development towards and away from cultural origins is a device also used by other writers such as Beatrice Culleton and Joy Kogawa.

Sky Lee's *Disappearing Moon Café* (1990) begins another new chapter in the Canadian female Bildungsroman as the main character Kae Yin Woo recounts her family history and confronts the narrative gaps and elisions of the past. In exploring the experience of first-generation Chinese immigrants in British Columbia, it dramatizes the sometimes fraught interaction of the two cultures and how this comes to affect Kae's life as she attempts to decode the past: "Maybe this is a chinese-in-Canada trait, a part of the great wall of silence and invisibility we have built around us. I have a misgiving that the telling of our history is forbidden. I have violated a secret code" (242). One of the most interesting aspects of Lee's investigation of inter-generational relations is the way in which the novel focuses on the relationships between women in the family. It is not unusual in the Bildungsroman that the female protagonist encounters snares and pitfalls both within and outside her own family unit and ethnic group. For Bonnie Hoover Braendlin, however, one of the most frequent internal obstacles to progress in the multicultural female Bildungsroman is visible in the form of sexist attitudes imposed by male peers: "Often marginal women must contend with prejudice and sexism not only from the dominant culture, but also from others of their group – particularly the males …" (76). *Disappearing Moon Café* provides an alternative perspective on this as the most absolutist and anti-individual doctrines are laid down and enforced by the rule-bound matriarch of the family.

Japanese-Canadian writer Joy Kogawa's *Obasan* is less about reconciling an originary and Canadian sense of home and more about the trauma of disenfranchisement and exile in Canada. Published in 1981, *Obasan* is a hugely influential chronicle of Japanese-Canadian internment during the Second World War. The narrative of dislocated identity in the novel is largely concerned with the struggle to define a Japanese-Canadian identity in the face of a hostile and overtly racist wartime government policy. It is an historical document of the confiscation and forced relocation of Japanese-Canadian citizens from Canada's west coast to the interior and, like the fiction and critical writings of Dionne Brand, comments on and engages with a number of discourses of Canadian identity associated with the work of many Anglo-Canadian writers and critics.

In *Obasan*, individual and community identities merge and are at every point determined by real historical events. Nancy J. Peterson's reading of *Obasan* stresses how

> Kogawa's novel occupies an interesting space between history and fiction. Her family was interned at Slocan in British Columbia, Canada, so personal history (autobiography) informs her novel, but Kogawa also drew on materials from the Public Archives of Canada, in particular using the letters of Muriel Kitagawa to her brother Wes as a source for the section of the novel that renders Aunt Emily's journal. (141)

This confluence of history, autobiography, and fiction is enhanced by the interpolation of official government letters regarding the confiscation of property and newspaper articles exemplifying the overtly racist rhetoric of media representation of the internment of Japanese-Canadians. Real political figures feature in the chronology of events leading up to the programme of forced internment and relocation such as the Prime Minister of the time, McKenzie King, and other government ministers. As described by Karin Quimby, this interpolated material is also important to Naomi's deconstruction of recorded history and reconstruction of her own family and personal history: "As an adult woman, Naomi rereads newspaper clippings Aunt Emily had collected during the war. Naomi counters the 'official' facts with her memory of living and working in the Alberta beet fields in a way that reasserts her experience on the land and constructs a specific history from this position" ("'This is my own, my native land'" 269). It is pertinent that the novel should have a double conclusion. The revelation of Naomi's mother's death in Nagasaki is followed by an extract from a memorandum sent by the "Co-operative Committee on Japanese Canadians" to the House and the Senate of Canada in April 1946, which denounced the treatment of Japanese Canadian citizens as "an adoption of the methods of Naziism" (300). This was to be the first step on the road to redress for the violation of human and civil rights perpetrated against the Japanese-Canadian community.

The extent of the novel's influence can be seen in the way that it is, in Guy Beauregard's terms, recognized as playing "a key role in mobilizing support for 1988 Redress Settlement, in which the federal government and the National Association of Japanese Canadians negotiated and signed an agreement providing a formal apology and compensation for Japanese Canadians for losses sustained in the 1940s" (5). Indeed, extracts from the novel were read aloud on the occasion of the announcement of the Redress Settlement (Peterson 168). Kogawa's sequel to *Obasan*, *Itsuka* (1992), records the struggle for and eventual achievement of Japanese-Canadian redress and Naomi's simultaneous awakening to the trauma of her individual and community's recent past. This recovery narrative draws on the same devices as *Obasan* in the way that it is situated somewhere between fiction, autobiography, and historical documentary.

Chapter 2 of this book considered the anglocentric construction of Canada as a victim in the 1970s, which traditionally located the victimizer very definitely outside Canada's national borders. According to Guy Beauregard, a number of critical responses have struggled to reconcile *Obasan* with this construction of Canadian identity, which has led to problematic readings of the Canadian wartime internment of citizens as:

> an irrational aberration in Canadian history, one that can be explained as an "error," or a "misunderstanding," or a result of wartime pressures on the Canadian state. What is unaddressed in these critical accounts – and what needs to be underlined in any serious discussion of racism in the 1940s – is the complex history of anti-Japanese racism in Canada, a history that extends far beyond the narrow and tumultuous window of 1942–49. (10)

Kogawa writes against the received version of Canadian victimhood. As noted by Quimby, Kogawa draws on the wilderness, an established motif in Canadian literature, in her articulation of the suffering of Japanese-Canadians:

> The landscape functions, in *Obasan*, to signify the problems of national and personal identity when the Japanese Canadians are forced into internal exile during World War II. Naomi, the young female protagonist and narrator, struggles, as an adult looking back on this experience, to arrive at a place of understanding what is perhaps an irreconcilable paradox – how she and her people could have been exiled upon their own native land. (258)

Kogawa reclaims the pioneer and wilderness mythologies of Canadian literature for the Japanese-Canadian community. She uses these motifs to emphasize the hostility of the prairies and beet fields where Naomi and her family are forced to work in unbearable conditions: "We are those pioneers who cleared the bush and the forest with our hands, the gardeners tending and attending the soil with our tenderness, the fishermen who are flung from the sea to flounder in the dust of the prairies" (*Obasan* 132). In *Obasan*, the wilderness becomes the inhospitable Alberta prairie, to which Naomi and her family are exiled: "The hardship is so pervasive, so inescapable, so thorough it's a noose around my chest and I cannot move anymore. All the oil in my joints has drained out and I have been invaded by dust and grit from the fields and mud is in my bone marrow" (232). While other writers such as Italian-Canadian Maria Ardizzi seem to restate the preoccupations and prescriptions of Canadian literature as outlined in pre-existing traditions – Ardizzi's *Made In Italy* (1982) is, for example, often read as being heavily influenced by Margaret Laurence's *The Stone Angel* (1966) – writers such as Kogawa are more concerned with deconstructing established narratives and revealing the misleading assumptions that lie behind the fictions of Canadian identity.

Thus, in terms of development, obstacles to development, and the struggle for survival, Kogawa, like the Canadian Native writers previously mentioned, explores the other side of Canadian victimhood and marks a departure in Canadian literature and literary criticism, as Canadian critical assumptions are interrogated and found to be problematic. Arnold Davidson's summary of the influence and achievement of *Obasan* could be taken as a statement of the importance of many of the writers discussed in this chapter:

> The novel is socially significant because it tells us something about ourselves that we long preferred not to hear. The novel is artistically significant because it tells us unpalatable truths with consummate art. The novel is culturally significant because, thanks to the very art with which it addresses large social questions, it claims a special place for the ethnic writer in the ostensibly bicultural context of Canada and thereby encourages us to rethink our paradigms for Canadian culture and literature. (*Writing Against the Silence: Joy Kogawa's 'Obasan'* 13)

The Canadian female Bildungsroman, then, renders personal and artistic growth and development according to the inflections of contemporary Canadian literature, as Canadian women writers revive and sustain the genre in new and diverse contexts. Moreover, it has brought to the surface challenging and difficult questions that have proved capable of altering the mainstream discourses of Canadian national identity.

Conclusion

This book has described a cultural renaissance in which Margaret Atwood played a major role; a major literary genre – the Bildungsroman – was both a key influence on this renaissance, and also found itself profoundly reshaped in the process. In a radio interview in 2002 (*Start the Week*), Atwood recalled her formative years as a writer in Canada and the privilege of being given "carte blanche" in the forging of a new literary tradition. In a short fragment called "The Page", written earlier in her career, Atwood confronted the other aspect of this challenge: the fear of journeying onto the blank page. Here, as for the aspiring Canadian writer in the 1960s, writing becomes a lonely, often hazardous, expedition or quest (*Murder in the Dark* 76). The tension between these two versions of Atwood's motivations as a writer are felt throughout her early work, including her critical writings, which are most concerned with reclaiming Canada's lost literary heritage and with securing a future for Canadian literature.

The significance of what critics such as Isabel Carrera Suarez identify as Atwood's vision of the "Survivor Self" (246) is most apparent, this book has shown, in Atwood's rendering of the progress of the subject in her early novels. In Atwood's early oeuvre, the representation of selfhood shifts from a state of embattlement in *The Edible Woman* to the discovery of devious and subversive means of escaping such entrapment in *Lady Oracle*. Whether exploring the difficulties and contradictions of female or Canadian national identity, or challenging the tyranny of language and ideology, Atwood's fiction is ultimately most interested in critiquing and overcoming these obstacles. From a position of apparently relentless negativity in her theory of survival and its impact on the Canadian literary imagination, Atwood's own writing, in particular her later novels, tests the limits of her early theory of Canadian literature; she designs, within her own fiction, the means of escape from what might have been a blind alley. Thus, Atwood's rendering of survival is, in this context, as concerned – in fact more concerned – with endurance than with victimhood.

This relates powerfully to Atwood's interest in the Bildungsroman: her fiction serves to question, rather than to invest in, conventional models of growth and development. Thus, the Canadian model of survival becomes the preferred template for development and progress, given that it refuses to invest in misleading constructions of the personal odyssey in literature, where coming of age holds the promise of victory or triumph. Instead, it interrogates the promise of cohesive selfhood associated with the original Bildungsroman and suggests that this kind of questioning method is the more useful and creative position from which to consider ideas of human subjectivity and development. This has much to say about what critics have identified as Canadian literature's inherent resistance to absolutist narratives.

There is a clear critical consensus that Atwood's fiction endorses the transformative potential of transgressive strategies in writing. Her method for narrating human development and progress is both to rehabilitate and to interrogate pre-existing traditions; this also leaves space to explore the nationalist and feminist concerns that are so central to her literary imagination. In *Their Own Worst Enemies: Women Writers of Women's Fiction*, Daphne Watson dismisses popular fiction by and about women as offering women only limiting stereotypes and draws attention to the alternatives offered by writers like Atwood. Watson ends her discussion of *Cat's Eye* (1988) with the conclusion: "Women, no less than men, need their *bildungsroman*, which is, as I hope to have indicated, out there, waiting to tell women the truth, not the sad and worn-out fiction; for they need to know that they, like Elaine, can survive the learning experience that is life, and they therefore need fiction that is rooted in the real world" (130–1). Published in 1995, *Their Own Worst Enemies* seems to sustain a certain nostalgia for the idea of life as a "learning experience" and is suggestive of the same faith in teleology and perfectibility celebrated in the early Bildungsroman. Watson cites Atwood as an example of a writer who, early in her career, provided a valuable alternative to existing stereotypes in women's fiction: she reads Atwood as ideally qualified to provide these "learning experiences" in her Bildungsromane. But what Watson – like so many earlier feminist critics – risks overlooking here is that Atwood does not just fill a gap in female literary culture, or simply provide the kind of positive, feminist reading experience that she describes, but in fact interrogates and, where necessary, dismantles literary convention and tradition at every level. She opens the genre up to the possibility that "multiple versions of our multiple selves populate our lives; we play Mr. Hyde constantly, to our various Dr. Jekylls; we supersede ourselves. We are our own broken puzzles, incomplete, scattered through time" ("Biographobia" 8). It might be said that the influence of her work, and that of contemporaries such as Alice Munro and Margaret Laurence, can be appreciated as having forged a distinctive Canadian female Bildungsroman – indeed a respected Canadian literature – in the last 30 years. So Atwood belongs to a generation of women writers who pioneered the genre and drew new attention to the possibilities of growing up Canadian. Atwood's value as a writer is, however, more profound, and perhaps difficult, than this suggests. Her playful, inconclusive, and ultimately highly subversive engagement with the female Bildungsroman results in an oeuvre, which forms part of a crucial strand in Canadian literary history and in the history of women's writing.

Works Cited

The Bildungsroman

Amrine, Frederick. "Rethinking the Bildungsroman." *Michigan Germanic Studies*, Ed. Amrine. Special Issue on the Bildungsroman 13.2 (1987): 119–39

Beebe, Maurice. *Ivory Towers and Sacred Founts: The Artist as Hero in Fiction from Goethe to Joyce*. New York: New York UP, 1964

Buckley, Jerome H. *Season of Youth: The Bildungsroman from Dickens to Golding*. Cambridge, MA: Harvard UP, 1974

Dickens, Charles. *David Copperfield*. 1849–50. Harmondsworth: Penguin, 1966

—. *Great Expectations*. 1861. Harmondsworth: Penguin, 2003

Enzensberger, Hans Magnus. "Wilhelm Meister auf Blech getrommelt." 1959. *Von Buch zu Buch – Günter Grass in der Kritik: Eine Dokumentation*. Ed. Gert Loschütz. Neuwied: Luchterhand, 1968. 8–12

Goethe, Johann Wolfgang. *Wilhelm Meister's Apprenticeship*. 1795–96. Trans. Eric A. Blackall. Princeton NJ: Princeton UP, 1995

Grass, Günter. *The Tin Drum*. 1959. Trans. Ralph Manheim. London: Vintage, 1998

Hardin, James N. *Reflection and Action: Essays on the Bildungsroman*. Columbia: U of South Carolina P, 1991

Hoffmann, E.T.A. *The Life and Opinions of the Tomcat Murr*. 1820–22. Trans. Anthea Bell. Harmondsworth: Penguin, 1999

Howe, Susanne. *Wilhelm Meister and his English Kinsmen: Apprentices to Life*. New York: Columbia UP, 1930

Japtok, Martin. *Growing Up Ethnic: Nationalism and the Bildungsroman in African American and Jewish American Fiction*. Iowa: U of Iowa P, 2005

Jost, François. "Variations of a Species: The Bildungsroman." *Symposium* 37 (1983): 125–44

Joyce, James. *A Portrait of the Artist as a Young Man*. 1916. Ed. Seamus Deane. Harmondsworth: Penguin, 1992

Kontje, Todd. *The German Bildungsroman: History of a National Genre*. Columbia: Camden House, 1993

Köhn, Lothar. *Entwicklungs- und Bildungsroman. Ein Forschungsbericht*. Stuttgart: Metzlersche Verlag, 1969

Mayer, Gerhart. *Der Deutsche Bildungsroman: Von der Aufklärung bis zur Gegenwart*. Stuttgart: Metzler, 1992

—. "Zum Deutschen Antibildungsroman." *Jahrbuch der Raabe Gesellschaft* (1974): 41–6

McKeon, Michael. *Theory of the Novel: A Historical Approach*. Baltimore: Johns Hopkins UP, 2000

Miles, David H. "The Picaro's Journey to the Confessional: The Changing Image of the Hero in the German Bildungsroman." *PMLA* 89.1 (1974): 980–92

Ratz, Norbert. *Der Identitätsroman: Eine Strukturanalyse*. Tübingen: Niemeyer, 1988

Sammons, Jeffrey L. "The German Bildungsroman for Nonspecialists: An Attempt at Clarification." Hardin 26–45

Steinecke, Hartmut. "The Novel and the Individual: The Significance of Goethe's *Wilhelm Meister* in the Debate about the Bildungsroman." Hardin 69–97

Swales, Martin. *The German Bildungsroman from Wieland to Hesse*. Princeton NJ: Princeton UP, 1978

Watt, Ian. *The Rise of the Novel: Studies in Defoe, Richardson and Fielding*. 1957. Harmondsworth: Pelican, 1972

The Female Bildungsroman/Writing the Self/Gender and Genre

Abel, Elizabeth, Marianne Hirsch and Elizabeth Langland, (eds) Introduction. *The Voyage In: Fictions of Female Development*. Hanover: UP of New England for Dartmouth Coll., 1983

Anderson, Linda. *Autobiography*. London: Routledge, 2001

—. "The Re-Imagining of History in Contemporary Women's Fiction." *Plotting Change: Contemporary Women's Fiction*. Ed. Anderson. London: Edward Arnold, 1990. 129–41

Barthes, Roland. "The Death of the Author." 1968. *Image Music Text*. Trans. Stephen Heath. London: Fontana, 1977. 142–8

Batz Cooperman, Jeannette. *The Broom Closet: Secret Meanings of Domesticity in Postfeminist Novels by Louise Erdrich, Mary Gordon, Toni Morrison, Marge Piercy, Jane Smiley, and Amy Tan*. New York: Peter Lang, 1999

Beckett, Samuel. *Trilogy: Molloy, Malone Dies, The Unnameable*. London: Calder, 1973

Beeton, Isabella. *Mrs Beeton's Book of Household Management*. 1861. Ed. Nicola Humble. Oxford, Oxford UP, 2000

Braendlin, Bonnie Hoover. "*Bildung* in Ethnic Women Writers." *Denver Quarterly* 17 (1983): 75–87

Brontë, Charlotte. *Jane Eyre*. 1847. Harmondsworth: Penguin, 1985

Butcher, Margaret K. "From *Maurice Guest* to *Martha Quest*: The Female Bildungsroman in Commonwealth Literature." *World Literature Written in English* 21 (1980): 254–62

Cardinal, Agnès. "Women's Writing under National Socialism." Catling 146–56

Catling, Jo, (ed.) *A History of Women's Writing in Germany, Austria and Switzerland*. Cambridge: Cambridge UP, 2000

Chopin, Kate. "The Awakening." 1899. *The Awakening and Selected Stories*. Ed. Sandra M. Gilbert. Harmondsworth: Penguin, 1984. 43–176

Christ, Carol P. *Diving Deep and Surfacing: Women Writers on Spiritual Quest*. 1980. Boston: Beacon, 1995

Cixous, Hélène. 1988. "The Two Countries of Writing: Theater and Poetical Fiction." *The Other Perspective in Gender and Culture: Rewriting Women and the Symbolic*. Ed. Juliet Flower MacCannell. New York: Columbia UP, 1990. 191–208

Coren, Stanley. *The Left-Hander Syndrome: The Causes and Consequences of Left-Handedness*. London: John Murray, 1992

Cranny-Francis, Anne. *Feminist Fiction: Feminist Uses of Generic Fiction*. Cambridge: Polity, 1990

Eagleton, Mary, (ed.) *Feminist Literary Theory: A Reader*. 2nd edn Oxford: Blackwell, 1996

Eliot, George. *Adam Bede*. 1859. Ed. Stephen Gill. Harmondsworth: Penguin, 1980

Elliott, Anthony. *Concepts of the Self*. Cambridge: Polity, 2001

Ellmann, Maud. *The Hunger Artists: Starving, Writing and Imprisonment*. Cambridge, MA: Harvard UP, 1993

Felski, Rita. *Beyond Feminist Aesthetics: Feminist Literature and Social Change*. Cambridge, MA: Harvard UP, 1989

—. "The Novel of Self-Discovery: A Necessary Fiction?" *Southern Review* 19 (1986): 131–48

Feng, Pin-chia. *The Female Bildungsroman by Toni Morrison and Maxine Hong Kingston: A Postmodern Reading*. New York: Peter Lang, 1998

French, Marilyn. *The Women's Room*. London: Sphere, 1978

Fuderer, Laura Sue. *The Female Bildungsroman in English: An Annotated Bibliography of Criticism*. New York: MLA, 1990

Gaskell, Elizabeth. *The Life of Charlotte Brontë*. 1857. Ed. Elisabeth Jay. Harmondsworth: Penguin, 1997

Gilbert, Sandra M., and Susan Gubar, *The Madwoman in the Attic: The Woman Writer and the Nineteenth-Century Literary Imagination*. New Haven: Yale UP, 1979

Gilmore, Leigh. *Autobiographics: A Feminist Theory of Women's Self-Representation*. Ithaca: Cornell UP, 1994

Heilbrun, Carolyn. 1988. *Writing a Woman's Life*. London: Women's Press, 1989

Hirsch, Marianne. "Spiritual *Bildung*: The Beautiful Soul as Paradigm." Abel, Hirsch and Langland 23–48

Huf, Linda. *A Portrait of the Artist as a Young Woman: The Writer as Heroine in American Literature*. New York: Ungar, 1983

Jong, Erica. *Fear of Flying*. London: Granada, 1974

—. *How to Save Your Own Life*. London: Granada, 1978

Kafka, Franz. "Ein Hungerkünstler." *Das Franz Kafka Buch*. Frankfurt: Fischer, 1983

Kolodny, Annette. "Dancing Through the Minefield: Some Observations on the Theory, Practice and Politics of Feminist Literary Criticism." *Feminist Studies* 6.1 (Spring 1980): 1–25

Kontje, Todd. *Women, the Novel and the German Nation 1771–1871: Domestic Fiction in the Fatherland.* Cambridge: Cambridge UP, 1998

Kuhn, Anna K. "Women's Writing in Germany since 1989: New Concepts of National Identity." Catling 233–53

Labovitz, Esther Kleinbord. *The Myth of the Heroine: The Female Bildungsroman in the Twentieth Century.* New York: Lang, 1986

LeSeur, Geta. *Ten is the Age of Darkness: The Black Bildungsroman.* Columbia: U of Missouri P, 1995

Moers, Ellen. 1976. *Literary Women.* London: Women's Press, 1978

Moi, Toril. *Sexual/Textual Politics: Feminist Literary Theory.* London: Methuen, 1985

Morgan, Ellen. "Humanbecoming: Form and Focus in the Neo-Feminist Novel." *Images of Women in Fiction: Feminist Perspectives.* Ed. Susan Koppelman Cornillon. Bowling Green, OH: Bowling Green U Popular P, 1972. 183–205

Morrison, Toni. *Sula.* 1973. London: Vintage, 1998

Müller, Herta. *Reisende auf einem Bein.* 1989. Hamburg: Rowohlt, 1995

Munro, Alice. *Lives of Girls and Women.* 1971. Harmondsworth: Penguin, 1982

Özdamar, Emine Sevgi. *Die Brücke vom Goldenen Horn.* Köln: Kiepenheuer & Witsch, 1998

Ostriker, Alicia. "The Thieves of Language: Women Poets and Revisionist Mythmaking." Showalter, *The New Feminist Criticism* 314–38

Piercy, Marge. *Small Changes.* 1972. Harmondsworth: Penguin, 1987

Pratt, Annis, and Barbara White. "The Novel of Development". *Archetypal Patterns in Women's Fiction.* Brighton: Harvester, 1982. 13–37

Rich, Adrienne. *Adrienne Rich's Poetry and Prose.* Ed. Barbara Charlesworth Gelpi and Albert Gelpi. New York: Norton, 1993

—. "When We Dead Awaken: Writing as Re-Vision." 1971. *On Lies Secrets and Silence: Selected Prose 1966–1978.* London: Virago, 1980. 33–49

Rosowski, Susan J. "The Novel of Awakening." *Genre* 12 (1979): 313–32. Rpt. In Abel, Hirsch and Langland 49–68

Ruthven, K.K. *Feminist Literary Studies: An Introduction.* Cambridge: Cambridge UP, 1984

Sceats, Sarah. "Eating the Evidence: Women, Power and Food." *Image and Power: Women in Fiction in the Twentieth Century.* Ed. Gail Cunningham and Sarah Sceats. Harlow: Longman, 1996. 117–27

—. *Food, Consumption and the Body in Contemporary Women's Fiction.* Cambridge: Cambridge UP, 2000

Schweickart, Patrocinio P. "Reading Ourselves: Towards a Feminist Theory of Reading." 1984. *Courage and Tools: The Florence Howe Award for Feminist Scholarship 1974-1989.* Ed. Joanne Glasgow and Angela Ingram. New York: MLA, 1990. 155–75

Sharpe, Lesley. "The Enlightenment." Catling 47–67

Showalter, Elaine. *The Female Malady: Women, Madness, and English Culture, 1830–1980*. London: Virago, 1987

—, (ed.) *The New Feminist Criticism: Essays on Women, Literature and Theory*. 1985. London: Virago, 1986

Smith, John H. "Sexual Difference: Bildung and the Bildungsroman." *Michigan Germanic Studies* 13 (1987): 206–25

Smith, Sidonie. *Subjectivity, Identity, and the Body: Women's Autobiographical Practices in the Twentieth Century*. Bloomington: Indiana UP, 1993

Spencer, Sharon. "'Femininity' and the Woman Writer: Doris Lessing's *The Golden Notebook* and the *Diary of Anais Nin*." *Women's Studies* 1 (1973): 247–57

Toderov, Tzvetan. "The Origin of Genre." 1976. *Modern Genre Theory*. Ed. David Duff. Harlow: Pearson, 2000. 193–209

Watson, Daphne. *Their Own Worst Enemies: Women Writers of Women's Fiction*. London: Pluto, 1995

Waugh, Patricia. *Feminine Fictions: Revisiting the Postmodern*. London: Routledge, 1989

Winterson, Jeanette. *Oranges are not the Only Fruit*. 1985. London: Vintage, 2001

Wolf, Christa. *The Quest for Christa T*. 1968. Trans. Christopher Middleton. London: Virago, 1982

Woolf, Virginia. *A Room of One's Own*. 1929. Harmondsworth: Penguin, 2004

Worthington, Kim L. *Self as Narrative: Subjectivity and Community in Contemporary Fiction*. Oxford: Clarendon, 1996

Yaeger, Patricia. *Honey-Mad Women: Emancipatory Strategies in Women's Writing*. New York: Columbia UP, 1988

Zimmerman, Bonnie. "What Has Never Been: An Overview of Lesbian Feminist Criticism." Showalter, *The New Feminist Criticism* 200–24

Cultural and Critical Contexts/National Identity

Anderson, Benedict. *Imagined Communities: Reflections on the Origin and Spread of Nationalism*. 1983. London: Verso, 1991

Benson, Eugene, and William Toye, (gen. eds) *The Oxford Companion to Canadian Literature*. 2nd edn Oxford: Oxford UP, 1997

Bhabha, Homi K. *Nation and Narration*. London: Routledge, 1990

Bordo, Jonathan. "Jack Pine – Wilderness Sublime or the Erasure of the Aboriginal Presence from the Landscape." *Journal of Canadian Studies* 27:4 (Winter 1992–93): 98–128

Brown, E.K. "Is a Canadian Critic Possible?" *Responses and Evaluations: Essays on Canada*. Ed. David Staines. Toronto: McClelland & Stewart, 1977. 313–14

Brown, Russell Morton. "The Practice and Theory of Canadian Thematic Criticism: A Reconsideration." *University of Toronto Quarterly* 70:2 (Spring 2001): 1–21

Davidson, Arnold E., (ed.) *Studies on Canadian Literature: Introductory and Critical Essays*. New York: MLA, 1990

Frye, Northrop. *The Bush Garden: Essays on the Canadian Imagination*. Toronto: Anansi, 1971

Grace, Sherrill E. *Canada and the Idea of North*. Montreal: McGill Queen's UP, 2001

Henighan, Tom. *Ideas of North: A Guide to Canadian Arts and Culture*. Vancouver: Raincoast, 1997

—. *The Presumption of Culture: Structure, Strategy and Survival in the Canadian Cultural Landscape*. Vancouver: Raincoast, 1996

Howells, Coral Ann. "Disruptive Geographies: or, Mapping the Region of Woman in Contemporary Canadian Women's Writing in English." *Journal of Commonwealth Literature* 31.1(1996): 115–26

Hutcheon, Linda. "'Shape shifters': Canadian Women Novelists and the Challenge to Tradition." *A Mazing Space: Writing Canadian Women Writing*. Ed. Shirley Neuman and Smaro Kamboureli. Edmonton: Longspoon/Newest, 1986. 219–27

—. *The Canadian Postmodern: A Study of Contemporary English-Canadian Fiction*. Oxford: Oxford UP, 1988

—. "The Canadian Postmodern: Fiction in English since 1960." Davidson 18–33

Laurence, Margaret. "A Place to Stand On." *Heart of a Stranger*. Toronto: McClelland and Stewart, 1976. 13–18

—. *The Diviners*. 1974. Chicago: U of Chicago P, 1993

Mackey, Eva. *The House of Difference: Cultural Politics and National Identity in Canada*. London: Routledge, 1999

MacLennan, Hugh. *Two Solitudes*. New York: Duell, Sloan & Pearce, 1945

Mathews, Robin. *Canadian Literature: Surrender or Revolution*. Toronto: Steel Rail, 1978

McWilliams, Ellen. "Transatlantic Communities: The Joycean Influence in Alice Munro's *Lives of Girls and Women*". *Narratives of Community: Women's Short Story Sequences*. Ed. Roxanne Harde. Newcastle: Cambridge Scholars Press, 2007. 372–88

Miller, David. *On Nationality*. Oxford: Clarendon Press, 1995

Moodie, Susanna. *Life in the Clearings Versus the Bush*. 1853. Toronto: McClelland & Stewart, 1989

—. *Roughing it in the Bush*. 1852. London: Virago, 1986

Morton, W.L. *The Canadian Identity*. 1961. Madison: U of Wisconsin P, 1972

Moss, Laura. *Is Canada Postcolonial?: Unsettling Canadian Literature*. Waterloo: Wilfred Laurier UP, 2003

Said, Edward. *Culture and Imperialism*. London: Vintage, 1992

Schöpflin, George. "The Functions of Myth and a Taxonomy of Myths". *Myths and Nationhood*. London: Hurst & Co., 1997. 19–35
Smith, Anthony D. *National Identity*. Nevada: U of Nevada P, 1991
Solecki, Sam. "Novels in English 1960-1982." Benson and Toye 823–32
Thackeray, W.M. *The Irish Sketchbook*. 1843. Dublin: Gill & Macmillan, 1990

Works by Margaret Atwood

Atwood, Margaret. *Alias Grace*. 1996. London: Virago, 1997
—. "Biographobia". *Nineteenth-Century Lives: Essays Presented to Jerome Hamilton Buckley*. Ed. Laurence S. Lockridge, John Maynard, and Donald D. Stone. Cambridge: Cambridge UP, 1989
—. *Cat's Eye*. 1988. London: Virago, 1990
—. *Dancing Girls*. 1977. London: Vintage, 1996
—. "Hair Jewellery". *Dancing Girls* 101–18
—. "Dancing on the Edge of the Precipice: Interview with Joyce Carol Oates." *Waltzing Again: New and Selected Conversations*. Ed. Earl G. Ingersoll. Princeton, NJ: Ontario Review, 2006. 43–54
—. *Eating Fire: Selected Poetry 1965–1995*. London: Virago, 1998
—. 'Giving Birth'. *Dancing Girls* 225–40
—. "Great Unexpectations." Autobiographical Foreword. *Margaret Atwood: Vision and Forms*. Ed. Kathryn Van Spanckeren and Jan Garden Castro. Carbondale: Southern Illinois UP, 1988
—. "In Search of *Alias Grace*: On Writing Canadian Historical Fiction." *Writing with Intent: Essays, Reviews, Personal Prose: 1983–2005*. New York: Carroll & Graf, 2005
—. Interview. *Start the Week*, Radio 4. 24 June 2002
—. *Lady Oracle*. 1976. London: Virago, 1982
—. *Margaret Atwood Collection*, Thomas Fisher Rare Book Library. University of Toronto
—. *Margaret Atwood: Conversations*. (ed.) Earl G. Ingersoll. Princeton, NJ: Ontario Review, 1990
—. *Moral Disorder*. London: Bloomsbury, 2006
—. *Negotiating with the Dead: A Writer on Writing*. Cambridge: Cambridge UP, 2002
—. "On Being a 'Woman Writer': Paradoxes and Dilemmas." *Second Words*. 190–204
—. "Review of *Diving into the Wreck*". *Adrienne Rich's Poetry and Prose*. New York: Norton, 1993. 280–2
—. *Second Words: Selected Critical Prose*. Boston: Beacon, 1984
—. *Strange Things: The Malevolent North in Canadian Literature*. Oxford: Clarendon Press, 1995
—. *Surfacing*. 1972. London: Virago, 1979

—. *Survival: A Thematic Guide to Canadian Literature*. Toronto: Anansi, 1972
—. "Survival, Then and Now." *Macleans* 112.26 (1999): 54–8
—. *The Blind Assassin*. London: Bloomsbury, 2000
—. "The CanLit Food Book." *Literary Gastronomy*. Ed. David Bevan. Amsterdam: Rodopi, 1988. 51–6
—. *The Edible Woman*. 1969. London: Virago, 1980
—. "The Female Body". *Good Bones*. 1992. London: Virago, 1993
—. "The Page." *Murder in the Dark*. 1983. London: Virago, 1994
—. *The Robber Bride*. 1993. London: Virago, 1994
—. *The Tent*. London: Bloomsbury, 2006
—. "True North". *Writing with Intent: Essays, Reviews, Personal Prose: 1983–2005*. New York: Carroll & Graf, 2005. 31–45

Works about Margaret Atwood

Barzilai, Shuli. "'Say That I Had a Lovely Face': The Grimm's 'Rapunzel,' Tennyson's 'Lady of Shalott,' and Atwood's *Lady Oracle*." *Tulsa Studies in Women's Literature* 19.2 (2000): 231–54
Bouson, J. Brooks. "'A Commemoration of Wounds Endured and Resented': Margaret Atwood's *The Blind Assassin* as Feminist Memoir." *Critique: Studies in Contemporary Fiction* 44.3 (2003): 251–69
Carrera Suarez, Isabel. "'Yet I Speak, Yet I Exist': Affirmation of the Subject in Atwood's Short Stories." *Margaret Atwood: Writing and Subjectivity*. Ed. Colin Nicholson. Basingstoke: Macmillan, 1994. 230–47
Cooke, Nathalie. *Margaret Atwood: A Biography*. Toronto: ECW, 1998
Davey, Frank. "Atwood Walking Backwards." *Open Letter* 2.5 (1973): 74–84
Howells, Coral Ann. *Margaret Atwood*. Basingstoke: Macmillan, 1996
—. "The Robber Bride; or, Who is a True Canadian?" *Margaret Atwood's Textual Assassinations: Recent Poetry and Fiction*. Ed. Sharon Rose Wilson. Ohio: Ohio State UP, 2003. 88–101
McCombs, Judith. "Contrary Re-Memberings: The Creating Self and Feminism in *Cat's Eye*." *Canadian Literature* 129 (1991): 9–23
Nicholson, Colin, (ed.) *Margaret Atwood: Writing and Subjectivity*. Basingstoke: Macmillan, 1994
Nischik, Reingard M., (ed.) *Margaret Atwood: Works and Impact*. New York: Camden House, 2000
Parsons, Ann. "The Self-Inventing Self: Women Who Lie and Pose in the Fiction of Margaret Atwood." *Gender Studies: New Directions in Feminist Criticism*. Ed. Judith Spector. Bowling Green, OH: Bowling Green U Popular P, 1986. 97–109
Rao, Eleonora. *Strategies for Identity: The Fiction of Margaret Atwood*. New York: Peter Lang, 1993
Rigney, Barbara Hill. *Margaret Atwood*. Basingstoke: Macmillan, 1987

Thieme, John. "A Female Houdini: Popular Culture in Margaret Atwood's *Lady Oracle*." *Kunapipi* 14.1 (1992): 71–80

The Contemporary Canadian Female Bildungsroman

Primary Texts

Anderson-Dargatz, Gail. *The Cure for Death by Lightning*. 1996. London: Virago, 1998
Ardizzi, Maria. *Made in Italy*. 1982. Trans. Anna Maria Castrilli. Toronto: Guernica, 1999
Armstrong, Jeannette. *Whispering in Shadows*. Penticton, BC: Theytus, 2000
Barfoot, Joan. *Gaining Ground*. 1978. London: The Women's Press, 1980
Birdsell, Sandra. *The Chrome Suite*. Toronto: McClelland & Stewart, 1992
Brand, Dionne. *In Another Place, Not Here*. 1996. Toronto: Vintage, 1997
Campbell, Maria. *Halfbreed*. Toronto: McClelland & Stewart, 1973
Caspar, Claudia. *The Reconstruction*. Harmondsworth: Penguin, 1996
Culleton, Beatrice. *In Search of April Raintree*. 1983.Winnipeg, MB: Peguis, 1999
Gowdy, Barbara. *Falling Angels*. 1989. New York: Washington Square, 1991
Kogawa, Joy. *Itsuka*. New York: Anchor, 1992
—. *Obasan*. 1981. New York: Anchor, 1994
Kulyk Keefer, Janice. *The Green Library*. Toronto: Harper Collins, 1996
MacDonald, Ann-Marie. *Fall On Your Knees*. 1996. Toronto: Vintage Canada, 1997
Maracle, Lee. *Sundogs*. Penticton, BC: Theytus, 1992
Moore, Brian. *The Luck of Ginger Coffey*. 1960. London: Paladin Books, 1987
Swan, Susan. *The Biggest Modern Woman of the World*. Toronto: Lester & Orpen Dennys, 1983
Thomas, Audrey. *Intertidal Life*. New York: Beaufort, 1984
Urquhart, Jane. *Away*. Toronto: McClelland & Stewart, 1993

Secondary Texts

Adams, Howard. *A Tortured People: The Politics of Colonization*. Penticton, BC: Theytus, 1995
Armstrong, Jeannette, (ed.) *Looking at the Words of Our People: First Nations Analysis of Literature*. Penticton, BC: Theytus, 1993
Beauregard, Guy. "After *Obasan*: Kogawa Criticism and Its Futures." *Studies in Canadian Literature* 26.2 (2001): 5–22
Blaeser, Kimberly M. "Native Literature: Seeking a Critical Center." Armstrong, *Looking at the Words of Our People* 51–62

Boland, Eavan. *Object Lessons: The Life of the Woman and the Poet in Our Time.* Manchester: Carcanet, 1995

Brand, Dionne. *Bread out of Stone*. Toronto: Coach House, 1994

Buckman, Jacqueline. "Questions of Identity and Subjectivity: Audrey Thomas's *Intertidal Life*." *English Studies in Canada* 22.1 (1996): 71–87

Damm, Kateri. "Says Who: Colonialism, Identity and Defining Indigenous Literature." Armstrong, *Looking at the Words of Our People* 9–26

—. "Dispelling and Telling: Speaking Native Realities in Maria Campbell's *Halfbreed* and Beatrice Culleton's *In Search of April Raintree*." Armstrong 93–114

Davidson, Arnold E. *Writing Against the Silence: Joy Kogawa's 'Obasan'*. Toronto: ECW Press, 1993

Dumont, Marilyn. "Popular Images of Nativeness." Armstrong, *Looking at the Words of Our People* 45–50

Hall, Tony. "Blockades and Bannock: Aboriginal Protests and Politics in Northern Ontario, 1980–1990." *Wicazo Sa Review* 7.2 (Autumn 1991): 58–77

Lee, Sky. *Disappearing Moon Cafe*. Vancouver: Douglas and McIntyre, 1990

Maracle, Lee. *I am Woman: A Native Perspective on Sociology and Feminism.* 1988.Vancouver: Press Gang, 1996

MacPherson, Heidi Slettedahl. "From Housewife to Hermit: Fleeing the Feminine Mystique in Joan Barfoot's *Gaining Ground*." *Studies in Canadian Literature* 21.1 (1996): 92–106

Peterson, Nancy J. *Against Amnesia: Contemporary Women Writers and the Crises of Historical Memory*. Philadelphia: U of Pennsylvania P, 2001

Petrone, Penny. "Aboriginal Literature: Native and Métis Literature." Benson and Toye 6–15

—. *Native Literature in Canada: From the Oral Tradition to the Present*. Toronto: Oxford UP, 1990

Quimby, Karin. "'This is my own, my native land': Constructions of Identity and Landscape in Joy Kogawa's *Obasan*." *Cross-Addressing: Resistance Literature and Cultural Borders*. Ed. John C. Hawley. New York: State U of New York P, 1996. 257–73

Index